MEDICOLEGAL FORMS WITH LEGAL ANALYSIS

AMA
AMERICAN MEDICAL ASSOCIATION

Additional copies may be ordered from:
Order Department: OP630290
P.O. Box 2964
Milwaukee, WI 53201-2964

ISBN 0-89970-402-6

GF12:90-621:7.5M:1/91

Medicolegal Forms with Legal Analysis

Table of Contents

Table of Contents Continued

Table of Contents Continued

Preface

This is the latest edition of Medicolegal Forms with Legal Analysis, a publication first issued almost 35 years ago. the purpose and intention of this edition remains the same as with all previous editions, to be of assistance to the practicing physician.

This publication offers a brief legal analysis of some of the more common issues that confront physicians from time to time in thier practice. The legal analysis is supported by court decisions and statutes. The forms presented this book are very general in nature and must be specifically adapted to the particular facts of the case and to the legal requirements of each jurisdiction. All forms may not be able to be used in all states.

Before relying on the legal principles or the forms in this book, the physician should consult his or her own attorney for specific legal advice.

Acknowledgement

Several people, in particular, should be recognized for their contributions to the publication of this book.

Gayle Kumchy, Ph.D., J.D., LL.M. did the research and developed the basic format for this publication, producing the manuscript from which the work evolved. Gayle is a Clinical Psychologist and a lawyer. She has written articles in both fields and has teaching credentials at Northwestern University Medical School, Department of Psychiatry, and also at the University of Toronto Department of Rehabilitation Medicine.

Charles C. Renshaw, Jr. edited the text with dispatch and a great deal of expertise, for which he has long been justly recognized.

Marina L. Ramos typed the manuscript, and produced innumerable drafts. Her patience, skill and accuracy must be recognized, for without her efforts this publication would never have been produced.

William B. Smith, Senior Attorney in the Office of General Counsel, coordinated the efforts of the team.

Edward B. Hirshfeld, J.D.
Associate General Counsel for Health Law

1.1 Physician-Patient Relationship

A physician is not required to accept every patient who requests treatment.[1] Courts have also been reluctant to require physicians to undertake treatment of every patient who presents himself to the physician:[2]

The Supreme Court of Indiana noted that the legislative act regulating the practice of medicine provides for the Board of Examiners, standards of qualifications, examinations, licensure to qualified physicians,and penalties for practicing without a license. "The act is a preventive, not a compulsive, measure. In obtaining the state's license (permission) to practice medicine, the state does not require, and the licensee does not engage, that he will practice at all, or on other terms that he may choose to accept."

Even if no other physician is available, the physician may refuse to accept a patient.[3] The mere rendering of first aid services in an emergency does not give rise to the relationship but the physician nevertheless is required to use due skill and care in administering emergency treatment.[4] The physician may, by special agreement with the patient, limit his engagement to treat the patient to one particular treatment or procedure or to administering treatment at a particular time or place.[5]

Once the patient has requested treatment and the physician has assented, the physician-patient relationship is established and certain obligations are imposed on the physician.[6] If no relationship exists, or the relationship is terminated, these duties will not be imposed. Therefore, the physician should understand the nature of the physician-patient relationship and how it is created and ended.

---

1 *Opinion 9.05, Free Choice, Current Opinions of the Judicial Council of the American Medical Association, 1984.*

2 Oliver v. Brock, *342 So 2d 1 (Alabama, 1976);* Buttersworth v. Swint, *186 SE 770 (Georgia, 1936);* Childers v. Frye, *158 SE 744 (North Carolina, 1931);* Osborne v. Frazor, *425 S.W. 2d 768 (Tennessee, 1968);* Ricks v. Budge, *64 P. 2d 208 (Utah, 1937);* Lyons v. Grether, *239 S.E. 2d 103 (Virginia, 1977);* Miller v. Dumon, *64 P 804 (Washington, 1901).*

3 *This discussion does not include emergency medical care (ethical and sometimes legal requirements) or hospital emergency room situations. Some pre-existing contractual arrangements, such as an agreement with a HMO, may obligate the physician to accept a patient.*

4 Birmingham, Baptist Hospital v. Crews, *229 Ala. 398, 157 So. 224 (1934);* McNamara v. Emmons, *97 P.2d 503 (1939);* Dabney v. Briggs, *219 Ala. 127, 121 So. 394 (1929);* Nelson v. Farrish, *143 Minn. 368, 173 N.W. 175 (1919);* Urrutia v. Patino, *297 S.W. 512 (Tex. 1927).*

5 McNamara v. Emmons, *36 Cal. App. 2d 199, 97 P.2d 503 (1939);* Dabney v.

Briggs, 219 Ala. 127, 121 So. 394 (1929); Nelson v. Farrish, *143 Minn. 368, 173 N.W. 175 (1919);* Urrutia v. Patino, *297 S.W. 512 (Tex. 1927).*

6 Podvin v. Eickhorst, *128 N.W.2d 523 (1964);* Nelson v. Farrish, *143 Minn. 368, 173 N.W. 715 (1919);* Lawson v. Conaway, *37 W. Va. 159, 16 S.E. 564 (1892);* Oliver V. Brock, *342 So. 2d 1 (Alabama, 1976);* Keene v. Wiggins, *138 Cal, Rptr. 3 (California, 1977);* Buttersworth v. Swint, *185 S.E. 770 (Georgia, 1936);* Andrews v. Davis, *148 A. 684 (Maine, 1930);* Betesh v. United States, *400 F. Supp. 238 (Maryland, 1974);* Peterson v. Phelps, *143 N.W. 793 (Minnesota, 1913);* Young v. Crescente, *39 A.2d 449 (New Jersey, 1944);* Davis v. Tirrell, *443 N.Y.S.2d 136 (New York, 1981);* Childers v. Frye, *158 S.E. 744 (North Carolina, 1931);* Osborne v. Frazor, *425 S.W.2d 768 (Tennessee, 1968);* Lyons v. Grether, *239 S.E.2d 103 (Virginia, 1977);* Miller v. Dumon, *64 P 804 (Washington, 1901);* Nicholson v. Curtis, *452 N.E.2d 883 (Illinois, 1983);* Sullenger v. Setco Northwest Inc., *702 P.2d 1139 (Oregon, 1985).*

1.2 Nature of the Relationship

It is clear that the physician-patient relationship is a consensual one, a contract. This contract, however, is usually not a written document setting forth the terms, rights, and responsibilities of the parties. Rather, the contract is implied; the patient requests medical care and the physician agrees to provide it. The contract thus created is one based on a fiduciary, not a financial, relationship.

The Supreme Court of Virginia, for example, has held that in accepting an appointment to treat a particular patient, the physician had an implied agreement to provide a specific medical service at a specific date and time. Consequently, the relationship could be characterized as a consensual one between the physician and patient and gave rise to a duty to perform the services contemplated.[1]

In another instance, a patient called to indicate that he would be late for his second appointment with the physician. The doctor indicated that he would not treat the patient and did not refer him to another physician. The court of appeals concluded that the relationship between the patient and the physician was sufficient to impose a duty upon the doctor to conform to the usual standard of care in such a case. The court found that to guard against injury, the physician should have advised the patient of his condition and told him to consult another physician without delay.[2]

These rulings suggest that a duty of care exists, whether it arises from a formal physician-patient relationship or occurs simply as a result of the acceptance by a physician, or his or her office staff, of an appointment to see a patient with a specific medical problem. If the physician decides not to see the patient, he or she should notify the patient in writing by registered letter, with a return receipt requested, to seek other medical assistance and offer to help in finding such assistance.[3]

1 Lyons v. Grether, *218 Va. 630, 329 S.E.2d 103 (1977).*

2 Davis v. Hagman, *439 N.E.2d 660 (1982).*

3 E.A. Bianco, Legal Physician-Patient Relationship, legal aspects of medical practice, American College of Legal Medicine, Volume 11 No. 5, May 1983.

1.3 Creation of the Relationship

The physician-patient relationship is created when a physician responds to an express or implied request for treatment from a patient or the patient's guardian.[1] One issue that arises is whether the relationship may be created even if the doctor never actually sees the patient. Courts have divided over this issue.

In one instance,[2] the court held that no contract was created when a physician spoke to a nurse over the telephone and advised her to have a patient call the latter's regular doctor. In another case,[3] the court held that a physician on call in an emergency room was obligated by medical staff rules to provide emergency treatment to any emergency patient.[4] A useful rule of thumb is that if the patient is justifiably relying on the physician's advice, a relationship is assumed.[5]

In another instance, it was ruled that a physician-patient relationship did not occur when a woman telephoned a physician who had treated her previously for an unrelated condition. The physician listened to the woman's recital of symptoms, told her to see him the next morning, and recommended that that she continue the immediate course of treatment prescribed by another physician.[6]

In another case, no physician-patient relationship was found to exist between the recipient of a donated kidney and the doctor of the donor because the donor's doctor was never the recipient's doctor. That doctor did not have a duty to that patient. The donor's physician owed a duty to the donor and the recipient's physician owed a duty of care to the recipient patient.[7]

1 Stowers v. Ardmore Acres Hospital, *172 N.W.2d 497 (Mich. 1969);* Greenwald v. Grayson, *189 So.2d 204 (Fla. 1966);* State of North Carolina v. Hollingsworth, *139 S.E.2d 235 (N.C. 1964).*

2 Childs v. Weis, *440 S.W.2d 104 (Tex. 1969).*

3 Hiser v. Randolph, *617 P.2d 774 (Ariz.) reh. den. (1980).*

4 Id. *at 778.*

5 Katsetos v. Nolan, *368 A.2d 172 (Conn. 1976);* Johnson v. Vaughan, *370 S.W.2d 591 (Ky. 1955). See also cases where a relationship was established:* Duprey v. Shane, *249 P.2d 8 (California, 1952);* Stafford v. Shultz, *270 P.2d 1 (California, 1954);* Rule v. Cheeseman, *317 P.2d 472 (Kansas, 1957);* Barrios v. Sara Mayo Hospital, *264 So.2d 792 (Louisiana, 1972);* Peterson v. Phelps, *143 N.W. 793 (Minnesota, 1913);* Frazor v. Osborne, *414 S.W.2d 118 (Tennessee, 1966);* Lyons v. Grether, *239 S.E.2d 103 (Virginia, 1977). Relationship not established:* Greenwald v. Grayson, *189 So.2d 204 (Florida, 1966);* Sendjar v. Gonzales, *520 S.W.2d 478 (Texas, 1975);* Thomas v. Kenton, *425 So.2d 396 (Louisiana, 1982).*

6 Clanton v. Von Haam, *340 S.E.2d 627 (Georgia, 1986).*

7 Moore, et al v. Shah-New York, *458 NYS 2d, 33, 90 AD 3rd Depart., (December 30, 1982).*

1.4 Continuing the Relationship

Once a physician-patient relationship is created, a doctor is under an obligation to provide services as long as the patient requires them or until the relationship is properly terminated.[1] The patient's failure to pay a bill does not end the relationship because the contract that exists is based on a fiduciary, not a financial, responsibility.[2]

A physician may limit the scope of the relationship to a designated geographic area or medical specialty. In one such case, a woman had a cut treated by a physician's associate. The next day she left for vacation 20 miles away. While there, she decided that she needed additional treatment and asked the physician to come and treat her. Instead, the doctor gave her the name of a local physician. This action was upheld as proper.[3]

1 Johnson v. Vaughan, *370 S.W.2d 591 (Kentucky, 1963);* Coughlin v. Christoffersen, *431 P.2d 997 (Washington, 1967).*

2 Ricks v. Budge, *64 P.2d 208 (Utah 1937).*

3 McNamara v. Emmons, 97 P.2d 503 (Cal. 1940).

2.1 Physician Discharge Or Terminating The Relationship

A physician-patient relationship may be terminated by the patient, the doctor, or mutually. Once the relationship has ended, the physician is under no obligation to follow the patient's progress.[1] At least one court has held, however, that a duty continued after the relationship ended.

In that case,[2] the court imposed a responsibility on the doctor to inform the patient of the newly discovered hazards of an IUD. The physician nonetheless stated that he only saw the patient when he inserted the IUD. The court stated that the duty "... would arise by virtue of the confidential relationship between doctor and patient. It is ... a malpractice action from the imposed continuing status of physician-patient when the danger arose from that relationship.[3]

1 Fleishman v. Richardron-Merrell, Inc., *266 A.2d 843 (N.J. 1969).*

2 Tressmer v. Barke, *86 Cal. App. 3d 656, 150 Cal. Rptr. 389 Cal. 2d Div. (1978); see also,* Lee v. Dewbre, *362 S.W.2d 900 (Lexis 1962);* Johnson v. Vaughan, *370 S.W.2d 809 (Ky. 1955);* Carroll v. Griffin, *101 S.E.2d 764 (Ga. App. 1958);* Vann v. Horden, *47 S.E.2d 314 (Va. 1948);* Bolles v. Kenton, *263 P.2d 26 (Colo. 1928).*

3 Id. *at 394;* Tressmer v. Barke, *150 Cal. Rptr. 384 (2nd Div. 1978) (summary judgment review);* Lee v. Dewbre, *362 S.W.2d 900 (Lexis 1962);* Johnson v. Vaughan, *370 S.W.2d 809 (Ky. 1955);* Carroll v. Griffin, *101 S.E.2d 764 (Ga. App. 1958);* Vann v. Horden, *47 S.E.2d 314 (Va. 1948);* Bolles v. Kenton, *263 P.2d 26 (Colo. 1928).*

2.2 Termination by the Physician

A physician cannot withdraw from a case or discontinue practicing and thereby avoid liability by not seeing a patient without notifying the person of the withdrawal.[1] When a physician wishes to withdraw from a case, he or she must give the patient reasonable notice so that the person may secure other medical attention if that is desired.[2]

One way to determine what is a reasonable amount of time is to consult other physicians in the area. Factors to be considered include the condition of the patient, the size of the community, and the availability of other doctors.[3] The final decision must be made by the physician on the facts of each case. If proper notice is not given, and the patient therefore suffers damages, the doctor may be liable for abandonment.

To minimize liability exposure and to facilitate termination of a physician-patient relationship, when a physician intends to withdraw from a case, the patient should be clearly notified. The physician should send a letter preferably certified, to the patient explaining the situation. A copy should be kept in the doctor's files. The accompanying examples may be useful.

---

1 Carol v. Griffin, *96 Ga App 826, 101 SE 2d 764 (1958);* Vans v. Horden, *182 Va 555, 47 SE 2d 314 (1968);* Boeles v. Kinton, *83 Colo. 147, 263 P. 26 (1928).*

2 Katsetos v. Nolan, *368 A.2d 172 (Conn. 1972);* Collins v. Meeker, *424 P.2d 488 (Kan. 1967);* Norton v. Hamilton, *89 S.E.2d 809 (Ga. App. 1955);* Sibert v. Boger, *260 S.W.2d 569 (Mo. 1953);* McGulpin v. Bessmer, *43 N.W.2d 121 (Iowa 1950);* Groce v. Myers, *29 S.E.2d 553 (N.C. 1944);* Gray v. Davidson, *130 P.2d 341 (Wash. 1942);* Baird v. National Health Foundation, *144 S.W.2d 850 (Me. App. 1940);* Ricks v. Budge, *64 P.2d 208 (Utah 1937);* Fortner v. Koch. *261 N.W. 762 (Mich. 1935).*

3 Brandt v. Grubin, *329 A.2d 82, 88 (N.J. 1974).* See Sendjar v. Gonzales, *520 S.W.2d 478 (Tex. 1975) (coverage was adequate so no abandonment);* Medvecz v. Choi, *569 F.2d 1221 (3d Cir. 1977). In* Sibert v. Boger, *260 S.W.2d 569 (Mo. 1953), it was held that the physician did not abandon the case when the physician directed the patient to go to somebody else because she was consulting another physician at the time and the city was sufficiently large that medical services could have been obtained any day.* See also Urrutia v. Patino, *297 S.W. 512 (Tex. 1927).*

Letter of Withdrawal from a Case

Form 1a

Date:____________

Dear ____________:

I will no longer be able to provide medical care to (you/your children). If you require medical care within the next ____ days I will be available, but in no event longer than ____ days.

To assist you in continuing to receive medical care for (you/your children), we will make records available to a new physician as soon as you authorize us to send them to that physician.

Sincerely,

____________, M.D.

Form 1b

Date:____________

Dear __________:

I find it necessary to inform you that I am withdrawing from further professional attendance upon you because you have persisted in refusing to follow my medical advice and treatment. Since your condition requires medical attention, I suggest that you place yourself under the care of another physician without delay. If you desire, I shall be available to attend you for a reasonable time after you receive this letter, but in no event for more than ____ days.

This should give you ample time to select a physician of your choice from the many competent practitioners in this city. With your authorization, I will make available to this physician your case history and information regarding the diagnosis and treatment you have received from me.

Very truly yours,

__________, M.D.

Letter for Physicians Discontinuing Practice

Form 2

Date: ______________

Dear ______________:

Because of ________________ (my retirement, reasons of health, etc.) I am discontinuing the practice of medicine on __________, 19____. I will not be able to attend you professionally after that date.

I suggest that you arrange to place yourself under the care of another physician. If you are not acquainted with another physician, I suggest that you contact the __________ (local) Medical Society.

I shall make my records of your case available to the physician you designate. Since the records of your case are confidential, I shall require your written authorization to do so. For this reason, I am including at the end of this letter an authorization form. Please complete the form and return it to me.

I am sorry that I cannot continue as your physician. I extend to you my best wishes for your future health and happiness.

Yours very truly,

______________, M.D.

Authorization to Transfer Records

Form 3

Date: ______________

To: ______________, M.D.

I hereby authorize you to transfer or make available to ______________, M.D., ____________________ (address) all the records and reports relating to my case.

Signed ____________

Acknowledgement of Emergency Treatment

Form 4

Date: ______________

Time: ________ a.m. p.m.

I acknowledge that the medical care which (was) (is about to be) furnished to *(name of patient)* by Dr. ______________ (was) (will be) limited solely to emergency treatment. I understand that it will be necessary to select another physician and make immediate arrangements with that physician for a complete diagnosis and continuation of treatment.

Witness______________ Signed______________
(patient or person authorized to consent for patient)

*If the physician has agreed to provide only emergency treatment, the execution of this form before or immediately after treatment would be valuable as evidence against any later claim that the physician abandoned the patient by failing to continue treatment.

2.3 Termination by the Patient

A patient may unilaterally terminate a physician-patient relationship at any time. Since the patient's withdrawal is often unannounced or unexpressed a dispute may arise as to whether the physician had a continuing responsibility to attend the patient. If no further medical services are necessary for the particular injury or illness the physician was employed to treat, the relationship usually ceases without any formalities.

If a physician is discharged by a patient in need of further medical attention, or if the patient leaves the hospital against the physician's advice, the doctor should be in a position to establish that no abandonment occurred.[1]

There are several methods of protecting the physician from an abandonment lawsuit. These include obtaining a signed statement of the facts by the patient, or sending a letter to the person either confirming the discharge or the fact that the patient left against medical advice. Again, certified mail is preferable and a copy should be retained in the physician's files. The accompanying examples may be useful.

---

1 Pearson v. Norman, *106 P.2d 361 (Colo. 1940);* Muckleroy v. McHenry, *16 P.2d 123 (Okla. 1932);* Duke Sanitarium v. Hearn, *13 P.2d 183 (Okla. 1932).*

Letter Suggesting Follow-Up

Form 5

Date: ________________

Dear ________________:

As we discussed during your appointment today, I suggest that you make another appointment with me for a check-up in approximately ________________. Although my examination does not indicate the existence of any condition requiring treatment at this time, your condition should be monitored by me or another physician.

Sincerely,

________________, M.D.

Letter to Confirm Discharge by Patient

Form 6

Date: ________________

Dear ________________:

This will confirm our telephone conversation today during which you discharged me from attending you as your physician in your present illness. In my opinion, your condition requires continued medical treatment by a physician. If you have not already obtained the services of another physician, I suggest that you do so without delay. You may be assured that, upon your authorization, I will furnish that physician with information regarding the diagnosis and treatment that you have received from me.

Very truly yours,

________________, M.D.

Letter to Patient Who Fails to Follow Advice

Form 7

Date:________________

Dear________________:

At the time you brought your (*daughter/son*), to me for examination this afternoon, I informed you that I was unable to determine without X-ray pictures whether a fracture existed in (*his/her*) injured (right/left) arm. I strongly urge you to permit me or some other physician of your choice to make this X-ray examination without further delay.

Your refusal to permit a proper X-ray examination to be made of (*his/her*) arm may result in serious consequences if a fracture exists.

Very truly yours,

________________, M.D.

Statement of Patient Leaving* Hospital Against Advice

Form 8

Date: ______________

This is to certify that I am leaving______________Hospital at my own insistence and against the advice of the hospital authorities and my attending physician. I have been informed by them of the dangers of my leaving at this time. I release the hospital, its employees and officers, and my attending physician from all liability for any adverse results caused by my premature departure.

Signed ______________

I agree to hold harmless the______________Hospital, its employees and officers, and the attending physician from all liability, with reference to the discharge of the patient named above.

____
(Husband, wife, parent, etc.)

Date ______________

Witness ______________

* The patient may not be forced to sign this type of statement and cannot be restrained. If the patient refuses to sign the form, it should be filled out, witnessed by hospital personnel, and the statement "Signature Refused" included on the form.

Letter to Patient Who Fails to Keep Appointment

Form 9

Date: ______________

Dear ______________:

On ____________, 19____, you failed to keep your appointment at my office. In my opinion, your condition requires continued medical treatment. If you so desire, you may telephone me for another appointment, but if you prefer to have another physician attend you, I suggest that you arrange to do so without delay. You may be assured that, upon your authorization, I will make available my knowledge of your case to the physician of your choice.

I trust that you will understand that my purpose in writing this letter is out of concern for your health and well-being.

Very truly yours,

______________, M.D.

2.4 Patient Abandonment

Abandonment generally means unilateral severance of the professional relationship between a doctor and a patient without reasonable notice at a time when there is still a need for continuing medical attention.[1] Actionable abandonment, however, occurs only in the absence of reasonable notice or of failure to provide an adequate medical attendant.[2] When there is evidence that adequate medical care was available within a reasonable time after the physician left the case, or that no damage resulted from the abandonment, there is no cause for action.[3]

1 *Lee v. Dewbre, 362 S.W.2d 900 (Texas, 1962); Other cases recognizing that a physician has a duty not to abandon the case:* Carroll v. Griffin, *101 S.E.2d 764 (Georgia, 1958);* Kenney v. Piedmont Hospital, *222 S.E.2d 162 (Georgia, 1975);* Magana v. Elie, *439 N.E.2d 1319 (Illinois, 1982);* Capps v. Valk, *369 P.2d 238 (Kansas);* O'Neill v. Montefiore Hospital, *202 N.Y.S.2d 436 (New York, 1960);* Murray v. U.S., *329 F.2d 270 (Virginia, 1964);* Coughlin v. Christoffersen, *431 P.2d 997 (Washington, 1976).*

2 Id.

3 Carroll v. Griffin, *101 S.E.2d 764 (Georgia, 1958).*

3.1 Substitute Physician

A physician who has entered into a general agreement for treatment but is unable to care for a patient when services are needed, may arrange for another doctor to provide the services.[1] If the physician anticipates that he will be absent from his practice, however, he has an obligation to provide his patient with due notice and to arrange for a substitute to cover for him.[2] The substitute physician must be qualified and competent.[3]

Courts have held that a physician may send a substitute in an obstetrical case,[4] but because of the very personal nature of the physician-patient relationship in these situations, the physician should, when possible, obtain the written consent of the patient for a substitute if the doctor might not be available when needed. See form.

---

1 Jackowicz v. Knobloch, *265 N.W. 799 (Mich. 1936);* Jackson v. Burton, *147 So. 414 (Ala. 1933);* Stohlman v. Davis, *220 N.W. 247 (Neb. 1928);* Young v. Jordan, *145 S.E. 41 (W. Va. 1928);* Miller v. Dore, *148 A.2d 692 (Me. 1959);* Kenney v. Piedmont Hospital, *222 S.E.2d 162 (Ga. 1975).*

2 Stohlman v. Davis, *220 N.W. 247 (Neb. 1928).*

3 Tripp v. Pate, *271 S.E.2d 407 (N.C. App. 1980);* Stohlman v. Davis, *117 Neb. 178, 220 N.W. 247 (1928).*

4 Jackowicz v. Knobloch, *265 N.W. 799 (Mich. 1936);* Young v. Jordon, *145 S.E. 41 (W. Va. 1928);* See *also* Norton v. Hamilton, *89 S.E.2d 809 (Ga. App. 1955); Contra:* Hood v. Moffett, *69 So. 664 (Miss. 1915).*

Provision for Substitute Physician at Delivery

Form 10

Date ____________

Place ____________

To Dr.____________:

In engaging you as my obstetrician, I understand that if you are unavailable or unable for any reason to be present and to deliver me, at the time of my confinement, you will make a reasonable effort to refer me to another qualified physician to provide obstetrical care. I agree to hold you free from any responsibility in connection with any services that may be performed by any physician to whom you refer me or whom I may call.

Witness ____________ Signed ____________

** If the husband is present at the time arrangements are made, it is desirable that he witness the wife's execution of this form.

3.2 Consultants and Referrals

When a consultant is called into a case for the purpose of providing ongoing treatment for a patient, the original physician is generally under no obligation to continue treating the patient for that same condition. The primary physician may, however, be liable for negligence in selecting a particular consultant or in referring a patient to another physician.

If a physician exercises due care in making a recommendation for a referral to another physician and has no further involvement with the treatment, he or she is not liable for injuries caused by the other physician.[1] In an Illinois case, a doctor who initially examined an emergency room patient was informed that X-rays indicated that a lesion on the patient's knee indicated the possibility of a malignant primary bone neoplasm.[2] The physician conferred with a second doctor and referred the patient to him. The patient subsequently claimed that after he scheduled an appointment, the physician rescheduled it, and later told the patient he would not see him. The patient further alleged that no referral to another physician was made.

The court stated that the " ... determination of whether under the facts alleged the duty arose imposing an obligation on defendant for the benefit of plaintiff requires weighing of factors of foreseeability of subsequent occurrences, the likelihood of injury, the magnitude of guarding against it, and the consequences of placing that burden on the defendant."[3] The court stated that subsequent injury to the patient was reasonably likely and that the burden of guarding against it was slight. The court imposed a duty of reasonable conduct on the physician.

---

1 Graddy v. New York Medical College, *243 N.Y.S.2d 940 (1963).*

2 Davis v. Weiskopf, *439 N.E.2d 60 (Ill. 1982).*

3 Id. *at 65.*

4.1 Confidential Relationship

The physician-patient relationship is extremely confidential. Confidentiality is necessary so that a patient is free to make a full disclosure of facts and the physician can most effectively provide appropriate services. It is a breach of professional ethics for the physician to reveal confidential communications of a patient without the patient's express consent, unless required by law, as in the case of the communicable diseases, gunshot wounds, etc. This concept is embodied in the Current Opinions of the Judicial Council of the American Medical Association (1989).

The obligation to safeguard patient confidences is, however, subject to certain exceptions which are ethically and legally justified because of overriding social considerations. If there is a reasonable probability that a patient may inflict serious bodily harm on another person, for example, the physician in the case should take reasonable precautions to protect the intended victim. This might include notifying law enforcement authorities. Communicable diseases and gun shot and knife wounds, as noted above, should be reported as may be required by applicable statutes or ordinances.

The disclosure of a patient's confidential information may lead to the revocation of a physician's license.[1] Several courts have also held that if a physician reveals information obtained in a professional capacity, and does so without the consent of the patient, his action is a sufficient basis for awarding damages.[2] Therefore, a physician should obtain the express written consent of a patient before releasing confidential information. See forms.

Several courts have recognized this common law confidentiality. In one case,[3] the patient alleged that the doctor had disclosed information to the patient's employer, contrary to the patient's express instructions. The court found that even though there was no applicable state confidentiality statute, public policy requires " . . . that information obtained in the course of a doctor-patient relationship be maintained in confidence, unless the public interest, or the private interest of the patient, demands otherwise."[4]

Breach of this duty would give rise to a cause of action.[5] The same court also stated that the relationship between a doctor and a patient includes an implied provision that information will be kept confidential.[6] Some courts have based legal protection on the physician's ethical responsibility.[7] Other states have codified the confidentiality requirement.[8]

---

1 Simonsen v. Swenson, *104 Neb. 224, 177 N.W. 831 (1920);* Abelson's Inc. v. New Jersey State Board of Optometrists, *SNJ 412, 75 A.2d 867 (1950).* And see, Munzer v. Blaisdell, *183 Misc. 773, 49 NYS 2d 915 (1944).* See also *Kan. Stat. Ann. §65-2837 (1972) (Willful betrayal of confidential information is a basis for license suspension or revocation); repealed.*

2 Clark v. Geraci, *208 N.Y.S. 2d 564 (1961).* See also Berry v. Moench, *8 Utah 2d 191, 331 P.2d 814 (1958);* Simonsen v. Swenson, *104 Neb. 224, 177 N.W. 831 (1920);* Smith v. Driscoll, *94 Wash. 441, 162 P. 572 (1917);* Boyd v. Wynn, *286 Ky. 173, 150 S.W.2d 648 (1941);* People v. Leyra, *302 N.Y. 353, 98 N.E.2d 553, reversed 347 U.S. 556 (1951).*

3 Horne v. Patton, *287 So.2d 824 (1974).*

4 Id. *at 829.*

5 Id. *at 830.*

6 Id. *at 831.*

7 Orr v. Sievert, *292 S.E. 2d 548 (Ga. App. 1982).*

8 See e.g., *South Dakota 19-2-3 Cal. Civil Code §56.10; Ga. Code 38-418 Tex. Civil Statutes art. 4495B §3(h).*

4.2 Privileged Communications

The physician-patient privilege, although not recognized under common law,[1] is now recognized by statute in most states.[2] New York, in 1828, was the first state to pass such a statute.[3] The statutes that have been enacted throughout the country since then are far from uniform. States such as Arizona[4] make all communications between a physician and a patient privileged. Other states restrict the privilege to information that enables a doctor to treat a patient.[5]

Virginia and North Carolina allow the presiding judge to compel disclosure as he deems necessary for the proper administration of justice.[6] Since the privilege is founded on legislative action rather than common law, it may be revoked, modified or withdrawn by a legislature at any time.[7] It is also important to remember that the scope of the privilege in a particular state depends upon the express wording of the statute granting the privilege.

The statutes may vary somewhat in the particular language they employ, but the purpose behind them seems rather uniform. Their aim is to inspire confidence in the physician-patient relationship and to encourage the patient to disclose fully his or her sickness to the doctor.[8] The privilege is furthermore designed to encourage free disclosure in a hospital or a physician's office by preventing later disclosure in a courtroom.[9] The privilege also protects the patient from possible embarrassment and loss of privacy that public disclosure could cause.[10]

Typically, statutes delineate five requirements that must be met before a patient can successfully claim the physician-patient privilege. (1) Usually the patient can only silence a (physician or surgeon), and the person must have been a physician when he or she learned about the disputed communication. (2) The privilege is usually limited to information gained from the physician-patient relationship. (3) This information must come from a communication or an observation. (4) The communication must have been essential to the treatment of the patient. Lastly, the communication must have been confidential. The "privileged communication" statutes prevent disclosure in court and in other administrative proceedings of certain types of confidential information.

The privilege belongs to the patient, but the physician often may claim it on the patient's behalf.[11] The doctor may disclose information with the patient's consent, or if the latter waives the privilege, or if the privilege is inapplicable by law. A Colorado statute, for example, provides that the physician "... shall not be examined without the consent of his patient as to any information acquired in attending the patient which was necessary to enable him to prescribe or act for the patient ...' except as provided by law.[12]

A Nevada statute provides that "[a] patient has a privilege to refuse to disclose and to prevent any other person from disclosing confidential communications among himself, his doctor or persons who are participating in the diagnosis or treatment under the direction of the doctor, including members of the patient's family."[13] Again, statutory exceptions exist.

1 Quarles v. Sutherland, *389 S.W. 2d 249 (Tenn. 1965).*

2 *Only a few states do not have a physician-patient privilege statute. Georgia, Connecticut, and Florida only have a psychiatrist-patient privilege. South Carolina, Tennessee, and Texas law state that an attempt to unlawfully procure narcotics is not a privileged communication. Delaware and Rhode Island have no physician-patient privilege statute of any kind.*

3 *New York Rivised Statutes 1828, 406 (pt. 3, c7, art 9 Section 73).*

4 *Ariz. Rev. Stat. Ann. Sec. 12-2235.*

5 *Michigan Statutes Annotated Sec. 27A.2157; MCL Sec. 600.2157.*

6 *North Carolina Gen. Stat. Sec 8-53 (1953); Va. Code Ann. Sec. 8-289.1 (1950).*

7 Randolph v. Supreme Liberty Life Insurance Co., *221 S.W.2d 155, 156 (Missouri, 1948);* Bozicevech v. Kenilworth Mercantile Co., *58 Utah 458, 199 P. 406,*

409 (1921).

8 Massachusetts Mutual Life Insurance Co. v. Brei, *311 F.2d 463, 466 (California, 1963).*

9 McCormick Sec. 102 at 218.

10 Id. Sec. 98 at 213.

11 Osterman v. Ehrenworth, *256 A.2d 123 (N.J. 1969).*

12 Colo. Rev. Stat. 13-90-107 (1)(d) (1983).

13 Nev. Rev. Stat. §49.225; See also, e.g., *Mississippi* §13-1-21 (1983); Ohio Rev. Stat. §2317.02.

4.3 Exceptions or Required Disclosures

The exceptions usually cited are for disclosures pursuant to court or administrative orders,[1] court ordered examinations,[2] to procure a dangerous drug or controlled substance,[3] when the patient has made his or her own physical or mental condition the basis for lawsuit,[4] or to disclose the existence of a dangerous disease,[5] gunshot wounds,[6] or child abuse.[7] Several articles discuss child abuse statutes thoroughly.[8] In other situations, such as investigations by a board of medical examiners, disclosure may be required for that proceeding only.[9]

Other statutes allow disclosure without patient authorization in limited circumstances. For example, Montana law allows the physician to report to the Division of Motor Vehicles patients with conditions that impair their ability to safely operate a motor vehicle.[10] California law allows the physician to disclose information to an insurer, employer, and other specified groups, persons or entities responsible for paying for the patient's health care services, to the extent necessary to allow responsibility for payment to be determined and made.[11] Similarly, information may be disclosed to other health care professionals for the patient's diagnosis or treatment.[12]

Cases have arisen that question whether release only of a patient's name violates the confidentiality privilege. Often these cases turn on the particular factual situation; the court decisions have not been uniform. If release of the patient's name would identify the type of treatment received, the physician is advised to obtain the patient's consent prior to disclosure.[13] In some states, the statutory privilege has been extended to nurses,[14] psychologists, psychotherapists, marriage counselors, sexual assault counselors and others.[15]

The privilege also extends to hospital records insofar as they tend to disclose what the physician learned during the course of treatment.[16] Generally, it has been held that where a physician is employed by an adverse party to examine a claimant, with no contemplation of any treatment, the information thus acquired is not privileged and the physician may testify as to such information.[17] Some states have codified this requirement for physician[18] and hospital[19] records. Many states have judicial decisions to the same effect.[20]

---

1 *Cal. Civil Code §56.10 (b)(1); 29 U.S.C. §669-671 applied in G.M.C. v. Director of National Institute for Occupational Safety, 636 F.2d 163 (6th Cir. 1980).*

2 *Nev. Rev. Stat. §49.225.*

3 *Fla. Stat. Ann. §455.241.*

4 *Tex. Civil Stat. (Vernon) art. 4495b §5.08(g)(1983).*

5 *N.Y. Pub. Health Law §2101 (McKinney).*

6 *N.Y.P.L. 265.25.*

7 *Almost all states have mandatory reporting requirements for physicians in cases of suspected child abuse.*

8 Katz, S. et al., *1977. Legal Research on child abuse and neglect: past and future. Fam. Law Quart. 11(2): 151-1984; and Sussman, A. 1974. Reporting child abuse: A review of the literature. Fam. Law Quart. 11: 245-313 (1984*

9 *Tex. Civil Stats. (Vernon) art. 4495B §5.08(g)(1983) (Patient identity is protected).*

10 *Montana 1983 New Laws 353.*

11 *Cal. Civil Code §56.109c)(2) & §56.29;* See, *however,* Felis v. Greenberg, *273 NYS 2d 288 (1966), holding that the furnishing of information by a physician to an insurance company, without the patient's authorization constituted a violation of the patient-physician privilege.*

12 Id.

13 Rudnick v. Superior Court, *114 Cal. Rptr. 603 (1974);* Marcus v. Superior Court of Los Angeles, *95 Cal. Rptr. 545 (1971);* People v. Florendo, *447 N.E.2d 282 (Ill. 1983) (Release only to grand jury permitted);* Geisberger v. Willuhn, *390 N.E.2d 945 (Ill. 1979) (Release of name alone no violation).*

14 *Colorado Revised Statutes 13-90-107(1).*

15 *Utah Code Annotated 78-3C-4 (1984) (Limited disclosure only).*

16 State Of Iowa v. Bedel, *193 N.W.2d 121 (Iowa 1971); Unick v. Kessler Memorial Hospital, 257 A.2d 134 (N.J. 1969);* Koump v. Smith, *250 N.E.2d 857 (N.Y. 1969);* Toole v. Franklin Investment Co., *158 Wash. 696, 291 P. 1101 (1930);* Metropolitan Life Ins. Co. v. McSwain, *149 Miss. 455, 115 So. 555 (1928).* Contra: Sarrio v. Reliable Construction Company, Inc., *286 A.2d 183 (Md. 1972).*

17 Hardy v. Riser, *309 F.Supp. 1234 (Miss. 1970);* Hanlon v. Woodhouse, *113 Colo. 504, 160 P.2d 998 (1945);* McMillen v. Industrial Commission of Ohio, *37 N.E.2d 632 (Ohio 1941);* Bouligny v. Metropolitan Life Ins. Co., *133 S.W.2d 1094 (Mo. App. 1939);* Metropolitan Life Ins. Col. v. Evans, *183 Miss. 859, 184 So. 426 (1938);* City of Cherokee v. Aetna Life Ins. Co., *215 Iowa 1000, 247 N.W. 495 (1933);* Moutzoukos v. Mutual Benefit Health & Accident Assn., *69 Utah 308, 254 P. 1005 (1927);* Cherpeski v. Great Northern R. Co., *128 Minn. 360, 150 N.W. 1091 (1915);* Arnold v. City of Maryville, *110 Mo. App. 254, 85 S.W. 107 (1905).* Contra: Kramer v. Policy Holders' Life Ins. Assn., *5 Cal. App.2d 380, 42 P.2d 665 (1935);* Webb v. Francis J. Lewald Coal Co., *215 Cal. 182, 4 P.2d 532 (1931).*

18 See, e.g., *Cal. Welfare & Inst. Code §5152.1 (1983) (Mental Health Records); Fla. Stat. Ann. §455.241.*

19 *Fla. Stat. Ann. §395.017(3) (1983 Supp.);* Head v. Colloton, *331 N.W.2d 870 (Iowa 1983).*

20 *No privilege for court appointed physicians.* Massey v. State of Georgia, *177 S.E.2d 79 (Ga. 1970);* cert. den. *91 S. Ct. 984 (1971);* Illinois v. Lowe, *248 N.E.2d 530 (Ill. 1969);* New York v. Fuller, *248 N.E.2d 17 (N.Y. 1969).*

4.4 The Duty to Warn Third Parties Exception

A conflict regarding the physician-patient privilege sometimes arises when a patient tells a therapist that he or she intends to commit a criminal act such as murder. The physician/psychotherapist must then decide, on the basis of limited exposure to the patient, whether to report the threat or merely dismiss it as an attempt by the patient to get attention. If the doctor reports the threat a question arises as to whether the disclosure will create a liability for a breach of confidentiality.

A 1985 California law provided that a psychotherapist's duty to warn potential victims would be discharged if "reasonable efforts were made to communicate the threat to the victim(s) and to a law enforcement agency."[1] The law was passed primarily in response to a decision in a case in which a male student at the University of California became pathologically obsessed with a female student he had met at a dance.[2] After telling a psychiatrist about his fantasies of harming and perhaps even killing the woman, the young man carried out his threat. In the civil suit filed by the slain girl's parents, the court established a legal duty to warn.[3] In a subsequent ruling, the court held that the duty was to protect, rather than to warn, the intended victim(s).[4]

Beginning with this decision, numerous courts have considered the limitations of physician/psychotherapist-patient confidentiality when third parties are in danger of harm. (Table 1) The result, however, is that instead of clarifying the duty owed to the third parties, the law has become more clouded and cluttered with exceptions. Attorneys and physicians alike agree that society deserves protection from violence and that breaching the physician-patient privilege is sometimes necessary, but there is little agreement about the most effective way to protect innocent third parties.

Table 1

Limitations of Patient-Psychotherapist Confidentiality and Protection of Third Parties

Case	Location	Duty Owed	Liability	Victim Specificity	Violence Foreseeable
Tarasoff, (1974)[5]	California Supreme	Warn	No	Specified	Yes
Tarasoff, II 1976[6]	California	Protect	No	Specified	Yes
Macintosh, 1979[7]	New Jersey	Protect	No	Specified	Yes
Thompson, 1980[8]	California	None	No	Not Specified	No
Lipari, 1980[9]	Federal District	Protect	No Specified	Not	Yes
Leedy, 1981[10]	Federal District	None	No	Not Specified	No
Doyle, 1982[11]	Federal District	None	No	Not Specified	No
Jablonski, 1983[12]	Federal Circuit	Protect	Monetary Damages	Specified	Yes
Bradley, 1983[13]	Federal District	None	No	Not Specified	No
Hedlund, 1983[14]	California Supreme	Protect	No	Not Specified	Yes
Petersen, 1983[15]	Washington Supreme	Protect	Monetary Damages	Not Specified	No
Schrempf, 1985[16]	New York Appeals	None	No	Not Specified	Yes
Peck, 1985[17]	Vermont Supreme	Protect	No	Specified	Yes

1 *California Assembly Bill 1133, McAllister, 1984.*

2 Tarasoff v. Regents of University of California, *118 Cal. Rptr. 129 (Cal. 1974).*

3 Id.

4 Tarasoff v. Regents of University of California; *reargued 17 Cal. 3rd 425, 551 P.2d 334, 133 Cal. Rptr. 33 (1976).*

5 Tarasoff v. Regents of University of California, *118 Cal. Rptr. 129 (Cal. 1974).*

6 Tarasoff v. Regents of University of California; *reargued 17 Cal. 3rd 425, 551 P.2d 334, 133 Cal. Rptr. 33 (1976).*

7 MacIntosh v. Milano, *168 N.J. Super. 466, 403 A.2d 500 (1979).*

8 Thompson v. County of Alameda, *Cal. 614 P.2d 728 (1980).*

9 Lipari, et al. v. Sears Roebuck, U.S., *497, F Supp., 85 (July 17, 1980).*

10 Leedy v. Hartnett, *510 F. Supp. 425 (N.D. Penn. 1981).*

11 Doyle et al. v. U.S., *530 F. Supp. 1278, Jan. 28, 1982.*

12 Jablonski v. U.S., *712 F.2d 391 (9th Cir. 1983).*

13 Bradley v. Wessner et al., *161 Ga. App. 576, 287 S.E.2d 716 (1983).*

14 Hedlund v. Superior County, *34 California 3d 695 (1983).*

15 Peterson v. State of Washington, *671 P.2d 230 Oct 20, 1983.*

16 Sohrempf v. State of N.Y., *107 Ad.2d 1042 Jan. 29, 1985.*

17 Peck v. The Counselling Service of Addison County, Inc., *499 Atl.2d 422, June 14, 1985. See also Applebaun P.S. Tarasoff & the Clinician: Problems in Fulfilling the Duty to Protect American J. of Psychiatry 142:4 April (1985).*

4.5 Medical Records

The physician-patient privilege extends to hospital records that are prepared by physicians.[1] This prevents the privilege from being evaded by obtaining information from hospital medical records that could not be directly obtained from the physician. Hospital records prepared by nurses may or may not be included within the scope of the privilege; it depends upon the express language of the privilege statute in the particular jurisdiction. The Ohio privilege statute does not specifically include nurses. Thus, the Supreme Court of Ohio has permitted hospital records prepared by a nurse which did not contain any information from the attending physicians to be admitted.[2]

The medical records of physicians kept in their private offices are considered the personal property of the physician, absent an agreement to the contrary. The Current Opinions of the Judicial Council of the American Medical Association (1989) discuss medical records.

7.02 **Records of Physicians: Information and Patients.** Notes made in treating a patient are primarily for the physician's own use and constitute his personal property. However, on request of the patient a physician should provide a copy or a summary of the record to the patient or to another physician, an attorney, or other person designated by the patient . . .

The record is a confidential document involving the physician-patient relationship and should not be communicated to a third party without the patient's prior written consent, unless required by law or to protect the welfare of the individual or the community. Medical reports should not be withheld because of an unpaid bill for medical services . . .

In addition to the ethical responsibility, many states have enacted laws that define the patients access rights to the information in the records. Some states require that a copy or summary[3] of the record be given to the patient, while other statutes provide access to other people.[4] The statute usually defines the form of the authorization.

---

1 Kaplan v. Manhattan Life, *109 F.2d 463, 465 (Cal. D.C. 1939).*

2 Weis v. Weis, *72 N.E.2d 245, 252 (Ohio 1947).*

3 See, e.g., *Fla. Stat. Ann. §455.241; W. Va. Code §16-29-1; Cal. Civil Code §56.12; S.D. Codified Laws §36-2-16.*

4 See, e.g., *Ill. Rev. Stat. Ann 8-2001-2004 (Smith-Hurd).*

Authorization for Disclosure of Information by Patient's Physician

Form 11

1. I authorize Dr. ________________ to disclose complete information to ________________ concerning his medical findings and treatment of the undersigned from on or about ________________, 19____ until date of the conclusion of such treatment.

2. Further, I authorize him to testify, without limitation, as to all of his medical findings and the treatment administered to the undersigned, in any legal action, suit, or proceedings to which I am, or may become, a party; and I waive on behalf of myself and any persons who may have an interest in the matter, all provisions of law relating to the disclosure of confidential medical information.

Witness ________________

Signed________________

Place ________________

Date ________________

Authorization for Disclosure of Information by Examining Physician

Form 12

I authorize Dr. ________________ to disclose complete information to ________________ concerning the results of a physical examination of the undersigned made or to made on ________________, 19____, and to testify, without limitation, as to all findings of said physical examination, in any legal action or judicial proceedings to which I am, or may become, a party; and I waive on behlaf of myself and any persons who may have an interest in the matter, all provisions of law relating to the disclosure of information acquired through said examination.

Witness________________

Signed________________

Place ________________

Date ________________

Authorization for Examination of Physician's Records

Form 13

To Dr.________________:

I authorize you to furnish a copy of the medical records of ________________________________, covering the period
(state name of patient or "myself")
from ________________ 19____ to ________________ , 19____ or to allow those records to be inspected or copied by ________________.
I release you from all legal responsibility or liability that may arise from this authorization.

Witness________________ Signed________________

Date ________________

Authorization to Furnish Information

Form 14

Date________________ Time________________ A.M. P.M.

I authorize and request the ________________ Hospital, and the physicians who attended me while I was a patient in said hospital during the approximate period from ________________, 19____ to ________________, 19____, to furnish to ________________ all information concerning my case history and the treatment, examinations or hospitalization which I received, including copies of hospital and medical records.

Witness________________ Signed________________

Order for Taking of X-Ray Films

Form 15

Date ______________

Place ______________

1. I hereby order the taking of X-ray exposures and films of parts of the person of ______________ as follows: ______________.

2. I agree, in part consideration of Dr. ______________'s undertaking to render professional service to the person named above, that all such X-ray exposures taken and films made by Dr. ______________, or by any other person at his request, whether or not paid for by the undersigned, shall become a part of Dr. ______________'s professional records and shall be subject solely to his control and disposition.10

3. In addition to the foregoing, I agree to pay charges in the amount of $______________ for services rendered pursuant to this order.

Signed______________

Witness ______________

Medical Report Form

Form 16

Parent's Name ______________________________ Age ______

Address ____

Date of Injury ____________ Place ______________________

____

1. **First Aid Rendered by:** **Date:**
   Describe First Aid:
2. **Past History:**
3. **Nature of Injury** (describe complications if any):

Continued

Form 16 Continued

4. Physical Examination: **Date:**
Skin:
Eyes:
Ears:
Nose:
Mouth and throat:
Neck:
Chest:
Lungs:
Heart/Pulse:
Blood pressure:
Abdomen:
Genitalia:
Rectal:
Extremities:
Back:
Gross neurological:
Sensory tests:
Other:

5. Subsequent Examination(s): **Dates:**

6. Laboratory Test and Results:

7. X-Rays Taken and Results:

8. Consultations: *(names, dates, and results)*

9. Diagnosis:
What is the casual relationship between the injury and the patient's condition?

10. Treatment: **Dates:**

11. Surgery: **Dates:**

12. Prognosis:
Will the patient be partially or totally disabled?

13. Discussion:

14. Physician's Fee for Services *(itemize):*
Examinations:
Treatments:
Surgery:
Reports and Consultations:
Other:
Estimated Fees for Future Services:

______________________________, M.D. ______________
(Date) *(Signature)* *(Telephone No.)*

____
(Street) *(City or Town)* *(State)*

4.6 Third Persons Present

A communication remains privileged even if it is made in the presence of a third person who is assisting the physician or who is acting as a means of communication between the doctor and the patient.[1] If the communication is made in the presence of anyone else, however, the privilege is inapplicable.[2]

Some state courts have held that, in these situations, only the third person can testify about the communication.[3] In other instances, both the physician and third party were permitted to testify.[4] Still other courts regard the privilege as a statute which is intended to silence certain witnesses, and they therefore prohibit a doctor from appearing even though a third person can be compelled to testify.[5] The patient, however, cannot be compelled to give testimony.[6]

1 State of Washington v. Gibson, *476 P.2d 727 (Wash. 1970);* Franklin Life Insurance Company v. William J. Champion and Company, *353 F.2d 919 (1965);* cert. den. *384 U.S. 928;* North American Union v. Oleske, *64 Ind. App. 435, 116 N.E. 68 (1917).*

2 State v. Tornquist, *120 N.W.2d 483 (Iowa 1963);* Ryan v. Industrial Commission of Ohio, *72 N.E.2d 907 (Ohio 1946);* Iwerks v. People, *108 Colo. 556, 120 P.2d 961 (1941);* Leeds v. Prudenital Ins. Co. of America, *128 Neb. 395, 258 N.W. 672 (1935);* Horowitz v. Sacks, *89 Cal. App. 336, 256 P. 281 (1928);* Walmer-Roberts v. Hennessey, *191 Iowa 86, 181 N.W. 798 (1921);* In re Swartz's Will, *79 Okla. 191, 192 P. 203 (1920);* Cincinnati, Hamilton & Dayton R. Co. v. Gross, *186 Ind. 471, 114 N.E. 962 (1917);* Denaro v. Prudential Ins. Co. of America, *154 App. Div. 840, 139 N.Y.S. 758 (1913);* Indiana Union Traction Co. v. Thomas, *44 Ind. App. 468, 88 N.E. 356 (1909);* Masons' Union Life Ins. Assn. v. Brockman, *26 Ind. App. 182, 59 N.E. 40! (1901);* Springer v. Bryam, *137 Ind. 15, 36 N.E. 261 (1894).*

3 Walmer-Roberts v. Hennessey, *191 Iowa 86, 181 N.W. 798 (1921);* Cincinnati, Hamilton & Dayton R. Co. v. Gross, *186 Ind. 471, 114 N.E. 962 (1917);* Denaro v. Prudential Ins. Co. of America, *154 App. Div. 840, 139 N.Y.S. 758 (1913);* Indiana Union Traction Co. v. Thomas, *44 Ind. App. 468, 88 N.E. 356 (1909);* Springer v. Bryam, *137 Ind. 15, 36 N.E. 361 (1894).*

4 Horowitz v. Sacks, *89 Cal. App. 336, 265 P. 281 (1928);* In re Swartz's Will, *79 Okla. 191, 192 P. 203 (1920).*

5 Iwerks v. People, *108 Colo. 556, 120 P.2d 961 (1942).*

6 Indiana Union Traction Co. v. Thomas, *44 Ind. App. 468, 88 N.E. 356 (1909).*

4.7 Waiver of the Physician-Patient Privilege

The privilege belongs not to the physician but to the patient, who may waive it. When a patient brings a professional liability action against a physician, the action constitutes a waiver of the privilege.[1] This is also true when a patient claims worker's compensation for a work-related injury.[2] In some states, courts have held that the mere filing of a personal injury suit constitutes a waiver of the privilege,[3] but in other states courts have held that mere filing does not constitute a waiver.[4]

The privilege may be waived if a patient testifies about the communications or medical treatment provided,[5] or if he or she calls the doctor as a witness.[6] A waiver that pertains to one physician, however, does not necessarily extend to other physicians[7] unless the doctors jointly conducted a unified course of treatment.[8] In a few jurisdictions, this issue of whether a waiver of one physician extends to other physicians is controlled by statute.[9]

The patient-physician privilege exists not only during the patient's lifetime but also after death.[10] When a patient dies, the privilege may be waived by a surviving spouse[11] or personal representative.[12] This protection conforms to the fundamental purpose of the privilege which is to free the patient from embarrassment. Such embarrassment could extend to family members after the patient's death. The privilege, however, does not apply to an autopsy because there cannot be a physician-patient relationship between a physician and a dead body.[13]

The beneficiary of a deceased person who seeks to recover under the terms of a life insurance policy is generally permitted to waive the privilege of the deceased.[14] The Supreme Court of Oregon permitted such a waiver of privilege on the ground that the beneficiary was the representative of the deceased person.[15] Other courts have taken the same approach.

1 Callaham v. Burton, *487 P.2d 515 (Mont. 1971);* Gailitis v. Bassett, *146 N.W.2d 708 (Mich. 1966);* Terier v. Dare, *146 App. Div. 375, 131 N.Y.S. 51 (1911);* Fedell v. Wierzbieniec, *127 Misc.2d 124, 485 N.Y.S.2d 460 (1985);* Lane v. Boicourt, *27 N.E. 1111 (Indiana 1981);* Orr v. Sievert, *292 S.E.2d 548 (Ga. App. 1982) (Waiver by "--- filing a complaint placing in issue the nature and quality of treatment ---");* Caesar v. Mountanos, *542 F.2d 1064 (Cir. 1976).*

2 Acosta v. Cary, *365 So.2d 4 (La. App. 1978).*

3 State ex rel. McNutt v. Keet, *432 S.W.2d 597 (Mo. 1968);* Hill v. Huddleston, *263 F. Supp.2d 108 (Md. 1967);* Mathis v. Hilderbrand, *416 P.2d 8 (Alas. 1966).*

4 Arker v. Brodnitz, *413 N.Y.S. 2d 582 (1979) (Even though a complaint was*

filed, the third party physician could only be interviewed by the defendants within the formal discovery procedures unless the plaintiff consented otherwise.); Eberle v. Savon Food Stores, Inc., *186 N.W.2d 837 (Mich. 1971);* State ex rel. Lambdin v. Brenton, *254 N.E.2d 681 (Ohio 1970);* Nielson v. Bryson, *477 P.2d 714 (Ore. 1970);* Phipps v. Sasser, *445 P.2d 624 (Wash. 1968);* Boyd v. Wrisley, *228 F. Supp. 9 (Mich. 1964).*

5 Mauro v. Tracy, *380 P.2d 570 (Colo. 1963);* Moutzoukos v. Mutual Benefit Health and Accident Assn., *69 Utah 309, 254 P. 1005 (1927);* Blish v. Greer, *74 Ind. App. 469, 120 N.E. 606 (1918);* Roeser v. Pease, *37 Okla. 222, 131 P. 534 (1913);* Epstein v. Pennsylvania R. Co., *250 Mo. 1, 156 S.W. 699 (1913).* See also, In Re Roberto, *151 N.E.2d 37 (Ohio 1958).*

6 Fields v. State of Georgia, *144 S.E.2d 339 (1965);* Whitmore v. Herrick, *205 Iowa 621, 218 N.W. 334 (1928);* Albers v. Wilson, *201 App. Div. 775, 195 N.Y.S. 145 (1922);* Epstein v. Pennsylvania R. Co., *250 Mo. 1, 156 S.W. 699 (1913).*

7 Orlich v. Buxton, *177 N.W.2d 184 (Mich. 1970);* Hill v. Stewart, *209 So.2d 809 (Miss. 1968).* See also Stauffer v. Karabin, *492 P.2d 862 (Colo. 1971);* Chaffee v. Kaufman, *113 Kan 254, 214 P. 618 (1923);* State v. Long, *257 Mo 199, 165 S.W. 748 (1914);* Steinberg v. New York Life Ins. Co., *263 NY 45, 188 N.E. 152 (1933);* Dahlquist v. Denver & R.G.R. Co., *52 Utah 438, 174 P 833 (1918);* Re Quick's Estate, *161 Wash 537, 297 P 198 (1931).*

8 Barnard v. Cedar Rapids City Cab Co., *133 N.W.2d 884 (Iowa 1965).*

9 Aetna Life Ins. Co. v. Gordy, *248 F.2d 129 (Arkansas 1957);* De Groff v. Clark *358 Mich. 274, 100 N.W.2d 214 (1960);* La Count v. Von Platen-Fox Co., *243 Mich. 250, 220 N.W. 697;* Mulvena v. Alexander, *278 Mich. 265, 270 N.W. 291 (1936).*

10 Massachusetts Mutual Life Ins. Co. v. Brei, *311 F.2d 463 (1962);* Aetna life v. McAoloo, *106 F.2d 618, 621 (CA 8, 1939).*

11 Application of Hofberg, *269 N.Y.S.2d 919 (1966).* See also Dick v. John Hancock Mutual Life Insurance Company, *434 F.2d 808 (1970).*

12 Lembke v. Unke, *171 N.W.2d 837 (N.D. 1969);* Grant v. Norwood, *161 So.2d 189 (Miss. 1964).*

13 Carmody v. Capital Traction, *43 App. DC 245, 249 (1915).*

14 State ex rel. Calley v. Olsen, *532 P.2d 230 (Oregon 1975).*

15 Id.

16 Maryland Casualty v. Maloney, *178 S.W. 387 (Arkansas 1915);* Penn Mutual v. Wiler, *100 Ind. 92 (1894);* Johnson v. Fidelity & Casualty, *151 N.W. 593 (Michigan 1915);* Olson v. Court of Honor, *110 N.W. 374 (Minnesota 1907);* U.S. National Life v. Heard, *298 P. 619 (Oklahoma 1931).*

4.8 The Medical Report to Lawyer

The medical report that a physician makes to a lawyer about the condition, and prognosis of a patient-client in a personal injury lawsuit is extremely important to all concerned. The same is true of any litigation involving the health and well being of any other party in such a case. The lawyer uses the medical report as the basis for planning the conduct of the case and as the starting point in the research needed to prepare for trial. The medical report, moreover, assumes great weight during settlement negotiations and can be the most important factor in determining whether a fair and just settlement is reached.

The medical report is also the initial and perhaps final step the physician takes to assist the patient in obtaining any compensation due, or to convey findings and conclusions to the attorneys. The report can also be used by the physician before giving trial testimony and as a reference, when the doctor is on the witness stand. In addition, the report serves to notify the opposing party, including its medical witnesses, of the physician's professional views on the matters in dispute.

A Patient's Right to Privacy

5.0

There has been a trend among the courts in recent years to provide a tort remedy for the violation of an individual's right of privacy. The individual has a right to be "left alone" and to be free of unwarranted and unwanted publicity with possible attendant shame, mortification, and humiliation.[1]

A patient has the same right of privacy as any other individual. Information about a person's condition must be kept secret and must not become the subject of publicity.[2] When a patient disrobes for an examination or any other medical procedure, for example, the person does so for the professional benefit of the physician. He or she does not expect to be subjected to examination by anyone else, medical or nonmedical, who is not a part of the medical procedure. The presence of nonessential persons, without the patient's specific consent, is a violation of the his or her right of privacy.[3]

When considering violations of an individual's privacy, courts often focus on the nature and content of the disclosure involved. In one case,[4] a court held that the physician's disclosure of certain medical facts about an employee was not an invasion of privacy since the information was already present in the individual's employment record.

In another instance,[5] however, the court determined that there was a cause of action because the physician had told a newspaper reporter about a patient's illicit drug use and had also disclosed the fact that the individual was a patient of the Narcotics Treatment Administration.

There are other cases in which no right of privacy exists. These have included an instance in which an employee claimed compensation for a work-related injury[6] and another in which a physician revealed information about a patient's mental condition.[7] There was also a case in which the physical condition of the patient was an issue and information was disclosed,[8] and another case in which the physician released the identity of an adoptee's natural mother.[9]

The unauthorized taking of a patient's picture, even though the photograph is not published, can give rise to a cause of action.[10] The unauthorized use of a patient's picture is, in fact, one of the most frequent violations of the right to privacy.[11]

The patient who submits to a medical procedure does not consent to the taking of pictures for future publication. It is immaterial that the patient's condition is made public because it is newsworthy,[12] or that unessential persons are allowed to observe the patient, or that the photographs are taken and published to advance medical science[13] or educate the public.

Only if a patient consents to publicity, may pictures may be taken and published. To facilitate proof, such consent should be in writing, and it should specify what the patient consents to regarding observers, pictures, etc. Any limitations on the consent must be strictly observed.[14]

In sum, a patient can expect his or her right of privacy to be respected by the physician. The indiviudal can also expect to receive decent and considerate treatment at all times from his or her doctor.[15]

---

1 Commonwealth v. Wiseman, *249 N.E.2d 610 (Mass. 1969).*

2 *The publication of a news story about the patient's unique ailment which story included the patient's name and picture, was held, in* Barber v. Time, Inc., *348 Mo. 1199, 159 S.W.2d 291 (1942), to be a violation of the patient's right of privacy.* See also Bazemore v. Savannah Hospital, *171 Ga. 257, 155 S.E. 194 (1930).*

3 *In* DeMay v. Roberts, *46 Mich. 160, (1881), the physician took a young, unmarried man, who was not a doctor, to the plaintiff's confinement. This was held to be actionable. The defendant, in* Carr v. Shifflette, *82 F.2d 874 (D.C. Cir. 1936), had a layman perform a catheterization on the plaintiff. The case was tried on the theory that there was negligence in the doing of the catheterization. Judgment was for the defendant but it was suggested, in both the court's opinion and a concurring opinion that the plaintiff could have had a cause of action for the exposure of her body to one who was not a doctor.* See also Savage v. Boies, *77 Ariz. 355, 272 P.2d 349 (1954).*

4 Valencia v. Duval Corp., *132 Ariz. 348, 645 P.2d 1262 (1982).*

5 Logan v. District of Columbia, *447 F. Supp. 1328 (D.C. Dist. Court 1978).*

6 Acosta v. Cary, *365 So.2d 4 (La. App. 1978).*

7 Schwartz v. Thiele, *51 Cal. Rptr. 767 (Cal. 2nd District 1966);* Werner v. Kliewer, *238 Kan. 289, 710 P.2d 1250 (1985);* Bratt v. International Business Machines Corp., *785 F.2d 352 (Massachusetts 1986).*

8 Glenn v. Kerlin, *248 So.2d 834 (La. App. 1971).*

9 Humphers v. First Interstate Bank, *298 Or 706, 696 P.2d 527 (1985).*

10 Clayman v. Bernstein, *38 Pa. D. & C. 543, 548 (1940). The court said: 'While the court appreciates the development of the art of photography generally, and in the medical profession particularly, not only as a means of diagnosis and treatment, but also as means of instruction, its progress has not yet reached a stage at which physicians have been accorded the right to photograph their patients without their consent, nor has medical jurisprudence recognized the unlimited right of a physician to perform any test, administer any treatment, or perform any operation without the authority of the patient."* See also Vassitiades v. Garfinckel's, Brooks Bros., *492 A.2d 580 (D.C. App. 1985);* Feeney v. Young, *181 N.Y.S. 481 (1920).*

11 Barber v. Time, Inc., *348 Mo. 1199, 159 S.W.2d 291 (1942);* Burks v. King Features Syndicate, *30 F. Supp. 352 (S.D.N.Y. 1939);* Griffin v. Medical Society of State of New York, *11 N.Y.S.2d 109 (1939);* Bazemore v. Savannah Hospital, *171 Ga. 257, 155 S.E. 194 (1930).*

12 Barber v. Time, Inc., *348 Mo. 1199, 159 S.W.2d 291 (1942);* Bazemore v. Savannah Hospital, *155 S.E. 194 (1930).*

13 Clayman v. Bernestein, *38 Pa. D. & C. 543 (1940);* Griffin v. Medical Society of the State of New York, *111 N.Y.S.2d 109 (1939);* Doe v. Roe, *400 N.Y.S.2d 668 (1977).*

14 Griffin v. Medical Society of the State of New York, *111 N.Y.S.2d 109 (1939);* Doe v. Roe, *400 N.Y.S.2d 668 (1977);* Feeney v. Young, *191 App. Div. 501, 181 N.Y. Supp. 481 (1920). The plaintiff had consented to the taking of motion pictures of a Caesarean section performed on her which were to be exhibited for scientific purposes only. Publicly showing these pictures, as part of a film called "Birth," was held actionable.*

15 Estate of Bethraume v. Pratt, *395 N.Y.S.2d 343 (1977) (Patient manifested by motions non-consent to taking of pictures.). In* Stone v. Eisen, *114 N.E.2d 44, 45 (N.Y. 1916), the court said: "Decent and respectful treatment is implied in the contract from the confidential relation of the parties and especially because of the necessary exposure of the person required of the patient in connection with the services to be performed pursuant to the contract. The implication arises whenever one person is placed in the control or protection of another."* See also Inderbitzen v. Lane Hospital, *124 Cal. App. 462, 12 P.2d 744 (1932), where the pregnant patient was subjected to some thirty or forty examinations by medical students to the accompaniment of levity and discourtesy.*

Authority to Admit Observers

Form 17

Patient________________ Place________________ Date____________

I authorize Dr.________________ and the______________________

________________ Hospital to permit the presence of such observers as they may deem fit to admit in addition to physicians and hospital personnel, while I am undergoing (operative surgery) (childbirth), examination, and treatment.

Signed________________

Witness________________

Consent to Taking and Publication of Photographs

Form 18

Patient________________________ Place________________ Date______

In connection with the medical services which I am receiving from my physician, Dr.________________, I consent that photographs may be taken of me or parts of my body, under the following conditions:

1. The photographs may be taken only with the consent of my physician and under such conditions and at such times as may be approved by him.
2. The photographs shall by taken by my physician or by a photographer approved by my physician.
3. The photographs shall be used for medical records and if in the judgment of my physician, medical research, education or science will be benefited by their use, such photographs and information relating to my case may be published and republished, either separately or in connection with each other, in professional journals or medical books, or used for any other purpose which he may deem proper in the interest of medical education, knowledge, or research; provided, however, that it is specifically understood that in any such publication or use I shall not be identifed by name.
4. The aforementioned photographs may be modified or retouched in any way that my physician, in his discretion, may consider desirable.

Signed________________
(Patient)

Witness ________________

Consent to Televising of Operation

Form 19

Patient ____________________ Place__________________ Date______

In the interest of medical education and knowledge, I consent to te televising of the operation which is scheduled to be performed upon me on or about________________, 19____. I authorize Dr.________________ and the ________________ Hospital to admit to the operating room, the cameraman and technicians who are to participate in the televising of this operation, in addition to the usual hosptial staff.

Signed________________

Witness ________________

Consent to Taking Motion Pictures of Operation

Form 20

Patient ______________________ Place________________ Date______

1. I consent to the taking of motion pictures of the operation which is scheduled to be performed upon me on or about ______________, 19____. I authorize Dr.________________ and the ________________ Hospital to admit to the operating room the cameraman and technicians who will participate in the filming of this operation.

2. I waive all rights that I may have to any claims for payment or royalties in connection with any exhibition, televising, or other showing of this motion picture film, regardless of whether such exhibition, televising, or other showing is under philanthropic, commercial, institutional, or private sponsorship, and irrespective of whether a fee of admission or film rental is charged.

3. I grant this consent as a voluntary contribution in the interest of medical education and knowledge and subject only to the condition that I will not be identified by name in this motion picture film.

Signed________________

Witness ________________

Unauthorized Treatment

6.0

A physician who treats a patient without the consent of the patient or someone legally authorized to speak for the individual engages in assault and battery. The doctor may be prosecuted civilly or criminally[1] even though the treatment or procedure is performed without any negligence.[2]

In one such case,[3] a first-year resident acted as the primary surgeon in a knee operation at a teaching hospital under the supervision of the patient's orthopaedic surgeon. The court held that there was no need to obtain a consent to operate because the patient had signed a consent form. In this case, however, the patient had withdrawn her battery and breach of contract counts, and the court therefore ruled that there was no basis for her claim of lack of "informed consent."

If a resident or attending physician substitutes a qualified physician in a particular instance, there is not necessarily a basis for a claim of battery if the patient did not object to the substitution and agreed to "the intended procedure".[4] An assault is [t]he apprehension of harmful or offensive contact with the person. . .[5] A physician can be subject to a charge of battery if a patient did not understand substantially the nature of a surgery and its probable results.[6]

Assault can occur without physical contact, while battery is the actual, unsolicited physical touching of a person or something closely associated with the person.[7] Pain and suffering are an element of damages for assault and battery, and some pain may be presumed to occur in any operation and recovery.[8] If the person upon whom the unauthorized procedure is performed cannot prove any actual harm, however, only nominal damages will customarily be recovered, but punitive damages may be assessed in certain circumstances.[9]

In *Perna v. Pirozzi*,[10] the Court discusses battery principles. A patient must prove initially that the physician deviated from a professional standard of care. Under a battery theory, the plaintiff is entitled to nominal damages by proving that there has been an unauthorized invasion of his or her person, even if it was harmless. In that case, the procedure was performed by a different doctor than the one who obtained the consent. The Court stated '[t]he point is that a patient has the right to know who will operate.[11] The Current Opinions of the Council on Ethical and Judicial Affairs of the American Medical Association set forth a similar requirement:

> 8.16 **Substitution of Surgeon Without Patient's Knowledge or Consent.** To have another physician operate on one's patient without the patient's knowledge and consent is a deceit. The patient is entitled to choose his own physician and he should be permitted to acquiesce in or refuse to accept the substitution...

It should be noted that it is the operating surgeon to whom a patient grants consent to perform an operation. A patient is entitled to the services of the particular surgeon with whom he or she contracts. A surgeon, in accepting a patient, is obligated to utilize his or her personal talents in performing the procedure to the extent required by the agreement creating the physician-patient relationship. The physician cannot properly delegate to another person the duties he or she is required to perform personally.

Under the customary arrangement with private patients, and consistent with the usual form of consent to operate, the surgeon is obligated to perform the operation. The physician may, however, use the services of assisting residents or other assisting surgeons if the operation reasonably requires such assistance. If another physician is to perform the operation under the guidance of the surgeon, full disclosure of this fact must be made to the patient. This disclosure should be evidenced by an appropriate statement in the consent.

If a surgeon merely assists a resident or other physician in performing an operation, the resident or other physician is considered to be the operating surgeon. If the patient is not informed of the identity of the operating surgeon, the situation is described as "ghost surgery." The physician is not employed merely to supervise the operation; he or she is retained to perform the procedure. The physician can properly utilize the services of an assistant but the doctor is not performing the operation if his or her participation consists merely of guidance, or standby responsibility in the case of an emergency.[12]

1 Perna v. Pirozzi, *442 A.2d 1016 (N.J. Super. 1982);* Gaston v. Hunter *588 P.2d 326, (1983);* Guebard v. Jabaay *452 N.E. 2d 751, 755, 756 (1983).*

2 Buie v. Reynolds, *571 P.2d 1230 (Okla. 1977);* Moos v. United States, *118 F.*

Supp. 275 (D.C. Minn. 1954); Church v. Adler, *350 Ill. App. 471, 113 N.E.2d 327 (1953);* Nolan v. Kechijian, *75 R.I. 165, 64 A.2d 866 (1949);* Physicians' & Dentists' Business Bureau v. Dray, *8 Wash.2d 38, 111 P.2d 568 (1941);* Dicenzo v. Berg, *240 Pa. 305, 16 A.2d 15 (1940);* Rogers v. Sells, *178 Okla. 103, 61 P.2d 1018 (1936);* Mully v. Hop Sang, *1 W.W.R. 714 (1935);* Jackovach v. Yocom, *212 Iowa 914, 237 N.W. 444 (1931);* Franklin v. Peabody, *240 Mich. 363, 228 N.W. 681 (1930);* Hively v. Higgs, *120 Ore. 588, 253 Pac. 363 (1927);* Hershey v. Peake, *115 Kan. 562, 223 Pac. 1113 (1924);* Throne v. Wandell, *176 Wis. 97, 186 N.W. 146 (1922);* Schloendorff v. Society of New York Hospital, *211 N.Y. 125, 105 N.E. 92 (1914);* Mohr v. Williams, *95 Minn. 261, 104 N.W. 12 (1905). See also Comment 4, U.C.L.A. L. Rev. 627 (1957).*

3 Guebard v. Jabaay, *452 N.E. 2d 751, 755, 756, (1983).*

4 Forlana v. Hughes, *471 N.E. 2d 1315 (Mass. 1984).*

5 *W. Prosser, Law of Torts, §10, p. 37 (4th ed. 1971).*

6 Riedisser v. Nelson *534 p.2d 1052 (1975).*

7 Id. *§9, at 34-37.*

8 Schmeltz v. Tracy, *119 Conn. 492, 177 A. 520 (1935). The physician removed moles from the patient's face without her consent. Scars developed where the moles had been removed. The jury found that the scars were the result of intervening acts of the patient, rather than a direct result of the unauthorized operation. The court said, "proof of the assault entitles the plaintiff to a verdict for at least nominal damages." See also* Ebaugh v. Rabkin, *99 Cal. Rptr. 706 (1972).*

9 *Prosser at §9, at 35. (4th ed. 1971). Franklin v. Peabody*, 249 Mich. 363, 228 N.W. 681 (1930); Perry v. Hodgson, *168 Ga. 678, 148 S.E. 659 (1929);* Hershey v. Peake, *115 Kan. 562, 233 Pac. 1113 (1924);* Zotorell v. Repp, *187 Mich. 319, 153 N.W. 692 (1915);* Mohr v. Williams, *95 Minn. 261, 104 N.W. 12 (1905). See also* Dow v. Kaiser Foundation, *190 Cal. Rptr. 747 (App. 1970).*

10 *457 A.2d 431, 438 (N.J. 1983).*

11 Id. *at 440.*

12 *Current Opinions of the Council on Ethical and Judicial Affairs of the American Medical Association, (1989) see also American Hospital Association Patients Bill of Rights.*

Consent to Treatment

7.0

A physician who administers treatment or performs an operation without a patient's express or implied consent may incur liability for damages. This general rule includes an operation that is different than the one for which consent was given.[1]

The patient decides whether to undergo the procedure or treatment the doctor recommends. Expressed or implied consent must, therefore, be given before the physician may proceed.[2] A competent adult patient who has been informed of the treatment proposed and who knows that it can be refused or accepted, gives implied consent to the treatment if he or she then cooperates with the physician.[3]

This implied consent is the type of consent usually obtained in routine office practice.[4]

Implied consent to an operation always involves the possibility of a misunderstanding about the purpose and scope of the undertaking. If a controversy does arise, proof is sometimes difficult to obtain.[5] Implied consent often occurs in emergency medical situations. If a person is, for example, injured or unconscious, and if his injuries require prompt attention, a physician is justified in undertaking treatment to preserve the patient's life or limb without express consent.[6]

Oral consent to a procedure is usually supplemented by implied consent. This would occur, if for example a patient orally consented to a procedure and then cooperated with the physician in its performance. Like implied consent, oral consent is open to misunderstanding and may be difficult to prove.

Written consent to treatment is not required by law, and no particular form is necessary to give a valid consent.[7] If a form is used, however, it should state the nature of the treatment or procedure authorized, and it should be signed by the person legally qualified to give consent. A surgical authorization, for example, should state who is responsible for administering the anesthetic[8] and the postoperative care[9] if these services are to be provided by a physician other than the operating surgeon. The place and date of the document's execution and the signature of a witness[10] should be included to facilitate proof.

The more vague and indefinite the terms of a consent are, the more specifically the agreement will usually be construed by a Court.[11] Even if the plaintiff read the form and understood its contents, that act is not considered blanket authority to proceed with treatment other than that which the patient anticipated.[12]

General or "blanket" consent forms purportedly giving a physician unlimited authority and discretion, without specifying the particular treatment or procedure contemplated, are not recommended.[13] The use of such blanket consent forms has given rise to medical liability claims for the performance of operations different from those orally contemplated. Some courts have construed blanket consent forms to permit only those procedures for which oral consent existed.[14] Others have held that a signed consent form constitutes only limited evidence of valid consent.

A question often arises as to whether a general consent form signed on admission to a hospital will cover all subsequent treatments and procedures. This reliance is not recommended. The general form will allow hospital personnel to provide routine treatment to a patient, but for additional procedures or treatments, a more specific form should be used. This recommendation applies to surgical procedures that involve anesthesia. The administration of anesthesia should be mentioned in the surgical consent form, but a separate form for the anesthesiologist would also be appropriate.

Some states have enacted laws that provide the terms under which a written consent will be presumed valid. Georgia law, for example, states that: "[A] consent to surgical or medical treatment which discloses in general terms the treatment or course of treatment in connection with which it is given and which is duly evidenced in writing and signed by the patient or other person or persons authorized to consent. . . shall be conclusively presumed to be a valid consent in the absence of fraudulent misrepresentations of material facts in obtaining the same."[15]

Furthermore, some states have recently enacted laws that establish additional consent requirements for mastectomies. The Minnesota Statute, for example, states that "every patient or resident suffering from any form of breast cancer shall be fully informed, prior to or at the time of admission and during her stay, of all alternative effective methods of treatment. . .and the risks associated with each of those methods."[16] These type of laws are intended to prevent "one-step" procedures, that is, after ordering a biopsy and discovering a malignancy, performing a mastectomy.[17]

---

1 Cross v. Trapp, *294 S.E.2d 446 (W.Va. 1982),* Adams v. EL-Bash, *338 S.E.2d 381 (W.Va. 1985),* Largey v. Rothman, *540 A.2d 504 (N.J. 1988).*

2 Perna v. Pirozzi. *442 A.2d 1016 (1982);* See *61 AMJUR. 2d Physicians, Surgeons, etc. §158 (1972), leading case absent valid written consent "Risk Case".*

3 See, i.e., LaCaze v. Collier, *434 So. 2d 1039 (La. 1983). Also see* Hundroulis v. Schumacher *531 S. 2d 450 (La. 1988);* Leonard v. New Orleans East Orthoclinic *485 So.2d 1008 (La App. 4 Cir. 1986)* Precourt *v.* Fredenck *481 N.W. 2d 1144 (Mass. 1985)* **Seals v. Pittman *499 S.2d 114 (La. App. Cir. 1986).*

4 Seals v. Pittman, *499 So.2d. 114 (La. App. I Cir. 1986).*

5 Haywood v. Allen, *406 S.W.2d 721 (Ky. 1966).*

6 Mohr. v. Williams, *95 Minn. 261, 104 N.W. 12 (1905).*

7 *But see footnotes 10 and 11 for presumptions of validity involving consent and footnotes Chapter 5 for informed consent.*

8 *A surgeon usually is not responsible for the negligence of an anesthetist who is not preforming those duties under the surgeons direction.* Woodson v. Huey, *216 P.2d 199 (Okla. 1953);* Wiley v. Wharton, *41 N.W.2d 255 (Ohio 1941).* See generally, *Surgeons and Anesthesiologists, Vicarious Liability and the Continued Trend Toward Specialization and Decentralization in the Operating Room, 9 Ohio Northern Univ. Law. Rev. 437 (1982). Also see, 90. A.L.R. 3d 788, Malpractice in connection with Anesthetist.*

9 See Saunders v. Lischkoff, *188 So. 815 (Fla. 1939);* Gross v. Partlow, *68 P.2d 1034 (Wash. 1937);* Reed v. Laughlin, *58 S.W. 2d 440 (Mo. 1933);* Hopkins v. Heller, *210 P.975 (Cal. App. 1922).* Bateman v. Rosenberg, *525 S.W. 2d 753, 756 (Mo. 1975).*

10 *In* Wheeler v. Barker, *298 P.2d 68 (Cal. 1949) and* Stone v. Goodman, *271 N.Y.S. 500 (1943), the plaintiff alleged that he signed the consent form while under sedation and that the consent was, therefore, invalid. A witness to the signing testified to the contrary.*

11 *The Court in* Valdez v. Percy, *96 P. 2d 142 (Cal. App. 1939), said with respect to a broad, general consent: "However, we do not understand such agreement to constitute a consent to perform operations other than the one for which the operating surgeons were engaged by plaintiff to perform unless necessity therefore arose during the authorized operation as hereinbefore mentioned."* See also Moore v. Webb, *345 S.W.2d 239 (Mo. 1961).*

12 Moore v. Webb, *345 S.W.2d at 243 (Mo. 1961).*

13 Rogers v. Lumbermens Mutual Casualty Co., *119 So.2d 649 (La. 1960). In this case the patient signed a vague consent form. The court stated: "We think this so-called authorization is so ambiguous as to be almost completely worthless, and, certainly, since it fails to designate the nature of the operation authorized, and for which consent was given, it can have no weight under the factual circumstances of the instant case---" Also* see Karl J. Pizzalotto, M.D., Ltd. v. Wilson, *437 So.2d 859, 865; (La. 1983).*

14 Pizzalotto v. Wilson, *437 So.2d at 865 (1983).*

15 *Ga. Code Ann. §31-9-6 (1981)* See also *Louisiana Revised Statutes §40:1299.40. A signed consent form that meets the statutory requirements for disclosure" ---shall be presumed to be valid and effective, in the absence of proof that execution of the consent was induced by misrepresentation of material facts."* See also, *Florida Medical consent law, Fla. Stat. Ann. §766.103 (4)(a) (1978 Supp). A consent which is evidenced in writing and meets the requirement---shall, if validly signed by the patient or another authorized person, raise a rebuttable presumption of a valid consent.* Also see, *Iowa code Annot. §147.137 (1979-80 Curr. Supp.)*

16 *Minn. Rev. Stats. §144.651 (Subd. 9.)*

17 *Cal. Health & Safety Code §1704.5 (Supp. 1984) requires the physician to inform the patient, through a standardized written summary, of alternative efficacious methods of medically viable treatment. Failure to do so constitutes unprofessional conduct. Cal. Bus. & Prof. Code §2257 (Supp. 1984). Massachusetts law requires that every patient or resident of a facility shall have complete information in non-medical language on all alternative treatment and possible adverse consequences. Hawaii enacted legislation to establish standards for physicians to follow in giving information to patients. Hawaii Rev. Stats. §671-3. Louisiana has adopted a resolution to urge and request all physicians to advise their patients, orally and in writing, of the alternatives to a radical mastectomy prior to performing this procedure. H. Concurrent Resol. 125.*

Consent to Operation, Anesthetics, and Other Medical Services

Form 21

A.M.
Date_______________ Time________P.M.

1. I authorize the performance upon ______________________
(*myself or name of patient*)

of the following operation ________________________________
(*state nature and extent of operation*)

to be performed by or under the direction of Dr.________________.

2. I consent to the performance of operations and procedures in addition to or different from those now contemplated, whether or not arising from presently unforeseen conditions, which the above-named doctor or his associates or assistants may consider necessary or advisable in the course of the operation.

3. I consent to the administration of such anesthetics as may be considered necessary or advisable by the physician responsible

for this service, with the exception of ______________________
(*state "none," "spinal anesthesia," etc.*)

4. The nature and purpose of the operation, possible alternative methods of treatment, the risks involved, the possible consequences, and the possibility of complications have been explained to me by Dr.________________ and by ________________.

5. I acknowledge that no guarantee or assurance has been given by anyone as to the results that may be obtained.

6. I consent to the photogaphing or televising of the operations or procedures to be performed, including appropriate portions of my body, for medical, scientific or educational purposes, provided my identity is not revealed by the pictures or by descriptive texts accompanying them.

7. For the purpose of advancing medical education, I consent to the admittance of observers to the operating room.

8. I consent to the disposal by hospital authorities of any tissues or body parts which may be removed.

9. I am aware that sterility may rsult from this operation. I know that a sterile person is incapable of becoming a parent.

10. I acknowledge that all blank spaces on this document have been either completed or crossed off prior to my signing.

(Cross Out Any Paragraphs Above Which Do Not Apply)

Witness________________ Signed________________
(*Patient or person authorized to consent for patient*)

Consent to Operation, Anesthetics, and Other Medical Services (Alternate Form)

Form 22

A.M.
Date_______________ Time_________P.M.

1. I authorize the performance upon___________________________
(myself or name of patient)

of the following operation__________________________________
(state name of operation)

to be performed by or under the direction of Dr.______________.

2. The following have been explained to me by Dr.___________:

A. the nature of the operation__________________________
(describe the operation)

____

____

B. The purpose of the operation_________________________
(describe the purpose)

____

C. The possible alternative methods of treatment__________

____
(describe the alternative methods)

D. The possible consequences of the operation____________

____
(describe the possible consequences)

E. The risks involved_______________________________

____
(describe the risks involved)

F. The possibility of complications______________________

____
(describe the possible complications)

3. I have been advised of the serious nature of the operation and have been advised that if I desire a further and more detailed explanation of any of the foregoing or further information about the possible risks or complications of the above listed operation it will be given to me.

4. I do not request a further and more detailed listing and explanation of any of the items listed in paragraph 2.

Witness________________ Signed_______________________
(Patient or person authorized to consent for patient)

Consent to Operation, Anesthetics, and Other Medical Services at Teaching Institution

Form 23

A.M.
Date________________ Time__________P.M.

1. I authorize the performance upon ______________________________
(myself or name of patient)

of the following operation ______________________________________
(state name operation)

2. I understand that the operation is to be performed at________________, a teaching institute.

3. I understand that the operation, the medical services rendered in conjunction with the operation, and the post-operative care are to be performed and rendered by those individuals selected and deemed qualified by the teaching staff of the ______________________________
(name of the institution)

Witness________________ Signed ________________________
(Patient or person authorized to consent for patient)

8.1 Informed Consent—The Doctrine

To be legally valid, the consent given for a treatment or procedure must be an informed consent given with an understanding of what is to be done and the risks involved. No universal, informed consent form exists since informed consent is a process, while the form serves merely to document the process.

Lawsuits that allege a lack of informed consent are based on the concept of negligence.[1] This concept stems from two principles of law. The first is the fiduciary relationship between the physician and the patient. The second principle is the concept that people have a right to make major decisions about their bodies. The often-cited statement of principle is derived from Judge Cordozo's opinion in *Schloendorff v. Society of New York Hospitals*: 'Every human being of adult years and sound mind has a right to determine what shall be done with his own body . . ."[21]

Informed consent may be defined as the physician's responsibility to give the patient the right kind and amount of information so that the patient can decide whether to undergo the proposed treatment or procedure. The kind and amount of information that must be given was originally defined by the courts, but most states have subsequently enacted legislation that attempts to define the facts that must be disclosed.[3] Because of the almost limitless number of diseases, procedures, treatments and patients, no definitive listing of elements of disclosure is possible. Several common elements can, however, be found in the laws and opinions.

1 Hodge v. Lafayette General Hospital, *399 So.2d 744 (La. 1981);* LaCaze v. Collier, *434 So.2d 1039 (La. 1983).* See generally, *Miller, L.S., Informed Consent, 244:18 Journal of the American Medical Association, 2100 et seq. (Nov. 7, 1980);* Leonard v. New Orleans Orthopedic Clinic, *485 So.2d 1018 (1986);* Hondrouus v. Schumacher, *531 So.2d 450 (1988);* Seals v. Pittman, *499 So.2d 114 (1986);* Stafford v. LSU, *448 So.2d 852 (1984);* Jones v. Levy, *520 So.2d 457 (1988).*

2 *105 N.E.2d 92, 93 (N.Y. 1914);* Keogan v. Holy Family Hospital, *622 P.2d 1246 (1980);* Harbeson v. Parke-Davis, Inc., *656 P.2d 483 (1983);* Alexander v. Gonser, *711 P.2d 347 (Wash. App. 1985);* Pratt v. U. of Minn. Affiliated Hospitals, *(Minn. 1987).*

3 See *Alaska Stat. §09.55.556; Del. Code Ann. tit. 18, §6852 (Supp.); Idaho Code §39-4304; Iowa Code Ann. §147.137 (1983 Supp.); Ky. Rev. Stat. §304.20-320 (Supp.); Ohio Rev. Code §2317.54 (Page); Me. Rev. Stat. tit. 24 §2905 (Supp.); N.Y.Pub. Health Law §2805-d (McKinney); Pa. Stat. Ann. tit. 40, §1301.103 (Purdon) (Insurance Code); Utah Stat. Ann. §78-14-5; Vt. Stat. Ann., tit. 12, §1909 (Supp.); Wash. Rev. Code Ann. §7.70.050 (Supp.);* See also *Nev. Rev. Stat. §41A.110 (consent).*

8.2 Disclosure of Information for Informed Consent

There are several kinds of information that need to be disclosed.[1]

(a) *The Diagnosis.* Because informed consent involves the patient's right to decide, the disclosure of diagnosis should be as candid as possible.

(b) *The Procedure or Treatment.* The procedure or treatment should describe what will happen and whether the procedure is diagnostic or therapeutic.[2]

(c) *Risks and Consequences.* The risks and consequences involved in the procedure or treatment should be listed. A risk, it should be noted, is something that *might* occur, while a consequence is something that is *expected* to occur. Although this area has spawned many actions related to informed consent, it would be impractical to require a physician to disclose all possible risks.[3]

In one case, for example,[4] a patient brought a malpractice action against a physician and a nurse who were treating her because of an injury that had resulted from anesthesia. The court ruled that the doctor could not be expected to explain all the possible risks to the patient, but only those that were serious. The court held that a test must be applied to determine if a person in the patient's position could reasonably have expected to be informed of the risks associated with general anesthesia and also of the possibility of alternative treatment.[5]

In a similar case,[6] the court held that a physician's failure to inform a patient before performing a biopsy to determine whether a growth on her vertebra was malignant and perhaps incurable, was not a misrepresentation that would vitiate the plaintiff's consent to the biopsy. The purpose of the biopsy, the court pointed out, was to rule out an incurable malignancy and clear the way for treatment of the woman's back pain. The court further stated that a reasonable patient would have consented to such a diagnostic biopsy despite the slight chance of irreparable neurological injury.[7]

Risks that are very improbable or not serious can usually be omitted from disclosure since they would not be material to a patient's decision whether to undergo the proposed treatment.[8]

In one such case,[9] a plaintiff entered a hospital for a diagnostic outpatient angiogram as prescribed by his physician. The patient signed a consent form and was taken for the angiogram but was not informed of any serious risks. The patient died from an anaphylactic reaction to the angiographic dye contrast material. The plaintiff contended that failure to administer epinephrine intraveneously constituted negligence.[10] The court held that the test for determining whether a particular peril must be divulged is its relevance to the patient's decision. All risks potentially affecting the decision must be disclosed.

No uniform statistics indicate what degree of risk is too remote.[11] One court has stated that whenever a procedure involves a known risk of death or serious bodily harm, the physician must disclose that information;[12] risks that are commonly known to the reasonable patient do not require disclosure.[13]

(d) *Outcome Probability.* The possibility of successful treatment or of failure, should be discussed with a patient. In agreeing to provide treatment or perform an operation, the doctor does not, in the absence of a special contract, guarantee particular results or a cure.[14] The physician warrants only that he or she possesses the degree of knowledge and skill ordinarily common to a member of the medical profession in good standing in the community and has the ability to use that knowledge and skill in treating the patient.[15] When a physician agrees to perform a procedure, the agreement includes an implied warranty that the doctor has the skill required to perform the procedure.[16]

A physician may expressly agree to achieve a particular result or effect a cure. If the doctor enters into such a contract, however, and fails to achieve the promised result or effect a cure, liability for breach of contract may occur even though the highest professional skill was employed.[17]

(e) *Feasible Treatment Alternative.* Feasible alternative treatments should always be discussed with the patient. In one instance,[18] a patient was advised to undergo a kidney biopsy, but the physician failed to discuss the alternative of an open biopsy. The court stated that it required that "... all viable alternatives be disclosed, even though some involve more hazards than others."[19]

(f) *No Treatment Outcome.* Finally, the physician should discuss what could happen if nothing is done. In one such case, the patient declined to have a pap test and subsequently developed cervical cancer.[20] The doctor was found liable for negligently failing to warn her of the risks of failing to have to the diagnostic procedure.

1 *Razovsky, F.A. Consent to Treatment: A Practical Guide. Little, Brown & Co. Boston. Toronto p. 41-50 Generally.*

2 Gates v. Jensen, *595 P.2d 919 (Wash. 1979).*

3 Smith v. Shannon, *666 P.2d 351 (Wash. 1983);* In Re Schouler, *723 P.2d 1103 (Wash. 1986);* Brown v. Dahl, *705 P.2d 781 (1985).*

4 Brown v. Dahl, *705 P.2d 781 (Wash. App. 1985).*

5 Id. *at 788.*

6 Leonard v. New Orleans East Orthopedic Clinic, *485 So.2d 1008 (1986).*

7 Id. *at 1013.*

8 See *Utah Code Ann. §78-14-5 (2)(a).*

9 Jones v. Griffith, *688 F. Supp. 446 (N.D. Ind. 1988).*

10 Jones v. Griffith, *688 F. Supp. 446 (N.D. Ind. 1988).*

11 See, e.g., Stottlemire v. Cawood, *213 F.Supp. 897 (D.D.C. 1963) (1/800,000 chance of aplastic anemia);* Yeates v. Harms, *393 P.2d 982 (1964) (1.5% chance loss of eye);* Starnes v. Taylor, *158 S.E.2d 339 (1968) (1/250 to 1/500 chance of perforation of the esophagus). Disclosure required:* Bowers v. Talmage, *159 So.2d 888 (Fla. App. 1963) (3% chance of death, paralysis, or other injury);* Scott v. Wilson, *396 S.W.2d 532 (Tex. Civ. App. 1965)* aff'd *412 S.W.2d 299 (Tex. 1966) (1% chance of hearing loss).*

12 Cobbs v. Grant, *104 Cal. Rptr. 505, 515 (1972).*

13 See generally, Jones v. Griffith, *688 F. Supp. 446, (1988);* Petty v. U.S., *740 F.2d 1428 (1984).*

14 Dazet v. Bass, *254 So.2d 183 (Miss. 1971);* Custodio v. Bauer, *59 Cal. Rptr. 463 (1967);* Bishop v. Byrne, *265 F. Supp. 450 (W. Va. 1967);* Lane v. Cohen, *201 So.2d 804 (Fla. 1967);* Bria v. St. Joseph's Hospital, *220 A.2d 29 (Conn. 1966);* Hawkins v. McCain, *79 S.E.2d 493 (S.C. 1954);* Waynick v. Reardon, *72 S.E.2d 4 (N.C. 1952);* Vann v. Harden, *47 S.E.2d 314 (Va. 1948);* Piper v. Halford, *25 So.2d 264 (Ala. 1946);* Fritz v. Horsfall, *163 P.2d 148 (Wash. 1945);* Wall v. Brim, *138 F.2d 478 (C.C.A. 5 1943);* Lake v. Baccus, *2. S.E.2d 121 (Ga. 1939);* Keating v. Perkins, *293 N.Y.S. 197 (1937).* See *N.Y. Pub. Health Law §2805-d(4)(a) (McKinney); Utah Code Ann. §78-15-4(2)(b); Vt. Stat. Ann. tit. 12, §1909(c)(1).*

15 Creighton v. Karlin, *225 So.2d 288 (La. 1969);* Benson v. Mays, *227 A.2d 220 (Md. 1967).*

16 Wolfe v. Virusky, *306 F. Supp. 519 (Ga. 1969).*

17 Guilmet v. Campbell, *188 N.W.2d 601 (Mich. 1971);* Brooks v. Robinson, *163 So.2d 186 (La. 1964);* Camposano v. Claiborn, *196 A.2d 129 (Conn. 1963);* Noel v. Proud, *367 P.2d 61 (Kan. 1961);* Robins v. Finestone, *127 N.E.2d 330 (N.Y. 1955);* Colvin v. Smith, *92 N.Y.S.2d 794 (1949);* Hawkins v. McGee, *146 A. 641 (N.H. 1929);* Brooks v. Herd, *257 238 (Wash. 1927).*

18 Logan v. Greenwhich Hospital Association, *465 A.2d 294 (Conn. 1983);* see also, Jones v. Griffith, *705 P.2d 701 (Wash. App. 1985).*

19 Id. *at 302.*

20 Truman v. Thomas, *611 P.2d 902 (Cal. 1980).*

Refusal to Submit to Treatment

Form 24

A.M.
Date________________ Time__________P.M.

I have been advised by Dr.________________ that it is necessary for me to undergo the following treatment:____________________

____

____
(Describe operation or treatment)

The effect and nature of this treatment have been explained to me.

Although my failure to follow the advice I have received may seriously imperil my life or health, I nevertheless refuse to submit to the recommended treatment. I assume the risks and consequences involved and release the above-named physician, the hospital and its staff from any liability.

Witness________________ Signed________________

8.3 Standards for Disclosure

In addition to certain kinds of information, the physician has a responsibility to give the patient the appropriate amount of information. Two jurisdictional approaches exist.

(a) The first is the traditional or the professional standard approach. Most courts have held that in a lawsuit based on lack of informed consent, the patient must establish by expert medical testimony that the physician failed to disclose a risk which the reasonable medical practitioner would have disclosed in similar circumstances.[1] Expert medical testimony is required because the necessary extent of disclosure is not common knowledge or within the experience of laymen.[2] Without such testimony a jury would be unable to decide whether or not a physician breached a duty owed to a patient.[3] A few courts have held that, while a patient must produce expert medical testimony if the adequacy of the disclosure is at issue, the patient need not produce any expert medical testimony if the patient claims that no disclosure of any kind was made.[4]

(b) *Minority Approach.* Some courts have departed from the general rule and adopted the reasonable patient "patient need" or "material risk" approach. Expert medical testimony is not necessary to establish the adequacy of the scope of disclosure made by the physician in these jurisdictions. These courts have stated that the medical profession is not permitted to determine its own responsibilities to the public.[5] The question is whether or not the physician disclosed sufficient information to enable the patient to intelligently decide whether to consent to the treatment or procedure.[6] The necessary scope of disclosure is to be determined by applying the standards of the reasonable layman, not the reasonable medical practitioner.[7]

In *Cooper v. Roberts,*[8] a woman was admitted to a hospital for a gastroscopic examination. Although she was not informed of any of the risks of the procedure, she signed a "blanket consent form." Shortly after the examination was performed, it was discovered that her stomach had been punctured. The woman claimed that the examination had been performed without her informed consent. The medical evidence indicated that the incidence of such a puncture was only 1 in 2500 or .0004%.

The trial judge instructed the jury that the physician's duty to disclose risks to the patient is not determined by what the members of the jury would disclose to the patient in similar circumstances. The required scope of disclosure is determined by what the reasonable medical practitioner would do.

Reversing the judgment in favor of the physicians, the Pennsylvania appellate court said that any medical expert would only testify as to what the expert would do in similar circumstances or what the expert thinks another physician should do. The court ruled that the necessary scope of disclosure consists of those facts, risks, and alternatives which a reasonable layman in a similar situation would deem significant in deciding whether or not to consent to a treatment or procedure.

If a proposed treatment or procedure is novel or unorthodox, the physician has an additional duty of disclosure. The physician must inform the patient that the treatment or procedure is novel or unorthodox and then must inform the patient of the possible risks.

In *Fiorentino v. Wenger*, a physician recommended a specific procedure to correct a minor's scoliotic condition. He did not inform the boy's parents that the procedure was not the generally accepted medical treatment in the community for scoliosis. He also failed to inform them that he was the only physician in this country utilizing the procedure and that untoward results had occurred in five of the thirty-five instances in which the procedure was performed. The procedure was performed and resulted in an exsanguinating hemorrhage during which the boy died.[9] Affirming judgment for the parents, a New York appellate court ruled that the physician had a duty to disclose the fact that the procedure was novel and unorthodox and that there were risks incident to, or possible in its use.[10]

---

1 *That the physician's duty of disclosure is determined by a professional standard is still the majority rule. Arizona, Arkansas, Colorado, Delaware, Florida, Illinois, Iowa, Kentucky, Michigan, Mississippi, Missouri, Montana, New Jersey, North Carolina, Tennessee, Texas, Virginia, and Wyoming and by federal courts in Idaho and North Dakota, and some appellate courts in Louisiana.*

2 Aiken v. Clary, *396 S.W.2d 668 (Mo. 1965).*

3 Visingardi v. Tirone, *178 So.2d 135 (Fla. 1965).*

4 Collins v. Meeker, *424 P.2d 488 (Kan. 1967);* Williams v. Menehan, *379 P.2d 292 (Kan. 1963);* Natanson v. Kline, *354 P.2d 670 (Kan. 1960). See also* Woods v. Burmlop, *377 P.2d 520 (N.M. 1962).*

5 Getchell v. Mansfield, *489 P.2d 953 (Ore. 1971);* Berkey v. Anderson, *82 Cal. Rptr. 67 (1969);* Brown v. Dahl, *705 P.2d 781 (1985);* In Re Schouler, *723 P.2d 1103 (Wash. 1986).*

6 *At present the material risk approach has been adopted by courts in California, the District of Columbia, Louisiana, Maryland, Massachusetts, Minnesota, New York, Ohio, Oklahoma, Oregon, Pennsylvania, Rhode Island, Vermont, Washington, and Wisconsin, although in two such states, New York and Vermont, the professional standard approach has been reimposed by statute. By statute in Utah. Utah Code Ann. §78-14-5.*

7 Hunter v. Brown, *484 P.2d 1162 (Wash. 1971). See also* Mason v. Ellsworth, *474 P.2d 909 (Wash. 1970);* Jones v. Griffith, *688 F. Supp. 446 (N.D. Ind. 1988).*

8 *286 A.2d 647 (Pa. 1971).*

9 Fiorentino v. Wenger, *19 N.Y.2d 407, 227 N.E.2d 296, 280 N.Y.S.2d 373 (1967).*

10 *See also* Natanson v. Kline, *350 P.2d 1093 (Kan. 1960);* Hunter v. Burroughs, *96 S.E. 360 (Va. 1918);* See also, Karp v. Cooley, *493 F.2d 408 (1974);* Lambert v. Park, M.D., *597 F.2d 236 (1979).*

8.4 Exceptions to Informed Consent

(a) *Therapeutic Privilege.* There are exceptions to the requirement of informed consent. The doctrine of therapeutic privilege allows the physician to withhold information from the patient in some situations. A court discussed this concept in *Cantebury v. Spence:*[1]

> . . . when the risk-disclosure poses such a threat of detriment to the patient as to become unfeasible or contraindicated from a medical point of view. It is recognized that patients occasionally become so ill or emotionally distraught on disclosure as to foreclose a rational decision, or complicate or hinder the treatment, or perhaps even pose psychological damage to the patient. Where that is so, the cases have generally held that the physician is armed with a privilege to keep the information from the patient, and we think it is clear that portents of that type may justify the physician in action he deems medically warranted.
>
> The critical inquiry is whether the physician responded to a sound medical judgment that communication of the risk information would present a threat to the patient's well-being. The physician's privilege to withhold information for therapeutic reasons must be carefully circumscribed, however, for otherwise it might devour the disclosure rule itself. The privilege does not accept the paternalistic notion that the physician may remain silent simply because divulgence might prompt the patient to forego therapy the physician feels the patient really needs.

Some states have codified the therapeutic privilege exception.[2] Since this privilege is contrary to the assumptions underlying the informed consent doctrine, its use should be circumscribed. A physician should explain, in the medical record, why the information was withheld.

An Iowa court held that a doctor could not withhold any information from a patient contemplating a vasectomy for socioeconomic reasons.[3] The court noted that the patient was a well and normal person not requiring surgical intervention or therapy. The surgery was not corrective, but designed to interfere with a normal bodily function.[4] Similar reasons may apply to some cosmetic procedures.

(b) *Patient Waiver.* A second exception to an informed consent requirement occurs when a patient knowingly waives the right to receive any information. While a waiver may be valid, its use is not recommended. If a waiver is used, the physician should require the patient to sign a form acknowledging the latter's decision to refuse information.

(c) *Emergency Exception.* The third exception to informed consent occurs in the case of an emergency. Such a situation obviates the need for any consent at all.[6]

The law recognizes that in some circumstances a physician may perform a procedure different from the one to which the patient consented. These circumstances arise in emergencies and unanticipated situations.[7] A physician can usually act without consent if an unanticipated condition is found that requires immediate action. This is also true in an emergency situation where the life of the patient is endangered, and the doctor is unable to obtain the person's consent.[8]

---

1 *464 F.2d at 789.*

2 *Alaska Stat. §09.55.556(b)(4); Del. Code Ann. Stat. tit. 18, §6852(b)(3) (Supp.); N.Y. Pub. Health Law §2805-d(4)(d) (McKinney); Pa. Stat. Ann. tit. 40, §1301.103 (Purdon) (Insurance Code); Utah Code Ann. §78-15-4(2)(d); Vt. Stat. Ann. tit. 12, §1909(d) (Supp.) (provide information to immediate family).*

3 Cowman v. Hornaday, *329 N.W.2d 422 (Iowa 1983).*

4 *Id. at 427.*

5 *N.Y. PUb. Health Law §2805-d(4)(b) (McKinney); Utah Code Ann. §78-14-5(2)(c); Vt. Stat. Ann. tit. 12, §1909(c)(2)(Supp.).*

6 *See Chapter 4, fns. Ky. Rev. Stat. §304.40-320 (Supp.); Nev. Rev. Stat. §41A.120; N.Y. Pub. Health Law 2805-d(2)(a) (McKinney); Pa. Stat. Ann. tit. 40, §1301.103 (Purdon) (Insurance Code); Vt. Stat. Ann. tit. 12, §1909(b); Wash. Rev. Stat. Ann. §7.70.050(4) (Supp.).*

7 *Rozovsky, Consent to Treatment, A Practical Guide §1.6.4.*

8 *See generally, Lloyd v. Kull, 329 F.2d 168 (7th Cir. 1964);* Demers v. Gerety, *P.2d 645 (1973) remanded on other grounds 520 P.2d 869 (1974);* Lipscomb v. The Memorial Hospital, *733 F.2d 332 (4th Cir. 1984).*

9.1 Extension of Treatment

As a general rule, the extension of a procedure beyond the scope of the consent may expose a physician to liability for battery. The strict common law rule is that the right of a surgeon to extend an operation beyond the limits that the patient has authorized is confined to emergencies requiring immediate action. Some courts have departed from this common law rule. One approach allows a doctor to extend an operation to deal with any abnormal condition discovered during a procedure when an extension is advisable for the welfare of the patient and follows accepted medical practice.

In an Ohio case, a patient's fallopian tubes were removed during an authorized appendectomy.[1] The physician testified that "I found her tubes in bad shape . . . I could have treated them, but the chances were that she might have been in the hospital for two or three months, so I thought I'd better take them out." The Ohio Supreme Court reversed a directed verdict for the defendant doctor and remanded the case for further proceedings on the question of consent.[2]

In another case, a surgeon found some enlarged follicle cysts on a patient's ovaries.[3] Although there was no immediate emergency, the surgeon punctured the cysts. The court noted that where an internal operation is required, both the surgeon and the patient know that no definite diagnosis is possible until the incision has been made. The court said, therefore, that in the absence of proof to the contrary, a surgeon can extend an operation to correct any abnormal or diseased condition in the area of the original incision whenever proper surgical procedure requires such an extension. Under this reasoning, the extension of an operation is not limited to an emergency.

In one critical case,[4] the plaintiff was told by her family physician that a lacerated uterus was responsible for her frequent miscarriages. Subsequently, she told the defendant surgeon she wanted to be "fixed up" so she could bear children. When the doctor operated on her, he found that her fallopian tubes were sealed and full of pus. Her ovaries were also badly infected, and consequently could never bear children. The surgeon removed the diseased organs, though immediate removal was not necessary to protect the patient's life or health.

On appeal, the court interpreted the patient's request to be "fixed up" as authority to perform a diagnostic operation and such surgery as might be necessary to cure her ailment. Although the court spoke of consent implied from the existence of an emergency, it appears that the patient had expressly consented to any surgery the physician might find necessary, so long as it did not interfere with her ability to bear children. According to the facts of the case, the woman's condition before the operation already made it impossible for her to bear children and this condition could not be corrected.

In another case,[5] an ophthalmologist was held liable for extending a surgical procedure without the patient's consent. The patient's condition was diagnosed as an infection of the meibomian glands on the lower left eyelid. The patient consented to having the eyelid opened and drained. The ophthalmologist administered a local anesthetic, excised some meibomian glands and also removed a freckle from the eyelid. During the operation, the tarsus that supports the eyelid was cut, causing the lid to drop. The Michigan appellate court affirmed a $12,500 judgment in favor of the patient and noted that no claim of negligence was made. The court held that no emergency existed, and that the removal of the glands and the freckle constituted an unwarranted assault and battery since the patient was conscious, and his consent could have been requested.

In another instance,[6] a patient complained of a pain in her lower abdomen which the surgeon diagnosed as a tubal pregnancy. The doctor operated, but when he opened the patient's abdomen, he found instead that she had a double uterus, a normal pregnancy but very acute appendicitis. The patient's husband later testified that he was just outside the operating room and presumably could have been consulted, but there was no evidence that the surgeon knew it. The surgeon concluded that the acute appendicitis was responsible for the patient's pain and removed her appendix. The woman had an uneventful recovery and subsequently delivered a normal child. The patient's husband, however, refused to pay the surgeon's fee because the appendectomy was unauthorized. The judgment for the surgeon was affirmed.

The court queried: "What was the surgeon to do? Should he have left her on the operating table, her abdomen exposed, and gone in search of her husband to obtain express authority to remove the appendix? Should he have closed the incision on the inflamed appendix and subjected the patient, pregnant as she was, to a general spread of the poison in her system, or to the alternative danger and shock of a second independent operation to remove the appendix? Or should he have done what his professional judgment dictated . . .?"[7]

The court found that the surgeon had operated within the scope of the consent given him by the patient. The surgeon removed what he believed to be the cause of the patient's pain. It was essentially for this reason that the surgeon had been engaged.

A contrasting view was expressed in another case in which a 20-year-old woman submitted to an appendectomy.[8] During the operation, the surgeon discovered that the young woman's fallopian tubes were full of puss, swollen and sealed at both ends. Fearing that the swollen tubes eventually would break and cause peritonitis, the doctor removed them. It was impossible to obtain the consent of the unconscious patient, and the surgeon did not attempt to obtain the consent of the young woman's stepmother who was in the hospital at the time. At the trial, the surgeon testified that it would have been necessary to remove the tubes "within six months anyway if I was not mistaken."

The Kentucky appellate court ruled against the surgeon. The court ruled that while a surgeon may extend an operation in an emergency, the emergency must exist at the time of the operation and not merely endanger the patient's health or life at some future time. The court said that the evidence did not establish that, as a matter of law, there was an emergency of sufficient urgency to justify the removal of the tubes without the consent of the patient or her stepmother. Although the evidence did indicate that the tubes would have to be removed soon, and that in their infected condition were dangerous, their removal was not established as an emergency. Death was not likely to occur immediately if they were not removed.[9]

In another case, a patient brought an action against her physician for his removal of a vaccination mark without her consent. The court held that the woman's claim that she did not understand or otherwise consent to the removal of the vaccination mark was properly pleaded in battery, under a theory of lack of informed consent.[10]

As noted previously, a surgeon is entitled to extend an operation when the advisability of additional surgery becomes apparent during an operation. Embolism, infections, anesthesia deaths and paralysis are remote possibilities in modern surgery, but they do occur. Subjecting a patient to a second, separate operation just to obtain a consent the person would give anyway, if awake, is unconscionable. In the absence of specific prohibition by the patient, the physician should be privileged to perform such surgery as is justified by prevailing medical opinion.

When a bad result occurs, a plaintiff, unable to prove negligence, may resort to the theory of assault and battery to seek a recovery. A patient who would expect to be spared from an unnecessary, second operation may, nevertheless, react differently if an extension of the agreed operation proves unsuccessful. To hold a physician responsible under these circumstances may, however, penalize and thwart good medical practice.

The professional instincts of physicians should not be clouded by unreasonable threats of liability. Good surgery frequently requires additional procedures to correct conditions that are only discernible by visual inspection after the surgery has begun.[11]

---

1 Wells v. Van Nort, *125 N.E. 910 (Ohio 1919).*

2 Also see, Rubino v. DeFratias, M.D. *638 F.Supp. 182 (1986) (Patient brought a claim that she did not understand or otherwise consent to her physician's removal of her vaccination mark was properly pleaded in battery rather than negligence);* Samoilov v. Raz, *536 A.2d 275 (N.J. Super A.D. 1987).*

3 Kennedy v. Parrott, *90 S.E.2d 754 (N.C. 1954).* See also Barnett v. Bachrach, *34 A.2d 626 (D.C. 1943);* Bennan v. Parsonnet, *83 A. 948 (N.J. 1912).*

4 King v. Carney, *204 P. 270 (Okla. 1922). Appellate Ct. affirmed judgment on jury verdict for surgeon who removed facial tumor to recover for a nerve damage. Surgeon was held not to have committed battery; estate of* Leach v. Shapiro, *469 N.E. 2d 1047 (1989).*

5 Shulman v. Lerner, *141 N.W. 2d 348 (Mich. 1966).*

6 Barnett v. Bachrach, *34 A.2d 626 (D.D.C. 1943).*

7 *Id. at 629.*

8 Tabor v. Scobee, *254 S.W.2d 474 (Ky. 1952).*

9 Tabor v. Scobee, *254 S.W.2d 474 (Ky. 1952).*

10 Rubino v. DeFratias, *638 F. Supp. 182 (D. Ariz. 1986).*

11 Samoil v. Raz, 536 A.2d 275 (1987) (Patient brought medical malpractice action against surgeon who removed facial tumor to recover for a nerve damaged. The court held where patient consents to certain treatment and doctor undertakes that course, but undisclosed complications occur and the physician utilizes appropriate procedures there is no basis for claim of assault and battery.); Also see Rozovsky, F. Consent to Treatment, *Ch. 1 and 1987 Supp.*

9.2 Who May Consent

The authority to treat or operate usually arises from the valid consent of the patient or someone authorized to consent for the patient. Some state statutes define precisely who this may be.[1] Ohio, for example, provides that a consent must be signed by the patient, or if the patient is unable to sign then by a person who has legal authority to consent on his or her behalf.[2]

A consent may be invalid if the act consented to is unlawful,[3] if it is given by someone not authorized to do so,[4] or if it is obtained by misrepresentation or fraud.[5] The patient's consent to an operation is sufficient if the individual has reached the age of majority and, at the time of consent, is competent to understand the nature and purpose of the operation proposed and the risks involved.

The consent of a spouse is not necessary; the patient's consent is sufficient.[6] Nevertheless, it is advisable to have the spouse join in the consent whenever practicable. Spousal consent is particularly advisable if the operation involves danger to life, or may destroy or limit sexual functions, or may result in the death of any unborn child.

The law presumes patients are competent, rather than incompetent, to consent to care. The presumption may be rebutted, however, by evidence that the patient was drunk,[7] under the influence of drugs,[8] delirious or comatose,[9] or otherwise incapable of exercising rational judgment. Whether a patient is treated free or at someone else's expense, consent is still required.[10]

---

1 *For example, Georgia law defines who may give consent. The statute covers adults, minors, and those adjudicated incompetent. Ga. Code Ann. §88-2904.* See also *Del. Tit. 18, §6852; Idaho Code §39-4303; Iowa Code Ann. 147.137 Me. Rev. Code Tit. 24 §2905 (i)(1988 Supp.); Ohio Rev. Code §2317.54(c)(Page 90); Utah Code Ann. §78-14-5(4); and footnote Chapter 5.*

2 *Ohio Rev. Code §2317.54(c)(Page 90).*

3 Hancock v. Hullett, *82 So. 522 (Ala. 1919);* Miller v. Bayer, *68 N.W. 869 (Wisc. 1896).*

4 Moss v. Rishworth, *222 S.W.2d 225 (Tex. Civ. App. 1920);* Mohr v. Williams, *104 N.W. 12 (Minn. 1905);* Kinikin v. Heupel, *305 N.W.2d 589 (1981);* Kohoutek v. Hafner, *383 N.W.2d 195 (Minn. 1986).*

5 LaCaze v. Collier, 434 So. 2d 1039 (La. 1983). *In* Nolan v. Kechijian, 64 A.2d 866 (R.I. 1949), *the plaintiff's consent to abdominal surgery was based on the defendant's representation that the operation was intended "to build up the ligaments" that held the spleen in place. The court held that the defendant's representations were so inadequate as to border on deceit. The accidental tearing of blood vessels which required the removal of the spleen was therefore held to be sufficient to sustain an action for assault and battery. See also* Birnbaum v. Siegler, *76 N.Y.S.2d 173 (1948);* Keen v. Coleman, *20 S.E.2d 175 (Ga. 1942); Fla. Stat. Ann §768.46(4)(a)(Supp.); Ohio Rev. Code §2317.54.*

6 Jeffcoat v. Phillips, *417 S.W.2d. 903 (Tex. 1967). This rule applies even when it is likely that the operation will have some effect upon the sexual life of the individual, as for example, with sterilization operations. See* Kritzer v. Citron, *224 P.2d 808 (Cal. 1950);* Barker v. Heaney, *82 S.W.2d 417 (Tex. Civ. App. 1935);* Rytkonen v. Lojacono, *257 N.W. 703 (Mich. 1934);* Burroughs v. Crichton, *48 App. D.C. 596 (1919);* State v. Housekeeper, *16 A. 382 (MD. 1889). See* Coleman v. Coleman, *471 A.2d 1115 (Md. Ct. of Special App. 1984). The Maryland court denied the husband's petition to prevent his wife from having an abortion. The court held that "a woman in her first trimester of pregnancy, in consultation with her physician, may elect to terminate the pregnancy, and neither the state nor the woman's spouse nor the father of the child has any right to intervene so as to prevent her decision from becoming a fact."*

7 Barker v. Heaney, *82 S.W.2d 419 (Tex. Civ. App. 1935).*

8 Wheeler v. Barker, *208 P.2d 68 (Cal. App. 1949);* Demers v. Gerety, *529 P.2d 278;* Stone v. Goodman, *271 N.Y. Supp. 500 (1934).*

9 Arballo v. Nielson, *166 P.2d 621 (Cal. App. 1946).*

10 Bonner v. Moran, *126 F.2d 121 (D.C. Cir. 1941);* Kozup v. Georgetown Univ. *851 F.2d 437 (D.C. Cir. 1988; (Appeals court held as a material fact at issue as to whether transfusion was absolutely necessary to save child's life and thus whether patients gave implied consent for transfusion which resulted in the baby contacting aids).*

Consent

10.0

A patient has the right to withhold consent to lifesaving treatment, and thus can impose terms, conditions and limitations on the consent. A physician, however, does not have to agree to conditions that are incompatible with good medical practice. The prudent doctor will not agree to an arrangement that unduly circumscribes the exercise of a reasonable degree of professional judgment. The physician who does so, particularly in surgery when a patient is to be anesthetized, may later face the dilemma of choosing between poor medical practice or liability exposure for unauthorized treatment.

Any limitations on consent should be included in the consent form for a physician's protection if the limitations could cause an unsatisfactory result. If a patient insists on limitations that are clearly inconsistent with good medical practice, the physician would have justification for declining the case. Physicians should also be aware of the possibility that a patient may have a living will which specifically states that he or she does not want to undergo certain life prolonging techniques.[1] Many states today have legislation authorizing the execution of living wills, and the release of medical personnel from liability for honoring them.[2]

In a New York case,[3] a patient entered a hospital for an examination under anesthetic to determine the nature of a lump in her stomach. She subsequently claimed that she had notified the physician "that there must be no operation." While she was under the anesthetic, however, a fibroid tumor was removed from her abdomen. The court held that if the operation was performed without her consent, in the absence of an emergency, the procedure would be an assault by the surgeon. In another case,[4] a patient consented to an operation for hernia, but the surgeon also removed a testicle despite the patient's express prohibition. The surgeon contended that conditions warranted the removal, but it was held that this was an unauthorized extension for which he was liable.

A physician who administers a type of anesthetic expressly prohibited by a patient is responsible for damages caused by the anesthetic even though there is no negligence in administration. The frequency of medical liability claims involving the choice of anesthesia indicates the desirability of a statement in the patient's consent form indicating any restrictions on the anesthetics to be used.[5]

In one such case,[6] the plaintiff, an adult, expressly prohibited a spinal anesthetic. His mother later consented to the use of any anesthetic. At the start of the operation, sodium pentothal was injected. Because of an adverse reaction, a spinal block was administered. Since the operation had not begun, the jury found that there was no emergency which would justify a violation of the plaintiff's instructions.

Experimental procedures require a patient's consent, and such procedures usually impose greater disclosure responsibilities on physicians. Regulations of the Department of Health and Human Services (HHS) on the protection of human subjects limit the waiver of consent and the release from liability.

The regulations prohibit "exculpatory language through which the subject or the representative is made to waive or appears to waive any of the subject's legal rights, or releases or appears to release the investigator, the sponsor, the institution or its agents from liability for negligence."[7] Additional regulations apply to all research conducted or supported by HHS involving children as subjects.[8] Any research activity requires more thorough consent procedures than are required for clinical treatment.[9]

Another limitation that arises occurs when parents attempt to proscribe the type of treatment provided to their children. All states recognize that primary responsibility for the provision of medical necessities rests with the parents, but if the parents fail to provide adequate care, the state may step in to provide services necessary to preserve the life, health and welfare of a minor.[10] In situations where life-saving services are not required, however, or if a delay of treatment would not cause a serious deterioration of a child's condition, courts tend to defer to the parent's decision.[11]

Cases have discussed how parents should be dealt with in order to successfully treat a child.[12] In one case,[13] the court held that there was no legal duty on the physician's part to inform the parents of an infant suffering from a life-threatening condition that treatment could be withheld if they wished to let the child die. The court ruled that there were "no alternatives" to which the parents could consent.

1 *Gould, Linda,* Right to Die Legislation: *The* Effect On Physicians Liability, *39 Mercer Law Review 517 (1988)(article discusses situations in which a physician can withhold treatment, living will statutes as well as proposes a Model Act - Medical Decisions Act.* Also see, Gray v. Romeo, *697 F.Supp. 580*

(1988)(Declaratory judgment sought by husband to remove feeding tube from his wife. United States District Court for Rhode Island recognized the right to terminate nutrition and hydration.) Also see, *In Re:* Estate of Prange *520 N.E.2d 590 (1988).*

2 *Alabama: Ala. Code §§22-8A-1 to 10 (Supp. 1982); Arizona: Ariz. Rev. Stat. Ann §§36-3201 (West. 1985); Arkansas: Ark. Stat. §§ 82-3801 to -3804 (Supp. 1981); California: Cal Health & Safety Code §§7185 to 7195 (Supp. 1987); Colorado: Colo. Rev. Stat. §§ 15-18-101 to -113 (Supp. 1986); Connecticut: Conn. Gen. Stat. Ann. §§ 19a-570 to - 575 (Supp. 1987); Delaware: Del. code Ann. tit. 16, §§2501 (1983); District of Columbia: D.C. Code Ann. §§6-2422 to -2430 (Supp. 1987); Florida: Fla. Stat. Ann. 765.01-765.15 (West Supp. 1986); Georgia: O.C.G.A. §§ 31-32-1 to -12 (1982 & Supp. 1987); Idaho: Idaho Code § 39-4501 to -4508 (1985); Illinois: Ill. Rev. Stat. Ch. 110 1/2, §§ 701-710 (Supp. 1987); Indiana: Ind. Code §§ 16-8-11-1 to -22 (Supp. 1986); Kowa: Iowa Code Ann. §§144A.1-144A.10 (Supp. 1987); Kansas: Kan. Stat. Ann. §§ 65-28,101 to -28,109 (1985); Louisiana: La. Rev. Stat. Ann. §§ 40:1299.58.1-40:1299.58.10 (Supp. 1987); Maine: Me. Rev. Stat. Ann. tit. 22, §§ 2929-2931 (Cum. Supp. 1986); Maryland: Md. Health-Gen. Code Ann. §§ 5-601 to -614 (Supp. 1986); Missouri: Mo. Rev. Stat. §§ 459.010-459-055 (Supp. 1987); Nevada: Nev. Rev. Stat. §§ 449.540 to 449.690 (1986); New Mexico: N.M. Stat. Ann. §§ 24-7-1 to -10 (1978); North Carolina: N.C. Gen Stat. §3 90-320 to -323 (1985); Oklahoma: Okla. Stat Ann. tit. 63, §§ 3101-311 (Supp. 1987); Oregon: Or. Rev. Stat. §97.050 to .090 (1983 & Supp. 1987); South Carolina: S.C. Code Ann. §3 44-77-10 to -160 (Supp. 1986); Tennessee: Tenn. Code Ann. §32-11-101 to -110 (Supp. 1986): Texas: Tex. Civ. Rev. Stat. Ann. art. 4590h §§ 1 to 11 (Vernon Supp. 1987); Utah: Utah Code Ann. §§ 75-2-1101 to 1118 (Supp. 1987); Vermont: Vt. Stat. Ann. tit. 18, §3 5251 to 5262 (Supp. 1986); Virginia: Va. Code §§ 54-325.8.1 to 54-325.8:12 (Supp. 1987); Washington: Wash. Rev. Code Ann. §§ 70.122.010 to 70.122.905 (Supp. 1987); West Virginia: W. Va. Code §3 16-30-101 to -110 (1985); Wisconsin: Wis. Stat. §3 154.01 to .15 (Supp. 1986).*

3 Schloendorff v. Society of N.Y. Hospital, *105 N.E. 92 (N.Y. 1914).*

4 Markart v. Zeimer, *227 P. 683 (Cal. App. 1924).*

5 See, Malpractice - Liability of Anesthetist, *90 A. L.R 3d 775.*

6 Chambers v. Nottebaum, *96 So. 2d 716 (Fla. 1967);* Siegel v. Mt. Sinai Hospital, *403 NE.2d 202 (1978); (Court held that although signed consent form was evidence of decedents consent, it was not conclusive because it left open question for jury as to whether the decedent consented to added risk involved in administering anesthesia to an asthmatic).*

7 *45 C.F.R. §46.116. The information required in the written consent form and the documentation is specified in the regulations. 45 C.F.R. §46.116, §46.117. Each department of the Federal Government that supports research involving human subjects, to some extent, follows the HHS guidelines. Implementing Human Resource Regulations, President's Commission for the Study of Ethical Problems in Medicine and Biomedical and Behavioral Research, Ch. 1, March 1983.*

8 See, e.g., Bang v. Miller Hospital, *88 N.W. 2d 186, 190 (1958); Delgado, Richard,* Informed Consent in Human Experimentation Bridging the Gap Between Ethical Thought, *and* Correct Practice, *34 U.C.L.A. 67 (1986).*

9 *45 C.F.R. §346.401-46.409.*

10 *There are statutes in some states that authorize the juvenile court to order necessary medical and surgical care for a minor whose parents or guardian refuse to provide it when able to do so. See, e.g., Mich. Stat. Ann §§27.3178 (598.2)(b)(1), 27.3178 (598.18)(h)(1980 Rev. Vo.); N.Y. Unconsol. Laws Tit. I, §§2 (17)(g)(McKinney, Supp. 1955). The New York statute was held constitutional in* In Revasko, *263. N.Y. Supp. 552 (1933). The statute was said to be a valid method by which the state could protect its interest in the health of its infants.*

11 In Interest of Cooper, *631 P.2d 632 (Kan. 1981);* Muhlenberg Hospital v. Patterson, *320 A.2d 518 (N.J. 1974);* State v. Perricone, *181 A.2d 751 (N.J. 1962)(Jehovah's Witness);* Custody of a Minor, *379 N.E.2d 1053 (Mass. 1978) (Court ordered continuation of chemotherapy over parents' objection). If the child already has been declared a ward of the state, the court may be more willing to authorize treatment.* See, e.g., In Re Karwarth, *199 N.W.2d 147 (Iowa 1972).* But see In Re: Phillip B. *156 Cal. Rptr. 48 (1979).*

12 See, e.g., Raleigh Fitkin-Paul Morgan Memorial Hospital v. Anderson, *201 A.2d 537 (N.J. 1964) (Blood transfusion for the mother ordered);* Jefferson v. Griffin Spaulding County Hospital Authority, *274 S.E.2d 457 (Ga. 1981) Mother order to submit to a caesarean, rather than a vaginal, delivery over her religious objections.) In the interest of A.W., a child under the age of eighteen 740 P.2d 82 (Kan. 1987)(Court had the inherent power to accept relinquishment of parental rights by natural mother in lieu of a proceeding with an action to sever parental rights where all of the statutory requirements for the protection of the mother were met.)*

13 Iafeuee v. Luchs, *501 A.2d 1040.1048 (N.J. Super L. 1985).*

11.1 Minors

The general rule for consent when a minor is the patient is that the operation or treatment requires the consent of a parent or guardian except in an emergency where immediate treatment is imperative and any delay involves serious risk to the patient.

In one such case,[1] two adult sisters took an eleven-year old to a hospital for removal of badly diseased tonsils and adenoids. The child died while under the anesthetic. The court held that the child's father could recover from the operating surgeon for the child's death. Although the operation might have been necessary, no immediate emergency existed to excuse the need for parental consent.

In another instance,[2] a seventeen-year-old boy, accompanied by his aunt and two adult sisters, consulted a surgeon who recommended surgery to remove a tumor. Preparations were then made for an operation, with apparent knowledge of the boy's father with whom the youngster lived. Subsequently, while under an anesthetic, the boy died and his father sued. Recovery was denied. The court ruled that since the father was aware of the preparations and did not object, his consent could be implied. Furthermore, the operation was not ordinarily hazardous, and the boy was close to the age of majority.

Emergencies remove the need for consent for minors as well as adults.[3] The problem arises in defining what constitutes a true emergency. One case stated that: "It is not to be presumed that competent surgeons will wantonly operate, nor that they will fail to obtain the consent of parents to operations where such consent may be reasonably obtained in view of the exigency."[4] In that case, the decision to amputate a minor's foot was made after extensive consultation among the physicians involved. Doctors should always attempt, however, to contact the parents.

In one instance, in which a seventeen-year-old boy's arm was crushed by a freight train, efforts were made to reach the parents by telephone, but they failed.[5] After a consultation among physicians, the boy's arm was amputated. The consent of the parents was implied by the emergency.

In another case,[6] a seven-year old youngster died while anesthetized for treatment of a broken arm. Before administering the anesthetic, an unsuccessful attempt was made to contact the mother at her place of work. The court held that an emergency existed.

An extremely liberal view of what constitutes an emergency was taken by a court in the case of a twenty-year old man who fractured his ankle during a baseball game. The surgeon told the patient it would be necessary to put him under an anesthetic before the foot could be treated. The patient's response was: "Well, if you think best, go ahead." The young man's father brought suit charging that the anesthetic was administered without his consent. The court said the operation was necessary to stop needless pain and suffering; it held for the defendant.[7] Since it does not appear that a true emergency existed, the court probably was strongly influenced by the fact that the patient was nearly an adult, and that the operation ordinarily was not difficult.

In a Kansas case,[8] the court held that a minor who was near the age of majority could consent to a skin graft on her fingertip. The Kansas Supreme Court said that parental consent was not necessary if an emergency existed, if the minor was emancipated, if parental consent could not be obtained in time to accomplish proper results, or if the minor was able to understand the procedure and risks involved. The court found that the girl was conscious, capable of knowing what was taking place, and that no damage or disability resulted from the treatment.

The prudent physician should, as a general rule, obtain the consent of a parent or legal guardian before performing elective surgery or medical treatment for a minor. There are no reported cases which would indicate that the consent of both parents is necessary. In the absence of a controversy between parents as to whether the physician should provide treatment, the consent of one parent should suffice. If the parents are legally separated or divorced, consent on behalf of the child should be obtained from the parent who has legal custody.

Another exception to the parental consent requirement involves emancipated minors. What constitutes "*emancipation*" is defined by statute. Some states have enacted laws that relieve the physician of liability for lack of parental consent if the doctor, in good faith, relies on the minor's representation of emancipation.[9]

In one such instance,[10] an eighteen-year-old married man, the father of one child, was suffering from an incurable, progressive muscular disease. He and his wife decided to limit their family. After obtaining the couple's written consent, the doctor performed a vasectomy. When the man reached his majority, he sued the physician for operating without a valid consent.

Affirming the judgment in favor of the physician, the Washington Supreme Court said that the mental capacity necessary to consent was a fact question and should be determined from the circumstances of each case stating that "a married minor, eighteen years of age, who has successfully completed high school and is the head of his own family, who earns his own living and maintains his own home, is emancipated for the purpose of giving a valid consent to surgery."[11]

Some states have enacted statutes that lower the age of consent to obtain medical care in certain circumstances.[12] The Texas statute, for example, requires that the individual be at least sixteen years of age and reside separate and apart from his parents.[13]

Other exceptions to parental consent requirements are based in public policy. Treatment of venereal disease,[14] drug abuse,[15] alcohol dependency[16] or pregnancy[17] often do not require parental consent. A minor in Minnesota, for example, may give effective consent for medical services to determine pregnancy or to treat pregnancy.[18] Some statutes that eliminate the parental consent requirement add a corollary parental notification requirement.[19] Other statutes however prohibit informing the parents unless the minor consents or authorizes release of the information.

1 Moss v. Rishworth, *222 S.W.2d 225 (Tex. 1920).*

2 Baker v. Welsh, *108 N.W. 94 (Mich. 1906)*

3 See generally, Kozup v. Georgetown *851 F.2d 437 (D.C. Cir. 1988).*

4 Luke v. Lowrie, *136 N.W. 1106 (Mich. 1912).*

5 Jackovach v. Yocum *237 N.W. 444 (Iowa 1931).*

6 Wells v. McGehee, *39 So. 2d 196 (La. 1949).*

7 Sullivan v. Montgomery, *279 N.Y.S. 575 (N.Y. 1935).*

8 Younts v. St. Francis Hospital and School of Nursing, *469 P.2d 330 (Kan. 1970).* Also see, Cardwell v. Bechtol, *Supreme Court of Tennessee, S/C No. 36 2-6-87; seventeen-year old out on her own to seek osteopathic physician, Tennessee adopts the "mature minor" position.*

9 *N.Y. Pub. Health Law §2504; Pa. Stat. Ann. Tit. 35, §10105; Va. Code Ann. §32-137 (limited circumstances).*

10 Smith v. Seibly, *431 P.2d 719 (Wash. 1967).* see Planned Parenthood Association of Kansas City, Missouri v. Ashcroft, *103 S.Ct. 2517 (1983). A Missouri statute required either parental or judicial consent prior to performing an abortion on a minor. The Supreme Court stated that the state's interest in protecting immature minors will sustain a requirement of a consent substitute, either parental or judicial. However, "the state must provide an alternative procedure whereby a pregnant minor may demonstrate that she is sufficiently mature to make the abortion decision herself or that despite her immaturity, an abortion would be in her best interest."* Id. *at 2525 citing* City of Akron v. Akron Center for Reproductive Health, *103 S.Ct. 2481, 2497-98 (1983). The statute provided that the court would receive evidence about the emotional development, maturity, intellect and understanding of the minor. The provision was held constitutional;* Also *see,* Baird v. ATtorney General, *360 N.E. 2d 288 (1977)(minor parents must only consider what is in the best interest of the child in deciding whether to consent to abortion).*

11 Id. *431 P.2d at 723.*

12 *Code of Ala. §22-8-4; Alaska Stats. §§25.20.020 (1978 Supp.); 09.65.100 (1979 Supp.); Ariz. Rev. Stats. §44-132 (1988 Supp.); Ark. Stat. Ann. §82-363; Cal. Civil Code §34.10; Colo. Rev. Stat. §13-22-103 (Supp. 1981); Del. Code Ann. Tit. 13, §707; Fla. Stat. Ann. §743.01; Ga. Code Ann. §74-104.1; Haw. Rev. Stat. §§577-25, 577A-1; Ill. Rev. Stat. Ch. 111, §4501 (Smith-Hurd 1989); Ind. Stat. Ann. §16-8-12-2(2); Kan. Stat. Ann. §38-101 (1987 Supp.); Ky. Rev. Stat. §214.185; La. Rev. Stat. Ann., Art. 379, 366; Ann. Code of Md., §20-102; Mass. Gen. Laws Ann. Ch. 112, §12F; Mich. Comp. Law Ann. §722.4; Minn. Stat. Ann. §§144.341, 144.342; Miss. Code Ann. §41-41-3; Mo. Stat. Ann. §§475.010; 431.061; Mont. Code Annotate §41-1-402; Nev. Rev. Stat. §129.030; §129.010; N.J. Stat. Ann. §9:17A-1; 9:17A-4; N. Mex. §24-10-1; N.Y. Pub. H. Law §2504; N.C. Gen. Stat. §§90-21.1, 90-21.1(4); 90-21.1(5); Okla. Stat. Ann. Tit. 63, §§2601, 2602; Ore. Rev. Stat. §109.640; R.I. Gen. Laws. Ann. §23-51-1; S.C. Code Ann. §§44-45-10, 44-45-20; Tex. Code Ann. Family Code §35.03 (1989 Supp.); Wis. Stat. §51.47, Wyo. Stat. §14-1-101.*

13 *Tex. Code Ann. Family Code §35.03.*

14 *Code of Ala. §22-8-6;* Alas. Stat. *§09.65.100; Ariz. Rev. Stat. §44-132.01; Ark. Stat. Ann. §82-1606 (1979 Cumm. Supp.); Cal. Civil Code §34.7 (1989);* Conn. Gen. Stat. Ann. *§19a-216; Del. Code Ann. Tit. 13, §708 (1978 Cumm. Supp.).* D.C. Code Ann. *§6-129, (1973Bd. Vol.);* Ga. Code Ann. *§§74-104.2 to 74-104.4 (1988 Supp.); Haw. Rev. Stat. §577A-2; Idaho Code Ann. §39-3801 (1977); Ill. Rev. Stats. Ch. 111, §4504 (Smith-Hurd);* Ind. Stat. Ann. *§16-8-5-1; Iowa Code Ann. §140.9; Kan. Stat. Ann. §§65-2892, 2892a; Ky. Rev. Stat. §214.185; La. Rev. Stat. Ann. §40:1065.1;* Me. Rev. Stat. Ann., Tit. 32, §2595; *Ann.* Code of Md., Art. 43, *§135; Mass. Gen. Laws Ann., Ch. 111, §117;* Mich. Comp. Law Ann. §333.5257; *Minn. Stat. Ann. §144.343; Miss. Code Ann. §41-41-13; Mo. Stat. Ann. §431.061;* Mont. Rev. Code Ann. *§41-1-402; Neb. Rev. Stat. §71-1121; Nev. Rev. Stat. §129.060; N.H. Rev. Stat. ANn. §141.11-a; N.J. Rev. Stat. Ann. §9:17A-4; N. Mex. Stat. Ann. §24-N.Y. Pub. H. Law §2305; N.C. Gen. Stat. §90-21.5; N.D. Cent. Code Ann. §14-10-17; Ohio Rev. Code Ann. §2709.24.1; Okla.*

Stat. Ann. Tit. 63, §2602; Ore. Rev. Stat. §109.610, Pa. Stat. Ann. Tit. 35, §10103; R.I. Gen. Laws Ann. §23-11-11; S.C. Code Ann. *§44-45-10; S.C. Comp. Laws Ann. §34-23-16; Tenn. Code Ann. §29-31-101 to 105; Tex. Code Ann. - Family Code §35.03; Vt. Stat. Ann., Tit. 18, §4226; Va. Code Ann. §§32-137, 70.24.110; W. Va. Code Ann. §16-4-10; Wis. Stat. §143.07; Wyo. Stat. Ann. §35-4-151.*

15 *Code of Ala. §22-8-6, Alas. Stats. §44-133.01; Colo. Rev. Stat. §13-22-102; Conn. Gen. Stat. Ann. §19-382; D.C. Code Ann. Regulation No. 74-22, D.C. Register (Sept. 16, 1974); Ga. Code Ann. §§74-104.2 to 74-104.4 (1988 Supp.); Cal. Bus and Prof. Code §4211.5 Haw. Rev. Stat. §577-26 (1984 Supp.); Idaho Code Ann. §37-3201; Ill. Rev. Stat. Ch. 111, §4504 (Smith-Hurd); Ind. Stat. Ann. §16-13-6.1-23; Iowa Code Ann. §125.33; Kan. Stat. Ann. §§65-2892, 65-2892a; Ky. Rev. Stat. §214.185; La. Rev. Stat. Ann. §40:1096: Me. Rev. Stat. Ann. Tit. 32, §2595; Ann. Code of Md. §20-102; Mass. Gen Laws Ann., Ch. 112 §12F (need two physicians findings); Mich. Comp. Law Ann. §333.6121 (Public Health Code); Minn. Stat. Ann. §144.343; Mo. Stat. Ann. §431.061; Mont. Rev. Code Ann. §41-1-402; N.H. Rev. Stat. Ann. §318-B:12-a; N.J. Rev. Stat. Ann. §9:17A-4 (1988 Supp.); N.C. Gen. Stat. §90-21.5 (1988); N.D. Cent. Code Ann. §14-10-17; Ohio Rev. Code Ann. §3719.01.02; Okla. Stat. Ann. tit. 63, §2602 (1989); S.C. Code of Laws §20-7-280 (1976) rev'd 1981; Tenn. Code Ann. §63-6-220; Tex. Code Ann. - Family Code §35.03 (1989 Supp.); Tex Civ. Stats., Art 4447; Va. Code Ann. §32-137; Rev. Code. Wash. Ann. §60A-5-504.*

16 *Code of Ala. §577-26; Ind. Stat. Ann. §16-13-6.1-23; Ky. Rev. Stat. §214.185; Ann. Code of Md., Art. 43, §135; Mass. Gen. Laws. Ann., Ch. 111B §10; Minn. Stat. Ann. §144.343; Mont. Rev. Code Ann. §41-1-402; N.C. Gen. Stat. 90-21.5; N.D. Cent. Code Ann. §14-10-17; Okla. Stat. Ann. Tit. 63, §2602; S.C. Code Ann. §44-45-10; Vt. Stat. Ann. Tit. 18, §4226; Rev. Code Wash. Ann. §69.54-060; W. Va. Code Ann. §60-6-23.*

17 *Code of Ala. 22-8-6; Ark. Stat. Ann. 82-363 (not for abortions); Cal. Civil Code 34.5; Cal. Health and Safety Code §25958; Del. Code Ann. Tit. 13, §708 (Cumm. Supp. 1978); D.C. Code Ann. Regulation No. 74-22, D.C. Register (Sept. 16, 1974); Fla. Stat. Ann. §458.215; Ga. Code Ann. §31-9-2; Haw. Rev. Stat. §577A-2; Kan. Stat. Ann. §38-123 (1987) (if no parent or guardian is available); Ky. Rev. Stat. §214.185 (except for induced abortion or sterilization); Ann. Code of Md., Art. 43, §135; Mass. Gen. Laws Ann. Ch. 112, §125; Mich. Comp. Law Ann. §§333.5257, 333.6121 (discretionary for venereal disease or drugs); Minn. Stat. Ann. §144.343; Mo. Stat. Ann. §431.061; Mont. Rev. Code Ann. §41-1-402; N.J. Rev. Stat. Ann. §9:17B-1: N. Mex. Stat. Ann. §24-1-13; N.C. Gen. Stat. §90-21.5; Ohio Rev. Code Ann. §§3709.24.1, 3719.01.2 (parents responsible for payment if consent); Okla. Stat. Ann. Tit. 63, §2602; Pa. Stat. Ann. Tit. 35, §10103, S.C. Code Ann. §44-45-10; Tex. Code Ann. Family Code §35.03; Utah Code Ann. §78-14-5; Va. Code Ann. §32-137.*

18 Also *see Tenn Code Ann. 37-10-305 (parental consent to abortion, effective 07/01/89); Minn. Stat. Ann. §144.343.*

19 *Del. Code Ann. Tit. 13, §708 (1978 Cumm. Supp.) (for pregnancy discretionary); D.C. Code Ann. §6-119j-1 (Bd. Vol. 1973) for general disease services); Ga. Code Ann. §§74-104.2 to 74.104.4 (1973 Rev.) (discretionary for drug abuse or general disease); Haw. Rev. Stat. §577A-3 (physician must inform parents of minor's pregnancy); §755A-4 (physician's discretion to inform parents of positive general disease test); Ind. Stat. Ann. §61-13-6.1-23 (treatment disclosure within facilities discretion); Kan. Stat. Ann. §§65-2892, 65-2892a (physician's discretion); La. Rev. Stat. Ann. §40:1096 (provider's discretion); Me. Rev. Stat. Ann. Tit. 32, §2595 (practioner's discretion); N.J. Rev. Stat. Ann. §9:17A-5 (physician's discretion); Ore. Rev. Stat. §109.650 (discretionary); Pa. Stat. Ann. Tit. 71, §1690.112 (discretionary); Tenn. Code Ann. §63-624 (physician's discretion for general disease;* Also see *Shipers, William Medical Trial Technique Quarterly,* Informed Consent and the Child in Non-

therapeutic Human Experimentation: Evolution to Solution (discusses informed consent and minors generally, also discusses necessity of experimentation and ways to prevent abuse).

11.2 Minor Incompetent and Consent

When a patient is a minor and of unsound mind and incompetent to understand the nature, purpose and risk of a proposed operation, authority must come from one or both parents or a guardian.[1] If an incompetent patient has attained majority, authority must come from the spouse or legally appointed guardian.[2]

While some courts have held that if there is no spouse and no legally appointed guardian, the parent may give consent,[3] it is important to check the relevant state statute with respect to minors and incompetents since there is variability among the states.

---

1 Lester v. Aetna Casualty & Surety Co., *240 F.2d 676 (Cir. 1975);* In Re Green, *448 Pa. 338, 292 A.2d 382 (1972);* Rothe v. Hull, *180 S.W.2d 7 (Mo. 1944);* Barnett v. Bachvach, *34 A.2d 636 (D.C. 1934);* Pratt v. Davis, *161, 79 N.E. 562 (Ill. 1906).*

2 In Faber v. Olkon, *254 P.2d 520 (Cal. 1953), the court held that a parent who has the responsibility to maintain an adult incompetent child may authorize medical treatment where no guardian has been appointed.* Also see *88 Harvard Law Review, 1001 (1988) Parental Consent Requirements and Privacy Rights of Minors. The contraceptive controversy.*

3 Ritz v. Florida Patient's Compensation Fund, *436 So.2d 987 (Fla. App. 1983). Ritz involved an adult who had been mentally retarded since birth.* See also Farber v. Olkon, *254 P.2d 520 (Cal. 1953). These courts state that the parents have the responsibility to care for these children.* See Matter of Barbar C., *No. 21282-82 (N.Y. Sup. Ct., Sept. 23, 1982). Parents of a pregnant, profoundly retarded twenty-five year old woman could consent to an abortion for their legally incompetent daughter.* See also Public Health Trust of Dale Cty v. Valcin, *509 So.2d 596, 598 (Fla. 1982);* Superintendent of Belchertown State School v. Saikewicz, *373 Mass. 728, 370 N.E.2d 417 (1977) (court appointed guardian shall make a decision regarding whether an incompetent should be treated, but a hearing is required to review guardian's decision);* also see In Re Quinlan, *70 N.J. 10, 355 A2d 697 (1976).*

12.0

Informed consent requires that a patient understand and be able to weigh the positive and negative features of a proposed medical treatment.[1] An individual can only give valid consent if he or she is competent. The test in terms of mental capacity to consent has been stated as follows: "Does the patient sufficiently and reasonably understand the condition, the nature and effect of the proposed treatment, and the attendant risks in pursuing and not pursuing the treatment?"[2]

Various methods and theories have been set forth to aid physicians in determining whether a patient is competent to make a treatment decision.[3] Many state statutes also establish requirements for determining when an individual is not capable of informed consent.[4]

The state statutes, like the courts, are not uniform in their analysis of a patient's competence to consent to treatment. A doctor should therefore be aware of what the statute in his or her state requires. There are several definitions of incompetency including: (1) lack of capacity to consent to treatment; (2) lack of capacity to be informed of the treatment; and (3) individuals adjudicated as incompetent.[5]

State statutes use various phrases, such as: "unable to care for himself;' "lack of capacity to consent or to make responsible medical decisions for treatment; someone who may endanger himself;' "someone whose ability to receive and evaluate information is impaired;' "someone who because of the reason of illness lacks sufficient understanding or capacity to render a decision;' and, "someone who is in need of supervision."[6]

It is generally accepted by both the courts and the medical community that mental illness may affect only a specific area of function while leaving other areas unimpaired.[7] There is an almost unanimous consensus by courts that civil commitment does not mean that an individual is incompetent to make treatment decisions.[8]

In one such case, the court was confronted with one of the most common situations involving the right of institutionalized patients to refuse treatment.[9] The individual in this case was an involuntarily committed mental patient who was being treated with antipsychotic drugs without his consent.[10] In stating the institution's interest in medicating certain patients despite their objections, spokesmen for the institution acknowledged the right of competent adults to decide whether they will consent to certain treatment procedures.[11] The institution argued that an involuntarily committed mental patient is presumably incompetent to exercise this right. This argument was based on the theory that the court, in ordering involuntary retention, had implicitly determined that the patient's illness had impaired his judgment, and that he could not therefore make appropriate decisions regarding treatment and care. The court concluded, however, that neither mental illness nor the fact that a patient had been involuntarily committed was sufficient reason to deny an individual the opportunity to make his or her own treatment decision.[12]

In a similar case, the court approved the establishment of procedural safeguards to protect a patient's right to refuse treatment.[13] The court held that an involuntarily committed mental patient is competent to make treatment decisions until the individual is judged to be incompetent by a court.[14]

There are also situations in which a patient may be intermittently rational. In these circumstances, and whenever possible, the doctor should wait until the patient can give a valid consent. The physician should also document indications that the patient was competent when giving the consent.

When an immediate operation is imperative and the patient is unable to give a rational consent, an operation may be performed. This is also true when a delay in obtaining the act of someone legally authorized to consent on the patient's behalf would involve serious risk to the patient. The applicable legal theory is that of implied consent.[15] The law implies that the patient would, if competent, consent to whatever might be necessary in his or her own interests.[16]

---

1 *Andrews, Lori B.,* Informed Consent Statutes and the Decision Making Process, *Journal of Legal Medicine, Vol. 5, Num. 2, 1984.*

2 In the Matter of William Scheller, *148 N.J. Super. 168, 180-181, 372 A.2d 360, 367 (1977).*

3 *Andrews, Lori B.,* Informed Consent Statutes and The Decision Making Process, *Journal of Legal Medicine, Vol. 5, Num. 2, 1984; Parry John, A Unified Theory of Substitute Consent:* Incompetent Patients Right to Individualized Health Care Decision-Making, *11 Mental and Physical Disability Law Reporter 378 (1986); Parry John,* Psychiatric Care and the Law of Substitute Decision-Making, *11 Mental and Physical Disability Law Reporter 151 (1986); Solnick, John,* Proxy Consent for Incompetent Non-Terminally Ill Adult Patients, *The Journal of Legal Medicine, Vol. 6, No. 1 (1985).*

4 *Alabama, Al St. #26-2A-20(8); Alaska, Ak St. #13.26.0005; Arizona, Az St. #14-5101; Arkansas, Ar 5-11-101 (3); California, PH 3 #1880; Colorado, Unde-*

fined; Connecticut, Undefined; Delaware, Title 12 #3914 (1974); District of Columbia, Undefined; Florida, 744.102 (5); Georgia, 49-601; Hawaii, 560:5-304; Idaho, 15-5-101; Illinois, 110 #112, See also Chap. 111, par.; Indiana, #29-1-18-1 (c); Iowa, #229.1 (1)(2); Kansas, #59-3002; Kentucky, #304-40-320; Louisiana, General; Main, #18-A--#5-101; Maryland, #13-703; Massachusetts, General; Michigan, 700.8; Minnesota, 525.54; Mississippi, General; Missouri, #475.010 (8); Montana, General; Nebraska, #30-2610 (1); Nevada, General; New HampshireGeneral; New Jersey, N.J. S.A. 3B:1-2; New Mexico, #38-4-14; New York, E 172-17-A, Mentally Retarded defined; North Carolina, 35A-1101 (7); North Dakota, General; Ohio, E5101.60 (I); Oklahoma, General; Oregon, General; Pennsylvania, General; Rhode Island, Undefined; South Carolina, Undefined; South Dakota, #27B-6A-2; Tennessee, #34-4-102; Texas, Tex. Prob. Code #3(P); Utah, #78-14-5(F); Vermont, 1909 Sect. C4; Virginia, 37-1-128.01; Washington, 11-88-010; West Virginia, General; Wisconsin, #880.01; Wyoming, Undefined.

5 *Andrews, at 209.*

6 *Kumchy, C.I.G. The Competency Component of Informed Consent: Ethical, Legal & Clinical Perspectives Masters Thesis. Loyola University School of Law. May 1989. Appendix.*

7 *Plotkin, Limiting the therapeutic Orgy: Mental Patients Right to Refuse Treatment, 72 Northwestern University Law Review 461 (1978).*

8 Rennie v. Klein, *653 F.2d 836 (1981), vacated on other grounds, 458 U.S. 119 (1982);* Rogers v. Okin, *738 F.2d 1 (1 St. Cir. 1984);* Knecht v. Gillman, *488 F.2d 1136 (8th Cir. 1973);* Rivers v. Katz, *495 N.E.2d 337 (N.Y. 1986);* In Re the Mental Commitment of MP, *510 N.E.2d 645 (Ind. 1987);* Scott v. Plante, *532 F.2d 939 (3d Cir.);* Winters v. Miller, *446 F.2d 65 (2nd Cir.);* Davis v. Hubbard, *506 F. Supp. 915, 935 (Ohio);* Master of Anderson v. State of Arizona, *135 Arizona 578, 663 P.2d 570;* In Re Boyd, *403 A.2d 744, 747, n5 (D.C. Ct. App.);* Gundy v. Pauley, *619 S.W.2d 730, 731 (KY);* Rogers v. Commissioner of Dept. of Mental Health, *390 Mass. 489, 458 N.E.2d 308, 314;* Matter of K.K.B., *609.P.2d 747, 749 (Okla);* In Re Interest of Brande, *951 520 N.E.2d 946, (II App. 1st Dist. 1988); See, 82 Columbia L. Rev. 1720, 1722,* A Common Law Remedy for Forcible Medication of the Institutionalized Mentally Ill, But see, In Re Mental Commitment of M.P., *500 N.E.2d 216 (Ind. Ct. App. 1986) (in which the court allowed forcible medication on a patient who was not adjudicated incompetent).*

9 Rivers v. Katz, *459, N.E.2d 337, 341 (N.Y. 1986).*

10 Id. *at 341.*

11 Id. *at 341.*

12 Id. *at 341.*

13 Rogers v. Okin, *738 F.2d 1 (1st Cir. 1984).*

14 Id.

15 Wells v. McGee, *39 So. 2d 196 (La. App. 1949).*

16 Strunk v. Strunk, *445 S.W.2d 145 (K.Y. 1969). The brother of a 27 year old incompetent man was suffering from chronic glomerular nephritis. The incompetent was the only acceptable kidney donor. The guardian petitioned the court to allow the incompetent to act as a donor for a transplant. Noting the incompetent's dependence on his brother, the court ruled that the transplant would be in the incompetent's best interest.*

12.1 Proxy Decisionmaking

Many state statutes now provide that when a patient is incompetent to consent a proxy consent is required. Designation of a proxy decisionmaker is important because it attempts to assure that the treatment decision will closely resemble the decision the patient would make if competent.[1] Even if a proxy decisionmaker has been appointed, however, it is often beneficial to the patient's welfare to keep him or her as fully aware as possible of the treatment and its consequences.[2]

A number of states have statutes authorizing proxy decisionmaking; some have done this within their informed consent statutes.[3] Some statutes specify a specific person who can consent to treatment for the individual; others mention specific relatives.[4] It is important, therefore, to consult the applicable state statute rather than simply assuming that someone can validly act as a substitute decisionmaker for a patient.

The standards applied in the decisionmaking process when an individual is incompetent vary according to the test used. Many commentators and courts have attempted to spell out at least two theories.[5] These are the "substitute judgment" and the "best interest" tests. Both are designed to determine what treatment decision the patient would have chosen if he or she had been competent, and what treatment would be best in the particular instance. There has been much criticism and disagreement about which theory best protects the patient's rights.[6]

1 *Andrews, Lori B.,* Informed Consent Statutes And The Decisionmaking Process, *The Journal of Legal Medicine, Vol. 5, No. 2, 1984.*

2 Id. *at 211.*

3 *G.A. Code Ann. §88-2904 (1979); Idaho Code §39.4303 (1977); La Rev. Stat. Ann. §40.1299.53 (West. 1977); Me. Rev. Stat. Ann. Tit. 24, §2905(1) (Supp. 1983-1984); N.C. Gen. Stat. §40.21.13(a) (1981); Utah Code Ann. §78-14-5(4) (1977); Ark. Stat. Ann. §34-2614(B)(1) (Supp. 1983); Fla. Stat. Ann. §468.46(3)(a)(1)(4)(a) (West. Supp. 1983); Iowa Code Ann. §304.40-320(1) (1981); Nev. Rev. Stat. §414.120(2) (1979); Ohio Rev. Code Ann. §2317.54(c) (Page 1981); Tex. Stat. Ann. A.R. 4590i, §§6.03(a), 6.04(a), 6.05 (Vernon Supp. 1983); Wash Rev. Code Ann. §7.70 066 (Supp. 1983); Vt. Stat. Ann. Tit. 12 §1909(c)(3), (d) (Supp. 1984); Hawaii Rev. Stat. §671.3(a), (b) (Supp. 1984); Minn. Stat. Ann. §§144.651(2) (West. Supp. 1984).*

4 *For example, these 8 statutes mention relatives, such as a spouse, parent or adult children. Ga. Code Ann. §§88-2904 (1976); Idaho Code §39-4363(a), (b) (1977); La. Rev. Stat. Ann. §40.1299.53 (West 1977); Me. Rev. Stat. Ann. Tit. 24, §2905(1) (Supp. 1983); Miss. Code Ann. §§41-41-3 (1972); Neb. Rev. Stat. §44-2208 (1978); N.C. Gen. Stat. §90.21-13(a) (1981); Utah Code. Ann. §78-14-5(4) (1977). See also Ala. Code Sec. 26-1-2(c)(2) (Repl. 1986); Alaska Stat. Sec.*

13.26.145(D)(1) (1985); Rasmussen v. Fleming, *154 Ariz. 207, 221 n.21 741 P.2d 674, 688 n.21 (1987); Ark. Stat. Ann. Sec. 28-68-203(b) (1987); See Secs 2410(b), 2411(h), 2411(i), 2412.5, 7 2417(h), 2421(c), 2421(d), 2430-44, 250-08 (West Sup. 1988); Cal. Civ. Code Sec. 2401(b) (West Supp. 1988); Colo. Rev. Stat. See 15-14-501 (Repl. 1987); Colo. Rev. Stat. Sec. 15-14-311(2)( ) (Repl. 1987); Colo. Rev. Stat. Sec. 15-18-107 (Repl. 1987); Conn. Gen. Stat. An. Sec. 45-70 (West 1969); Del. Code Ann. tit. 12, Sec. 4903(a) (Repl. 1987); Del. Code Ann. tit. 16, Sec. 2502(b) (Repl. 1983); D.C. Code Ann. Secs. 21-2043(b), 21-2083(b) (Supp. 1988); Fla. Stat. Ann. Sec. 765.05(2) (1986); Ga. Code Ann. Sec. 29-5-2(c)(1) - Secs. 10-6-5 (1986); Hawaii Rev. Stat. ch. 327D-26 (Supp. 1987); Idaho Code Sec. 15-5-503(2) (Supp. 1988); Idaho Code Sec. 39-4505 (Supp. 1988); Ill. Ann. Stat. ch. 110 , Sec. 11a-6 (Smith-Hurd Supp. 1988); Ind. Code Ann. Sec. 30-2-11(3)(b) (Burns. Sup. 1988); Ind. Code Ann. Sec. 16-8-11-14(g)(2) (Burns Supp. 1988); Iowa Code Ann. Sec. 144.A.7(1)(a) (Supp. 1988); Kan. Stat. Ann. Sec. 58-612(b) (1983); Kan. Stat. Ann. Sec. 58-612(b) (1983); La. Code Civ. Proc. Ann. art. 4550 West Supp. 1988); Me. Rev. Stat. Ann. tit. 18-A, Sec. 5-501 (Supp. 1987); Me. Rev. Stat. Ann. tit. 18-A, Sec. 5-311(b)(1) (1981); Md. Est. & Trusts Code Ann. Sec. 13-707(a)(1) (Supp. 1987); Mass. Gen. Laws Ann. ch. 201B, Sec. 3(b) (West Supp. 1988); Mich. Comp. Laws Ann. Sec. 700.454(2) (West 1988); Minn. Stat. Ann. Sec. 525.544(1)-Ann. Secs. (West Supp. 1987); Mo. Stat. Ann. Sec. 475.050(1) (Vernon Supp. 1988); Mont. Code Ann. Secs. 72-5-312(2)(a), 72-5-501(2) (1987); Neb. Rev. Stat. Sec. 30-2667(2) (1985); Nev. Rev. Stat. Sec. 159.061(1) (1986); N.Y. Mental Hyg. Law Sec. 78.05 (McKinney 1978); N.C. Gen. Stat. Secs. 32A-1(9) (Nov. 1987); N.C. Gen. Stat. Sec. 32A-10(b) (Nov. 1987); N.D. Cent. Code Secs. 30.1-30-03.2 (Supp. 1987); Ohio Rev. Code Ann. Secs. 1337.09(B) 211.02, 2111.121(A) (Page Supp. 1987); Okla. Stat. Ann. tit. 58, Sec. 896 (West 1965); Or. Rev. Stat. Sec. 126.035(1) (Repl. 1987); Pa. Stat. Ann. tit. 20, Sec. 5604(c)(2) (Purdon Supp. 1988); R. I. Gen. Laws Sec. 23-4.10-2 (Supp. 1987); S.C. Code Ann. Sec. 44-77-50 (am. 1988 P.A. No. 586); S.D. Codified Laws Ann. Sec. 30-27-25 (Repl. 1984); Tex. Prob. Code Ann. Sec. 118A (Vernon Supp. 1988); Tex. Rev. Civ. Stat. Ann. art. Sec. 4590h(3)(e) (Vernone Supp. 1988); Utah Code Ann. Sec. 75-2-1106 (Supp. 1986); Vt. Stat. Ann. tit. 14, Sec. 3072(b)(1) (Supp. 1987); Va. Code Secs. 54-325.8:4, 54-325.8:6.2 (Supp. 1987); Wash. Rev. Code Ann. Sec. 11.94.010(1) (1987); W. Va. Code Sec. 39-4-3(b) (Supp. 1988); Wis. Stat. Ann. Sec. 243.07(3)(b) (West 1987); Wyo. Stat. Sec. 35-22-102(d) (Supp. 1987).*

5 *Parry John,* A Unified Theory of Substitute Consent, *11 Mental and Physical Disability Law Reporter 378 (1986); Solnick, Paul* Proxy Consent for Incompetent Non-Terminally Ill Adult Patients, *The Journal of Legal Medicine, Vol. 6, No. 1 1985.*

6 *Parry John,* A Unified Theory of Substitute Consent, *11 Mental Health and Disability Law Reporter 378 (1986).*

12.2 Living Wills

A person can appoint someone to make health care decisions on his or her behalf by the living will statutes in Arkansas, Delaware, Florida, Idaho, Louisiana, Texas, Utah, Virginia and Wyoming.[1] A person can also specifically authorize the appointment of a health care proxy who can decide whether life-sustaining treatment should be withheld or withdrawn. Two other states' statutes — Indiana's and Iowa's — do not directly address proxy appointments, but by providing for consultation between the attending physician and the patient's representative, they inferentially authorize such appointments.[2] The Colorado Medical Treatment Decision Act authorizes proxy involvement in health care decisions. Under certain circumstances, the attorney-in-fact under a durable power of attorney must be notified that the sustaining procedures may be withheld in accordance with a living will declaration.[3]

Some jurisdictions with living will statutes do not require that a specific form be followed, and this practice may permit proxy appointments.[4] Without a specific proxy reference in the law itself, however, the proxy appointment might be questionable.

Some states allow people to nominate a person to be their court-appointed fiduciary in the event that they become incapacitated and a judicial proceeding is required. Although judicial involvement is clearly a last resort, this nomination option at least allows the individual's preferences to be considered if a court proceeding becomes necessary.[5]

States have other statutes authorizing patients to appoint health care proxies. New York enacted a statute allowing proxy appointments for "do not resuscitate" decisions.[6] Indiana and Washington passed laws authorizing people to select health care consent proxies,[7] and Minnesota's patient rights statute allows a person to select a "chosen representative" to participate in his or her treatment plan.[8]

States may explicitly endorse the living will proxy (Virginia), while in others (e.g., California and Rhode Island) the durable power has greater authority. Since most states have not yet directly addressed the issue of appointing medical treatment proxies, maximum protection is achieved by naming the same person as proxy in all documents authorizing appointment (e.g., durable power, living will, and fiduciary nomination).[9]

---

1 *Arkansas Stat. Anot. Sec. 20-17-201(10), -202 (1987); Del. Code Ann. tit. 16, Sec. 2502(b) (Repl. 1983); Fla. Stat. Ann. Sec. 765.05(2) (1986); Idaho H.B. 514, as amended, ch. No. 262, adopted by the 49th Legislature, 2nd Regular Session; La. Rev. Stat. Ann. Sec. 40:1299.58.3(c)(1) (West Supp. 1987); Tex. Rev. Civ. Stat. Ann. art. Sec. 4590h(e)(e) (Vernon Supp. 1987); Utah Code Ann. Sec. 75-2-1106 (Supp. 1986); Va. Code Sec. 54-325.8:4, 54-325.8:6.2 (Supp. 1985); Wyo. Stat. Sec. 35-22-102(d) (Supp. 1987).*

2 *Indiana Code Ann. Sec. 16-8-11-14(g)(2) (Burns Supp. 1986); Iowa Code Ann. Sec. 2144.A.7(1)(a) (Supp. 1986).*

3 *Col. Rev. Stat. ff115-18-107 (Supp. 1986).*

4 *The states allowing declarations "substantially" similar to the form provided in the statute are: Arkansas, Alabama, Alaska, Arizona, Colorado, Connecticut,*

District of Columbia, Florida, Georgia, Hawaii, Idaho, Illinois, Indiana, Iowa, Kansas, Louisiana, Maine, Maryland, Mississippi, Missouri, Montana, Nevada, New Hampshire, North Carolina, Oklahoma, South Carolina, Tennessee, texas, Utah, Vermont, Virginia, Washington, West Virginia, Wisconsin and Wyoming. Two states (Delaware and New Mexico) do not provide sample forms. The states requiring that the statutory declaration form be precisely followed are: California and Oregon.

5 *Durable Power of Attorney Statutes, Society for the Right to Die, New York, 5-9 (1988).*

6 *'Orders Not To Resuscitate," N.Y. PUb. Health Law 2965(b), 1987 N.Y. Laws ch. 818.*

7 *Ind. Code Sec. 16-8-12 (P.L. 805 of 1987, Sec. 3, 6). 1987 Wash. Laws ch. 162 Sec. 2(1)(b).* See also *Uniform Laws Commissioners' Model Health Care Consent Act, 9 U.L.A. 489 Sec. 5, 6 (Supp. 1987).*

8 *Minn. Stat. Ann. Sec. 144-651(1), (9), (11), (19), Sec. 144.335(a) (Supp. 1987).*

9 *The Society for the Right to Die, New York (1988).*

Form 25

(e) The declaration may, but need not, be in the following form, and in addition may include other specific directions. Should any specific direction be determined to be invalid, such invalidity shall not affect other directions of the declaration which can be given effect without the invalid direction, and to this end the directions in the declaration are severable.

Declaration

This declaration is made this_______________ day of_______________ (month, year). I, _______________, being of sound mind, willfully and voluntarily make known my desires that my moment of death shall not be artificially postponed.

If at any time I should have an incurable and irreversible injury, disease, or illness judged to be a terminal condition by my attending physician who has personally examined me and has determined that my death is imminent except for death delaying procedures, I direct that such procedures which would only prolong the dying process be withheld or withdrawn, and that I be permitted to die naturally with only the administration of medication, sustenance, or the performance of any medical procedure deemed necessary by my attending physician to provide me with comfort care.

In the absence of my ability to give directions regarding the use of such death delaying procedures, it is my intention that this declaration shall be honored by my family and physician as the final expression of my legal right to refuse medical or surgical treatment and accept the consequences from such refusal.

Signed _______________

City, County and State of Residence___________________________

The declarant is personally known to me and I believe him or her to be of sound mind. I saw the declarant sign the declaration in my presence (or the declarant acknowledged in my presence that he or she had signed the declaration) and I signed the declaration as a witness in the presence of the declarant. I did not sign the declarant's signature above for or at the direction of the declarant. At the date of this instrument, I am not entitled to any portion of the estate of the declarant according to the laws of intestate succession or, to the best of my knowledge and belief, under any will of declarant or other instrument taking effect at declarant's death, or directly financially responsible for declarant's medical care.

Witness_______________

Witness_______________

Editor's Note: *This form is found in the Illinois Revised Statutes, Chapter 110½ Section 703(e). This form should be used only in Illinois, as the laws of other states may vary. Your own attorney or the State Medical Association of your state is the best source of information about a form for use in your state.*

12.3 Durable Power of Attorney

Legal authority for appointing the health care proxy lies in "durable power of attorney" statutes, proxy provisions in living will statutes and statutory provisions authorizing individuals to nominate their own court-appointed fiduciaries. Many states allow the appointment of health care agents even without specific statutory authority, but statutes provide important clarification of the proxy role.[1]

The traditional power of attorney ends when the appointer ('principal") becomes "disabled" (i.e., incompetent or otherwise incapacitated). A 'durable" power of attorney authorizes the attorney-in-fact to make decisions on the principal's behalf even after the person becomes disabled. All states (and the District of Columbia) have durable power of attorney statutes.[2]

Some durable powers of attorney are effective immediately and continue after the individual concerned becomes disabled, while others become effective only after the person becomes disabled. Some durable power of attorney laws restrict who may be appointed, or they have specific procedural requirements.[3]

Enacted primarily to authorize property decisions, most durable power of attorney statutes are silent about using the power of attorney for health care matters. Durable power of attorney appointments for health care are legally binding in these 'silent" statutes if the power of attorney explicitly authorize the attorney-in-fact to make health care decisions, and if it otherwise meets the durable power of attorney statutory requirements.[4]

Durable power of attorney appointments may allow proxies to provide, withhold or withdraw consent to specific medical procedures (e.g., surgery, antibiotics, blood transfusions, cardiac resuscitation, respiratory support, chemotherapy, dialysis, technologically supplied nutrition and hydration). Proxies may also be authorized to grant releases to medical personnel, or to employ and discharge such personnel, or to provide access to, and disclose, medical records and other personal information. They may be allowed to discuss the appointer's medical condition and prognosis with physicians, or resort to court, if necessary, to obtain the court's authorization in treatment decisions, and to request civil damages for failure to honor the appointer's or proxy's preferences. They may be authorized to expend or withhold funds necessary to carry out medical treatment, or to interpret the living will, or to delegate the decisonmaking authorization to another proxy, and to communicate any treatment decisons the appointer made.[5]

States that have explicitly addressed the use of durable powers of attorney for health care are: Alaska, Arizona, California, Colorado, Connecticut, Hawaii, Idaho, Illinois, Iowa, Maine, Maryland, Nevada, New Jersey, New York, North Carolina, Pennsylvania, Rhode Island, Texas, Vermont and Virginia. California, Illinois, Rhode Island, Nevada and Vermont have separate statutes authorizing powers of attorney for health care.[6]

---

1 *For a discussion of common law authority,* see, e.g., *Note,* Appointing an Agent to Make Medical Treatment Choices, *84 Colum. L. Rev. 985, 1009-12 (1984); New York Task Force on Life and the Law,* Life-Sustaining Treatment: Making Decisions and Appointing a Health-Care Agent *(1987).*

2 *Alabama, Ala. Code Sec. 26-1-2 (Repl. 1986); Alaska, Statutory Form Power of Attorney Act, ch. 109, 1988 Alaska Sess. Laws 1-38; Arizona, Ariz. Rev. Stat. Ann. Sec. 14-5501 14-5502 (1975); Arkansas, Ark. Stat. Ann. Secs. 28-6-201 to 28-68-203 (1987); California, Cal. Civ. Secs. 2400-24500-47, 2460 2500-08, 2510-13 (West Supp. 1988); Colorado, Colo. Rev. Stat. Secs. 15-14-501, 15-14-502 (Repl. 1987); Connecticut, Conn. Gen. Ann. Secs. 1-42 to 1-56 (West Supp. 1988); Deleware, Del. Code. Ann. tit. 12, Secs. 4901 to 4905 (Repl. 1987); District of Columbia, D.C. Code Ann. Secs. 21-2081 to 21-2085 (Supp. 1988); Florida, Fla. Stat. Ann. Sec. 709.08 (West 1988); Georgia, Ga. Code Ann. 10-6-36 (1982); Hawaii, Hawaii Rev. Stat. Secs. 560:5-501, 5-502 (Repl. 1985); Idaho, Idaho Code Secs. 15-5-501 to 15-5-507 (Supp. 1988); Illinois, Ill. Ann. Stat. ch. 110½ Secs. 801-1 to 804-12 (Smith-Hurd Supp. 1988); Indiana, Indiana Code Ann. Secs. 30-2-11-1 to 30-2-11-7 (Burns Supp. 1988); Iowa, Iowa Code Ann. Secs. 633,705 633,706 (West Supp. 1988); Kansas, Kan. Stat. Ann. Secs. 58-610 to 58-617 (1983); Kentucky, KY. Rev. Stat. Ann. Sec. 386.093 (Michie 1984); La. Civ. Code Ann. art. 3027; Maine, Me. Rev. Stat. Ann. tit. 18-A Secs, 5-501, 5-502 (1981 & Supp. 1987); Maryland, Md. Est. & Trusts Code Ann. Secs. 13-601 to 13-603 (1974); Massachusetts, Mass. Gen. Laws Ann. ch. 201B Secs. 1 to 7 (West Supp. 1988); Michigan, Mich. Comp. Laws Ann. Sec. 700.495 (West 1980); Minnesota, Minn. Stat. 523.01 to 523.25 (West Supp. 1988); Mississippi, Miss. Code Ann. Sec. 87-3-13 (Supp. 1988); Missouri, Mo. Ann. Stat. Secs. 486,550 to 486,595 (Vernon 1987); Montana, Mont. Code Ann. Secs. 72-5-501, 72-5-502 (1987); Nebraska, Neb. Rev. Stat. Secs. 30-2664 to 30-2672; Nevada, Nev. Rev. Stat. Secs. 111.460; New Hampshire, N.H. Rev. Stat. Ann. Sec. 506:6 (Supp. 1987); New Jersey, N.J. Stat. Ann. Secs. 46:2B-8 2B-9 (West Supp. 1988); New Mexico, N.M. Stat. Ann. Secs. 45-5-501, 45-5-502 (1978); New York, N.Y. Gen. Oblig. Law Secs. 5-1501 5-1601 (McKinney 1978 and Supp. 1988); North Carolina, N.C. Gen. Stat. Secs. 32A-1 to 32A-14 (Nov. 1987); North Dakota, N.D. Cent. Code Secs. 30.1-30-01 to 30.1-30-05 (Supp. 1987); Ohio, Ohio Rev. Code Secs. 30.1-30-01 to 30.1-30-05 (Supp. 1987); Oklahoma, Okla. Stat. tit. 58, Secs. 1051 to 1062 (West Supp. 1988); Oregon, Or. Rev. Stat. Secs. 126.407 126.413 (Repl. 1987); Pennsylvania, Pa. Stat. Ann. tit. 20, Secs. 5601 to 5607 (Purson Supp. 1988); RI, R.I. Gen. Laws Sec. 34-22-6.1 (1984) Secs. 23-4.10-1 to 23-4.10-2 (Supp. 1987); South Carolina, S.C. Code Ann. Secs. 62-5-501 62-5-502 (1987); South Dakota, S.D. Codified Laws Ann. Secs. 5907-2.1 to 59-7-2.4 (Repl. 1978); Tennessee, Tenn. Code Ann. Secs. 34-6-101 to 34-6-197 (Repl. 1984); Texas, TEx. Prob. Code Ann. Sec. 36A (Vernon 1980); Utah, Utah Code Ann. Secs. 75-5-501 75-5-502 (Repl. 1978); Vermont, Vt. Stat. Ann. tit. 14, Sec. 3451-67 (Supp. 1987); Virginia, Va. Code Secs. 11-9.1 to 11-9.4 (Repl. 1984 Supp. 1988); Washington, Wash. Rev. Code Ann. Secs.*

11.94.010 to 11.94.900 (1987); West Virginia, W. Va. Code Secs. 39-4-1 to 39-4-7 (Supp. 1988); Wisconsin, Wis. Stat. Sec. 243.07 (West 1987); Wyoming, Wyo. Stat. Secs. 3-5-101 to 3-5-103 (1985).

3 *The Society for the Right to Die, New York 1988.*

4 *President's Commission for the Study of Ethical Problems in Medicine and Biomedical and Behavioral Research,* Deciding to Forego Life-Sustaining Treatment *126-36, 145-49 (1983); F. Collin, Jr., J. Lombard, Jr., A. Moses and H. Spitler,* Drafting the Durable Power of Attorney *22 (1987); Note,* Appointing an Agent to Make Medical Treatment Choices, *84 Colum. L. Rev. 985, 1012-25. (1984).*

5 *The Society for the Right to Die, New York (1988).*

6 *Cal. Civ. Code Sec. 2500 (West Supp. 1987); 1987 Ill. Public Act No. 85-701; R.I. Gen. Laws Sec. 23-4.10-1, 23-4, 10-2 (Supp. 1986); 1987 Nev. Stat. ch. 396 Vt. Stat. Ann. tit. 14 Sec. 3451-67.*

Form 26

Notice to Person Executing This Document

This is an important legal document. Before executing this document, you should know these facts:

This document gives the person you designate (the attorney-in-fact) the power to make **MOST** health care decisions for you if you lose the capacity to make informed health care decisions for yourself. This power is effective only when you lose the capacity to make informed health care decisions for yourself and, notwithstanding this document, as long as you have the capacity to make informed health care decisions for yourself, you retain the right to make all medical and other health care decisions for yourself.

You may include specific limitations in this document on the authority of the attorney-in-fact to make health care decisions for you.

Subject to any specific limitations you include in this document, if you do lose the capacity to make an informed decision on a health care matter, the attorney-in-fact **generally** will be authorized by this document to make health care decisions for you to the same extent as you could make those decisions yourself, if you had the capacity to do so. The authority of the attorney-in-fact to make health care decisions for you **generally** will include the authority to give informed consent, to refuse to give informed consent, or to withdraw informed consent to any care, treatment, service, or procedure to maintain, diagnose, or treat a physical or mental condition.

However, even if the attorney-in-fact has general authority to make health care decisions for you under this document, the attorney-in-fact **never** will be authorized to do any of the following:

(1) Refuse or withdraw informed consent to health care necessary to maintain your life (unless you are suffering from an illness or injury that is likely to result in imminent death, regardless of the type, nature, and the amount of health care provided);

(2) Refuse or withdraw informed consent to health care necessary to provide you with comfort care (except that, if he is

Continued

Editor's Note: *The Office of the General Counsel is grateful to D. Brent Mulgrew, J.D., General Counsel of the Ohio State Medical Association, for making this form available for publication in this book.*

Because of variances in the provisions of the law in the several states, this form should be used only in Ohio. Your own attorney, or the State Medical Association in your state is the best source of information about a form for use in your state.

not prohibited from doing so under (4) below, the attorney-in-fact could refuse or withdraw informed consent to the provision of nutrition or hydration to you);

(3) Refuse or withdraw informed consent to health care for you if you are pregnant and if the refusal or withdrawal would terminate the pregnancy (unless the pregnancy or health care would pose a substantial risk to your life, or unless your attending physician and at least one other physician determine, to a reasonable degree of medical certainty, that the fetus would not be born alive);

(4) Refuse or withdraw informed consent to the provision of nutrition or hydration to you, unless, prior to the refusal or withdrawal of that informed consent, your attending physician and at least one other physician record their opinions that the provision of nutrition or hydration would not provide comfort to you, and additionally that either of the following situations exists: Your death is imminent whether or not nutrition or hydration is provided to you, and the nonprovision of nutrition or hydration to you is not likely to result in your death by malnutrition or dehydration; **OR** if nutrition or hydration were provided to you, it could not be assimilated or would shorten your life.

(5) Withdraw informed consent to any health care to which you previously consented, unless a change in your physical condition has significantly decreased the benefit of that health care to you, or unless the health care is not, or is no longer, significantly effective in achieving the purposes for which you consented to its use.

Additionally, when exercising his authority to make health care decisions for you, the attorney-in-fact will have to act consistently with your desires or, if your desires are unknown, to act in your best interest. You may express your desires to the attorney-in-fact by including them in this document or by making them known in another manner.

When acting pursuant to this document, the attorney-in-fact **generally** will have the same rights that you have to receive information about proposed health care, to review health care records, and to consent to the disclosure of health care records. You can limit that right in this document if you so choose.

Generally, you may designate any competent adult as the attorney-in-fact under this document. However, you **cannot** designate a physician who is treating you, an employee or agent of a physician who is treating you, or an employee or agent of a health care facility at which you are being treated as the attorney-in-fact under it.

Continued

Unless you specify a shorter period in this document, the document and the power it grants to the attorney-in-fact will be in effect for seven years from the date of its execution. However, if you lack the capacity to make informed health care decisions on the date that the document and the power it grants to the attorney-in-fact otherwise would expire, the document and the power it grants wil continue in effect until you regain the capacity to make informed health care decisions for yourself.

You have the right to revoke the designation of the attorney-in-fact by giving him oral or written notice of the revocation. You have the right to revoke the authority of the attorney-in-fact to make health care decisions for you by giving oral or written notice of the revocation to your physician or another physician who is providing you with health care. You have the right to revoke this document and the authority granted to the attorney-in-fact under this document by canceling, obliterating, or destroying it with the intent to revoke it, or by doing anything else that clearly communicates your intent to revoke the document.

If you execute this document and create a valid durable power of attorney for health care with it, it will revoke any prior, valid durable power of attorney for health care that you created, unless you indicate otherwise in this document.

This document is not valid as a durable power of attorney for health care unless it either is acknowledged before a notary public or it is attested and signed by at least two adult witnesses who personally know you and who are present when you sign or acknowledge your signature. No person who is related to you by blood, marriage, or adoption, and no person who is entitled to benefit in any way from your death may be a witness. The attorney-in-fact, physicians, and employees or agents of a physician or a health care facility are ineligible to be witnesses.

If there is anything in this document that you do not understand, you should ask your lawyer to explain it to you.

Your attorney-in-fact may need this document immediately in case of an emergancy that requires a decision concerning you health care. Either keep this document where it is immediately available to your attorney-in-fact and alternate attorneys-in-fact (if designated) or give each of them an executed copy of this document.

1. **Designation of attorney-in-fact.** I, ______________________
(your name)

Continued

of ______________________________
(your address)

do hereby designate and appoint:

____
(name of your attorney-in-fact)

of ______________________________
(address of your attorney-in fact)

Phone: ______________________________
(telephone of your attorney-in-fact)

as my attorney-in-fact to make health care decisions for me as authorized in this document. For the purpose of this document, "health care decision" means informed consent, refusal to give informed consent or withdrawal of informed consent.

2. **Creation of durable power of attorney for health care.** By this document I intend to create a durable power of attorney for health care under Section 1337.11 **et seq.** of Ohio Revised Code.

3. **General statement of authority granted.** Subject to any limitations in this document, I hereby grant to my attorney-in-fact full power and authority to make health care decisions for me to the same extent that I could make such decisions for myself if I had the capacity to do so subject to the limitations imposed by law. In exercising this authority, my attorney-in-fact shall make health care decisions that are consistent with my desires as stated in this document or otherwise made known to my attorney-in-fact.

4. **Special provisions and limitations.** In exercising the authority under this durable power of attorney for health care, my attorney-in-fact shall act consistently with my desires, subject to the special provisions and limitations stated below:

____

____

____

(You may attach additional pages if you need more space to complete your statement. If you attach additional pages, you should date and sign each of the additional pages at the same time you date and sign this document.)

Continued

5. **Inspection and disclosure of information relating to my physical or mental health.** Subject to any limitations in this document (see paragaph 4), my attorney-in-fact has the power and authority to do all of the following:
(a) request, review, and receive any information, verbal or written, regarding my physical or mental health, including, but not limited to, medical and hospital records;
(b) Execute on my behalf any releases or other documents that may be required in order to obtain this information;
(c) Consent to the disclosure of this information.

6. **Signing documents, waivers, and releases.** Where necessary to implement the health care decisions that my attorney-in-fact is authorized by this document to make, my attorney-in-fact has the power and authority to execute on my behalf all of the following:
(a) Documents purporting to be a Refusal to Permit Treatment or an Intent to Leave Hospital Against Medical Advice;
(b) Any necessary waiver or release from liability required by a hospital or physician.

7. **Duration.** This durable power of attorney for health care expires on ________________ (Fill in this space ONLY if you want the authority of your attorney-in-fact to end **earlier** than the seven (7) year period described above.)

8. **Optional designation of alternate attorneys-in-fact.** If the person designated as my attorney-in-fact in paragraph 1 is not available or becomes ineligible to act as my attorney-in-fact to make a health care decisions for me or loses the mental capacity to make health care decisions for me, or if I revoke that person's appointment or authority to act as my attorney-in-fact to make health care decisions for me, then I designate and appoint the following persons to serve as my attorney-in-fact to make health care decisions for me as authorized in this document, such persons to serve in the order listed below:

A. First Alternate Attorney-in-Fact:__________________________
(name)

of______________________________ Phone:______________
(address)

Continued

B. Second Alternate Attorney-in-Fact:____________________
(name)

of__________________________Phone:____________
(address)

9. **Prior designations revoked.** I revoke any prior durable power of attorney for health care.

I sign my name to this Durable Power of Attorney for health care on ____________________ at ________________
(date) (city)

______________ and have attached ____ additional pages
(state)

hereto each of which is signed and dated by me.

____
(you sign here)

(This power of attorney will not be valid unless it is (1) signed by two qualified witnesses who are present when you sign or acknowledge your signature or (2) acknowledged before a notary public. If you have attached any additional pages to this form, you should date and sign each of the additional pages at the same time you date and sign this power of attorney.)

I declare that the person who signed or acknowledged this document is personally known to me to be the principal, that the principal signed or acknowledged this durable power of attorney in my presence, that the principal appears to be of sound mind and under no duress, fraud, or undue influence, that I am not the person appointed as attorney-in-fact by this document, and that I am not a physician or an employee or agent of a physician or of a health care facility. I further declare that I am not related to the person who signed or acknowledged this document by blood, marriage or adoption and that, to the best of my knowledge, I am not entitled to benefit from that person's death.

Signature:______________ Residence Address:______________

Print Name:____________________ ____________________

Date:________________________ ____________________

Signature:______________ Residence Address:______________

Print Name:____________________ ____________________

Date:________________________ ____________________

Continued

Form 26 Continued

Or
Acknowledgement

State of Ohio
County of ______________, S.S.

On this the ____ day of ______________, 19____, before me, the undersigned Notary Public, personally appeared ______________________, known to me or satisfactorily proven to be the person whose name is subscribed to the above Durable Power of Attorney for Health care, and acknowledged that (s)he executed the same for the purpose expressed therein. Further, said person appeared to be of sound mind and under no duress, fraud or undue influence.

My Commission
Expires:____________________ ____________________________
Notary Public

This form has been provided to your doctor as a public service of the Ohio State Medical Association. Any legal questions you may have about the execution or operation of a Durable Power of Attorney for Health Care should be directed to a lawyer.

Warranties as to Results of Treatment

13.0

In agreeing to render treatment or to perform an operation, the physician does not, in the absence of a special contract, guarantee particular results or a cure.[1] The doctor warrants only that he or she possesses the degree of knowledge and skill common to a member of the profession in good standing in the community, and that he or she will use that knowledge and skill in treating the patient.[2] Once a physician undertakes to perform a procedure, there is an implied warranty that he or she has the skill commonly required to perform that procedure.[3]

A physician may expressly agree to accomplish a particular result or effect a cure. If the doctor enters into such a contract, however, and fails to bring about the result or to effect a cure, he is liable for breach of contract even though the highest possible professional skill was employed.[4]

In a Michigan case,[5] two surgeons performed a gastric resection on a patient with a bleeding ulcer. The day after the operation, a thoracic surgeon diagnosed a ruptured esophagus due to surgical trauma. The patient underwent three subsequent operations, contracted hepatitis and lost over eighty pounds.

In the lawsuit against the two surgeons, the patient not only alleged negligence on the part of the surgeons, but also charged that they breached their promise to cure him. The patient claimed that the surgeons had told him that there was "no danger at all in this operation," that the operation "takes care of all your troubles," and that the patient would be able to return to work in "approximately three to four weeks at the most." The jury found that the surgeons had not been negligent, but that they had breached their contract to cure the patient.

The Supreme Court of Michigan, affirming a $50,000 verdict in favor of the patient, ruled that it was for the jury to determine whether the surgeons had entered into a contract to cure the patient and whether they breached that contract. Whether a physician enters into a special agreement to cure, or guarantees a specific result, depends upon the words that were spoken, and the circumstances under which they were spoken. This determination, the court held, is always a question for the finder of fact, usually the jury.[6]

The court also referred to an earlier Michigan case,[7] in which the defendant osteopath promised to perform a caesarean section. In that instance, the woman patient had previously had two stillbirths and was convinced that she could not normally deliver. When she was ready to deliver, the attending osteopath turned her over to the head of the obstetrics department at the hospital but apparently failed to inform the department head of his agreement to perform a caesarean operation. The baby was unfortunately born dead, although hospital records showed that it had been alive near term.

On appeal, a verdict and judgment of $5,000 was affirmed for pain and mental suffering and for loss of wages due to the plaintiff's nervous condition resulting from the osteopath's failure to perform the promised caesarean section. Negligent treatment on the osteopath's part was not established, and recovery was solely on the basis that he failed to fulfill his promise.[8]

The court cautioned, however, that a physician's therapeutic reassurances that a patient will be all right must not be converted into a binding promise by the disappointed or quarrelsome.[9] In the Michigan case, referred to earlier, the court interpreted this statement as meaning that a jury, in order to find the surgeons liable, must find that the surgeons made a specific, clear and express promise to cure or effect a specific result.[10]

In another case,[11] a man who had suffered a severe burn from an electric wire consulted a physician concerning the removal of scar tissue from the palm of his right hand. He subsequently claimed that the doctor said that he would be in the hospital only three or four days and would return to work with a perfect hand. The New Hampshire Supreme Court ruled that this statement did not constitute a promise to cure, but was only the physician's opinion. The court also ruled, however, that the doctor's guarantee that he would make the patient's hand perfect did constitute a promise to cure.[12]

In a more recent case,[13] the plaintiff alleged that the physician had assured her that she did not have cancer in any part of her body. She claimed that he had therefore contracted with her that she would not be discharged with evidence of cancer. On appeal, she alleged that the trial court had erred in not submitting a special interogatory to the jury regarding whether or not there was a contract entered into between the patient and her physician.

The court held that there is no basis in law and no facts to indicate that there was a contract and thus the trial court did not err.[14]

The court in this case refused to consider a physician's reassurances and treatment as a contract guaranteeing the patient that she did not have cancer.

The same rules of consent apply to surgery or treatment for cosmetic reasons as apply to medical procedures for therapeutic reasons. the surgeon performing reconstructive surgery to correct the disfigurement of accident victims, or those who are born with handicaps or pronounced abnormalities of appearance, is not judged differently than his colleagues. On the other hand, the courts are not very sympathetic toward doctors who undertake questionable operations to satisfy a vain patient's quest for beauty.[15]

Optimistic statements by a surgeon assuring a desirable outcome have sometimes been construed by the courts as contractual guarantees of a promised result. Similar statements by a physician to a patient requiring therapeutic surgery tend, however, to be interpreted as mere words of encouragement to the sick.

The surgeon who engages in cosmetic surgery must be particularly careful to avoid any statements that might be technically interpreted as a guarantee of result. The patient who has had a bad result from cosmetic surgery frequently has the advantage of visual evidence with which to elicit the prejudices and sympathies of a jury.

---

1 Walker v. Skiwski, *529 So.2d 184 (Miss. 1988);* Thompson v. Caner, *518 So.2d 609, 611 (Miss. 1988);* Dazet v. Bass, *254 So.2d 183 (Miss. 1971);* Custodio v. Bauer, *59 Cal. Rptr. 463 (1967);* Bishop v. Byrne, *265 F. Supp. 460 (W. Va. 1967);* Lane v. Cohen, *201 So.2d 804 (Fla. 1967);* Bria v. St. Joseph's Hospital, *220 A.2d 29 (Conn. 1966);* Hawkins v. McCain, *239 N.C. 160, 79 S.E.2d 493 (1954);* Waynick v. Reardon, *236 N.C. 116, 72 S.E.2d 4 (1952);* Vann v. Harden, *187 Va. 555, 47 S.E.2d 314 (1948);* Piper v. Halford, *247 Ala. 530, 25 So.2d 264 (1946);* Fritz v. Horsfall, *24 Wash. 2d 14, 163 P.2d 148 (1945);* Wall v. Brim, *138 F.2d 478 (C.C.A. 5 1943);* Lake v. Baccus, *59 Ga. App. 656, 2 S.E.2d 121 (1939);* Keating v. Perkins, *250 App. Div. 9, 293 N.Y.S. 197 (1937).*

2 Creighton v. Karlin, *225 So.2d 288 (La. 1969);* Benson v. Mays, *227 A.2d 220 (Md. 1967), but see* Steinbeich v. Barfield, *428 So. 2d 915 (6 App. 1 Cir. 1983).*

3 Wolfe v. Virusky, *306 F. Supp. 519 (Ga. 1969).*

4 Guilmet v. Campbell, *188 N.W.2d 601 (Mich. 1971);* Brooks v. Robinson, *163 So.2d 186 (La. 1964);* Camposano v. Claiborn, *196 A.2d 129 (Conn. 1963);* Noel v. Proud, *367 P.2d 61 (Kan. 1961);* Robins v. Finestone, *306 N.Y. 543, 127 N.E.2d 330 (1955);* Colvin v. Smith, *276 App. Div. 9, 92 N.Y.S.2d 794 (1949);* Hawkins v. McGee, *84 N.H. 114, 146 Atl. 641 (1929);* Brooks v. Herd, *144 Wash. 173, 257 Pac. 238 (1927).*

5 Guilmet v. Campbell, *188 N.W.2d 601 (Mich. 1971).*

6 *In a strenuous dissenting opinion, one judge said that the decision would deprive a physician of the opportunity to make therapeutic reassurances which he deems medically necessary for the benefit of his patient. He denounced the imposition of liability on the surgeons for failing to do that which "none but the Deity could possibly agree to perform." He also denounced the court's 'unwarned, un-*

precedented, wholly gratuitous and destructively witless war of 'contract liability' upon a brother profession which, by the manifold harassment of malpractice actions, has been forced already to undertake what is professionally known as 'defensive medicine.'."

7 Stewart v. Rudner, *349 Mich. 459, 84 N.W.2d 816 (1957). See also* Hackworth v. Hart, *474 S.W.2d 377 (Ky. 1971);* Schork v. Huber, *649 S.W.2d 86 (1983).*

8 Stewart v. Rudner, *349 Mich. 459, 84 N.W.2d 816 (1957).*

9 Stewart v. Rudner, *349 Mich. 459, 84 N.W.2d 816 (1957).*

10 Guilmet v. Campbell, *188 N.W.2d 601 (Mich. 1971).*

11 Hawkins v. McGee, *84 N.H. 114, 146 Atl. 641 (1929).*

12 *In* Noel v. Proud, *367 P.2d 61 (Kan. 1961) the physician stated that while the Stapes Mobilization might not improve the patient's hearing, it would not make his hearing any worse. The court ruled that the physician breached his promise to obtain a specific result when the patient's loss of hearing worsened after the operation.* See also, Werner v. Kliewer, *710 P.2d 1250, 1257 (Kan. 1985).*

13 Steinbach v. Barfield, *428 So.2d 915, 923 (La. App. 1 Cir. 1983).*

14 Id. *at 923.*

15 *In* Bailey v. Harmon, *74 Colo. 390, 222 Pac. 393 (1924), the defendant physician was held liable for breach of contract where he assured the plaintiff that she would be made into "a model of harmonious perfection." See also* Hirsch v. Safian, *257 App. Div. 212, 12 N.Y.S.2d 568 (1939);* Safian v. Aetna Life Ins. Co., *260 App. Div. 765, 24 N.Y.S.2d 92 (1940), aff'd 286 N.Y. 649, 36 N.E.2d 692;* Gluckstein v. Lipsett, *93 Cal. App.2d 391, 209 P.2d 98 (1949);* Lacey v. Laird, *166 Ohio St. 12, 139 N.E.2d 25 (1956).*

Consent to Operation for Cosmetic Purposes

Form 27

A.M.
Date________________ Time__________P.M.

1. I authorize Dr.________________to perform an operation upon me for the purpose of attempting to improve my appearance with respect to the following condition:__________________________

____

2. The nature and effect of the operation to be performed, risks involved, as well as possible alternative methods of treatment, have been explained to me.

3. I also authorize the operating surgeon to perform any other procedures which he may deem desirable in attempting to improve the condition stated in paragraph 1 or any unhealthy or unforeseen condition that he may encounter during the operation.

4. I consent to the administration of anesthetics to be applied by or under the direction of Dr.________________, and to the use of such anesthetics as he may deem advisable.

5. I know that the practice of medicine and surgery is not an exact science and that therefore reputable practitioners cannot guarantee results. No guarantee or assurance has been given by anyone as to the results that may be obtained.

Witness________________ Signed ______________________
(Patient or person authorized to consent for patient)

Consent to Operation and Grafting of Tissue

Form 28

A.M.
Date________________ Time________P.M.

1. I authorize Dr.________________, and such assistants as he may designate, to perform upon ______________________________
(Myself or name of patient)
the following operation ______________________________
(state nature and extent of operation)
and to do any additional or different procedure that his judgment may dictate during the above operation.

2. I am informed that the above operation will require the grafting of the following tissue____________________________, and that
(skin, bone, cartilage, etc.)
the tissue to be used will be supplied by ________________________ .
(name of donor or tissue bank)

3. The risks involved in the use of such tissue for grafting, the nature and effect of the operation, and possible alternative methods of procedure or treatment have been explained to me. No guarantee or assurance has been given anyone as to the results that may be obtained.

4. I understand that the operating surgeon will be occupied solely with the surgery, and that the administration of the anesthesia is an independent professional function and will be in charge of an anesthetist, whom I authorize to administer such anesthetics as he may deem advisable.

Witness________________ Signed ________________________
(Patient or person authorized to consent for patient)

Consent to Removal of Tissue for Grafting

Form 29

A.M.
Date________________ Time________P.M.

1. I authorize Dr.________________, and such assistants as he may designate, to perform an operation upon myself for the purpose of removing the following tissues______________________________
(skin, bone, cartilage, etc.)
from my person for donation to ______________________________
(name of recipient)
The operation is to include such procedures as may be necessary in the judgment of the operating surgeon for the purpose of attempting to graft tissues, and the use of such anesthetics as he may deem advisable.

2. I make this request with full knowledge that this attempt to graft tissue may not be successful. The risks and uncertainties involved as well as the possibility that I may be permanently injured, scarred, or disfigured as a consequence of this operation, have been explained to me. Nevertheless, I make this request and grant the authority set forth above, voluntarily and upon my own initiative, and with no assurances from anyone as to the results that may be obtained, either in respect to myself or the recipient.

Witness________________ Signed______________________
(Patient or person authorized to consent for patient)

14.1 Sterilization

States allow sterilization of competent adults who are capable of making an informed decision and of signing a consent document. Such sterilizations are commonly referred to as non-therapeutic sterilizations; that is, they are usually used as an elective means of birth control. When dealing with a competent adult, a physician needs only to obtain consent to the sterilization. Such consent should be in writing. In Kentucky, a person seeking non-therapeutic sterilization must wait 24 hours after written consent has been given.[1]

If a physician is dealing with an incompetent, an incapacitated person or a mentally retarded individual, then the doctor must take additional steps to acquire approval for a sterilization. In recent years, sterilization laws which deal with incompetents, incapacitated persons or mentally retarded people have changed radically. Prior to this transformation, many states allowed sterilizations of retarded persons without their consent or knowledge.

The primary reasons for the change in the laws are two-fold. First, modern law has been influenced by a distaste for eugenic sterilization. Second, the law has sought to protect the individual's right to make his or her own reproductive decisions; that is, the right to privacy has influenced the sterilization area. The focus on the right of reproductive privacy has often resulted in the unavailability of sterilization for retarded persons. This unavailability stems from the strict procedure guidelines which must be followed prior to performing a sterilization on an incompetent, an incapacitated person or a mentally retarded individual.[2]

State laws covering sterilization vary considerably. Many states simply have no such legislation. Of those that do, Colorado is the most conservative. It prohibits sterilization of persons with developmental disabilities unless the individual himself or herself consents to the procedure.[3]

Many states allow sterilization of mentally incompetent persons if the court finds that such a procedure would be in the best interest of the person. The best interest standard is broad and leaves considerable room for interpretation by the court of unique facts and circumstances. States that have best-interest standards include: Connecticut;[4] Hawaii, as long as the court finds the clear and convincing evidence that the ward is functionally incapable of giving consent;[5] Minnesota;[6] North Carolina, as long as the court finds by clear and convincing evidence that the ward is functionally incapable of giving consent;[7] Oregon;[8] Vermont;[9] Utah;[10] and West Virginia.[11]

A court can order a sterilization in Arkansas if it finds that a person is incapable of caring for himself or herself.[12] Idaho allows petitions; however, the court must find a preponderance of evidence that the person is beyond reasonable doubt irreversibly and incurably mentally retarded.[13] New Jersey allows a petition, but specifies no standard.[14] The most specific state is Virginia which requires the court to find by clear and convincing evidence that there is a need for contraception; that no reasonable alternative method of contraception is adequate; that no extreme risk to the patient is involved, and that the person is permanently incapable of caring for and raising a child.[15]

In Iowa, the person seeking sterilization for an incompetent must appeal to the Board of Eugenics.[16] In Mississippi, the appeal must be made to the Board of Directors of the mental institution where the incompetent resides. The Board of Directors must then find that sterilization is in the best interest of the patient. If the board denies sterilization, an appeal can be taken to chancery court.[17] In Oklahoma, the Board of Affairs of the State hears such a petition.[18]

In Montana and Nevada, the law states that minors cannot give self consent to sterilizations.[19] Tennessee simply requires consent.[20] Texas takes a different approach, affirmatively requiring consent by the patient or a court order. Therefore, no relative or other person may substitute consent.[21] New Mexico says that no special qualifications can be attached to sterilization; that is, that hospitals should treat it as a routine procedure.[22]

As noted above, sterilization laws vary considerably. In addition to the laws referred to here, the reader must remember that many states have repealed the eugenic approach to sterilization and have allowed courts to set guidelines through case law. Therefore, the reader should look to case law if the state does not specify guidelines in its legislation.

1 Kentucky Rev. Stat., §212.347 (1982).

2 See generally, Elizabeth S. Scott, "Sterilization of Mentally Retarded Persons: Reproductive Rights and Family Privacy," 1986 Duke Law Journal 806.

3 Colorado Revised Stats. §27-10.5-128(2) 1986.

4 *Conn. Gen. Stat. Ann. §45-78q (1958).*

5 *Hawaii Rev. Stat. 560:5-608 (1976).*

6 *Minn. Stat Ann. §252A.131 (1988).*

7 *Gen. Stat. of N. Carol. ch. 35 §35-36.*

8 *Ore. Rev. Stat. §436.305 (1987).*

9 *Ver. Stat. Ann. Ch. 204 §8712 (1987).*

10 *Utah Code Ann. ch. 6 §62A-6-108(3) (1988).*

11 *W. Va. Code §27-16.1 (1985).*

12 *Ark. Code §20-49-101-206 (1987).*

13 *Idaho Code §39-3903(e) (1987).*

14 *New Jer. Stat. Ann. 30:6D-5.*

15 *Code of Va. §54.1-2777 (1950).*

16 *Iowa Code Ann. §145.9 and 145.10 (1972).*

17 *Miss. Code of 1972 Ann. §41-45-7-11.*

18 *Okla. Stat. Ann. 43A §341-344 (1984).*

19 *Montana Code Ann. §41-1-405 (1987); Nev. Rev. Stat. Ann. §129.030 (1986).*

20 *Tenn. Code §68-34-108 (1987).*

21 *Vernon's Rev. Civ. Stat. of Texas, Art. 3174b-2 (1989).*

22 *New Mex. Stats. of 1978 Ann. §24-1-14.*

Request for Sterilization[15]

Form 30

A.M.
Date________________ Time__________P.M.

We the undersigned husband and wife, each being more than twenty-one years of age and of sound mind, request

Dr.________________, and assistants of his choice, to perform upon

______________________________, the following operation:
(name of patient)

____
(state nature and extent of operation)

It has been explained to us that this operation is intended to result in sterility although this result has not been guaranteed. We understand that a sterile person is NOT capable of becoming a parent.

We voluntarily request the operation and understand that if it proves successful the results will be permanent and it will thereafter by physically impossible for the patient to inseminate, or to conceive or bear children.

Signed ____________________
(Husband)

Signed ____________________[16]
(Wife)

Witness__________________

[15]This form is intended to be used where the primary purpose rather than the incidental result is sterilization.

[16]The question of the necessity of the consent of the patient's spouse to a voluntary sterilization has never been litigated. It would appear that such consent is not necessary, although it nay be desirable. The statutes in Georgia, North Carolina and Virginia which specifically authorize voluntary sterilization require the written consent of the patient's spouse.

Request for Sterilization (Alternate Form)

Form 31

A.M.
Date_______________ Time________P.M.

1. I authorize the performance upon myself of the following operation ___________________________ to be performed by or under
(state name of operation)

the direction of Dr.____

2. It has been explained to me that this operation is intended to result in my sterility, but no such result has been guaranteed.

3. I understand that a sterile person is NOT capable of becoming a parent.

4. I understand that if the operation proves successful the results will be permanent and it will thereafter by physically impossible for me to inseminate, or to conceive or bear children.

5. The nature of this operation, the possible alternative methods of treatment, the risks involved, the possible consequences, the possibility that the operation may be unsuccessful, and the possibility of complications have been explained to me by Dr.

_______________ and by _______________.

Signed_____________________

Witness_______________

I have read the above **Request for Sterilization** and do hereby consent to the operation under the terms therein set forth as the spouse of _______________.

Signed_____________________

Date_______________ Time__________

Form 32

Read this consent form carefully. Make sure you understand all of it before you decide to have a sterilization. Make your decision only after careful thought. The decision is your free choice. You are free to withdraw your consent at any time prior to the sterilization.

For patients receiving health services supported in whole or in part by Federal or State financial assistance, your decision at any time not to be sterilized wil not result in a withdrawal or withholding of any benefits provided by programs to projects to which you might otherside be entitled. The sterilization procedure wil not be performed until at least 72 hours after the date and time shown on this consent.

1. I__________________________hereby request and authorize

Dr. __________________________ and/or his associates to perform upon me at the hospital one of the followng elective (that is, optional) sterilization procedures. I have been informed that there is the possibiltiy that the above named physician may not be available to perform the sterilization procedure; in that event, I request and authorize that the sterilization procedure be performed by one of his associates.

[Cross Out Inapplicable Paragraph]

"Laparoscopic sterilization" is an operation to prevent a woman from ever becoming pregnant by sealing and, in some cases, cutting each of the fallopian tubes. These tubes normally carry the eggs from the ovaries to the uterus or womb. Cutting or severing each tube prevents eggs from reaching the uterus. The patient is placed under general, regional or, in very rare instances, local anesthesia. The abdomen is inflated with gas and an instrument called a "laparoscope" is inserted into a small cut near the navel. The laparoscope is a tube which allows the surgeon to look around the abdomen. Once the fallopian tubes are located, a second small cut may be made in the abdomen a few inches below the laparoscope and another instrument called "cautery forceps" are inserted. In some cases, all the instruments go through the one cut. The cautery forceps are

Continued

Editor's Note: *This form is reproduced with permission of Michael Reese Hospital and Medical Center, Chicago, Illinois.*

applied to each of the fallopian tubes in turn, and use electricity to seal each tube and, in some cases, divide it. (Some surgeons prefer to use clips or elastic bands to pinch the tube closed instead of severing it). The abdomen is then deflated and the cuts are sewn shut or closed with clips or tape.

A "tubal ligation sterilization" is an operation to prevent a woman from ever becoming pregnant by tying off and removing a section of each of the fallopian tubes. These tubes normally carry the eggs from the ovaries to the uterus or womb. Cutting a section out prevents eggs from reaching the uterus. The patient is placed under either general, regional or, in very rare instances, local anesthesia, depending upon the judgement of her physician and her preference. A cut is made in the lower abdomen or vagina and the fallopian tubes are located. The tubes are held and a portion of each tube is tied off with surgical suture. These portions of tube may then be cut off and removed. Following this, the cut in the abdomen or vagina is sewn shut.

2. **This operation is intended to result in permanent sterility. I fully understand that this operation is intended to be permanent and that if I want to become pregnant or bear children in the future I should not have this operation. I understand that the operation may not make me sterile. I acknowledge that no guarantees have been made to me that I will be sterile as a result of this operation.**

3. I authorize the administration of local anesthesia by the above named physician and/or his associates, or a regional or general anesthetic by or under the supervision of an anesthesiologist. My doctors have explained to me that whenever an operation is done which requires an anesthetic there are some risks to me associated wth the anesthetic, and not necessarily with the operation. These risks involve sore throat, mild tongue or mouth damage, severe headaches, pneumonia, or, in extremely rare instances, even death.

4. I have been informed that, as with any surgical procedure, there are risks which may occur, such as infection, bleeding, damage to the organs other than my tubes which may require additional surgical procedures on an emergency basis or, in extremely rare instances, death. I also understand that if there is a complication, I may have to stay in the hospital for a longer period of time.

Continued

5. I understand that there may be benefits associated with having sterilization performed. If the sterilization is succesful, I will never again have to use a temporary method of birth control (such as the pill or the IUD) and will not have to worry about becoming pregnant again.

6. I recognize that during the operation unexpected conditions may require my doctors to perform additional or different procedures than those described above. Since I may be under anesthiesia or otherwise unable to give my consent to this treatment during the sterilization, I hereby authorize and request that the physician performing this operation and his assistants or designees perfrom such other procedures as are, in the exercise of good professional judgment, necessary and desirable. I understand that these procedures may include surgery as well as other forms of treatment. The authority granted in this paragraph shall extend to remedy all conditions found during the operation that require treatment, whether or not known at the time this operation is commenced.

7. I have been told that there are a number of other ways than sterilization that may prevent pregnancy, such as birth control pills, intrauterine device, contraceptive foam, contraceptive diaphragm and condoms (rubbers). These methods, unlike sterilization, are not intended to be permanent. I also know that it is possible for a man to have a sterilization procedure.

8. This surgery is being done at my request. I am at least 21 years of age. I understand and it has been explained to me that I may change my mind about having this operation or the type of operation I wish at any time before the operation is done without prejudicing my future care and that no benefits to which I might otherwise be entitled may be withdrawn or withheld from me by reason of a decision not to be sterilized.

9. I understand that governemnt regulations require that this sterilization may not be performed sooner than 72 hours following my signing of this Consent. I understand that I should use this 72 hour period to think over my decision to be sterilized and that if I want to change my mind, I may do so. The above named physician has offered to answer any questions I may have at any time concerning the sterilization procedure.

10. I have read and fully understand this "Consent for Elective Female Sterilization" the nature and purpose of this procedure, its advantages and possible risks, discomforts and complications, if any, as well as possible alternative methods of family planning which were

Continued

Form 32 Continued

explained by the above physician. All blanks have been completed or crossed off prior to my signing.

Date	Signature of Patient
	Time____________ A.M. P.M.

Witness to the Explanation and Signature

Name of Witness—Please Print	Explainer's Signature
Signature of Witness	
Signature of Physician	

Consent to Vasectomy (Husband and Wife)

Form 33

We the undersigned, husband and wife, request

Dr. ________________ and assistants of his choice to perform upon

__________________________ the operation know as a vasectomy
(name of husband/patient)

which is a severance of the vas deferens which conducts sperm and to do such things as are deemed necessary to such operation including the administration of any anesthetic of his choice.

It has been explained to both of us that this operation is intended to result in sterility. We understand that a sterile person is not capable of inducing or causing conception or reproduction of a child. We also understand that the operation may not result in sterility and that no guarantee that sterility will be the result of the operation, has been given to either of us.

We give our consent and agreement, individually and jointly, to the performance of the vasectomy operation and understant that, if it proves successful, the results may be permanent and it will be impossible for the patient to beget or induce the conception or reproduction of a child.

We, individually and jointly, assume all rists and consequences to the vasectomy operation, whether or not it is successful in sterilizing the patient for a temporary or permanent period of time and further agree to indemnify and save blameless the aforementioned doctor, his assistants and the Hospital and its employees and agents in the event any action is brought against them or any of them because of a misrepresentation of our marital status, knowingly or otherwise. We further release said doctor, his assistants and the Hospital and its employees and agents from liability for any and all claims and demands whatsoever we or our heirs, executors, administrators or assigns may have against any of them by reason of any matter relative or incident to such operation.

______________________ 19____ ____________________________
Date Signature of Husband/patient

______________________ 19____ ____________________________
Date Signature of Wife

____
Witness

____
Witness

Editor's Note: *This form is reproduced with permission of Michael Reese Hospital and Medical Center, Chicago, Illinois.*

Consent to Vasectomy (Single Individual)

Form 34

I hereby request that Dr. ________________ and assistants of his choice, perform on me the operation know as a vasectomy which I understand consists of severing of the vas deferens which conducts sperm and to do such things as are deemed necessary to such operation including the administration of any anesthetic of his choice.

I represent and warrant that I am not lawfully married and am over the age of legal consent to such surgical operation under the law of the State of Illinois, and understand that the physician named above, others acting in collaboration with him, his assistants, and the Hospital and its employees and agents are acting in reliance upon my statements.

It has been explained to me that this operation is intended to result in sterility. I understand that a sterile person is not capable of inducing or causing conception or reproduction of a child. I also understand that the operation may not result in sterility and that no guarantee that sterility will be the result of the operation, has been given to me. If the operation is successful in causing sterility such condition may be permanent and irreversible.

I hereby give my consent and agreement to the performance of the vasectomy operation, assume all risks and consequences involved and further agree to indemnify and save blameless the aforementioned doctor, his assistants and the Hospital and its employees and agents in the event any action is brought against them or any of them because of a breach of the representations and warranties made by me herein. I further release said doctor, his assistants and the Hospital and its employees and agents from liability for any and all claims and demands whatsoever I or my heirs, executors, administrators or assigns may have against any of them by reason of any matter relative or incident to such operation.

Date:__________________________ ______________________________
Signature of Consenting Party

A.M.
Time:______________________P.M.

Witnesses:

____
Signature of Witness

____
Signature of Witness

If Consenting Party is other than patient:

____
Signature of Consenting Party

____
Relationship

Editor's Note: *This form is reproduced with permission of Michael Reese Hospital and Medical Center, Chicago, Illinois.*

14.2 Abortion

The procedural and consent requirements for abortion vary according to state, age of the patient, viability of the fetus and the individual's competence. Certain consent requirements exist. The accompanying chart indicates this consideration to date.

Chart 1

State	Minors Parental Consent Notice: Parental	Minors Parental Consent Notice: Judicial Consent	Reporting Requirements: Minors	Reporting Requirements: Adults	Hospital's Right to Refuse to do an Abortion	Residency Requirements	Miscellaneous
Code of Alabama (1975)	Required consent of either parent or guardian. §26-21-3 Except: No consent required if emergency. §26-21-5	Permitted if court finds that the abortion is in the best interest of the minor & the minor is mature enough & well-informed to make the abortion decision on her own. §26-21-3	Must report any abortion on a minor and indicate type of consent or if emergency §26-21-8(c)				
Alaska Statutes of 1962							The State Medical Board shall adopt Regs, & define ethical & dishonorable conduct as it relates to abortions. §08.64.105
Ariz. Rev. Stat. of 1956 Title 3€	Required consent of either parent or guardian §36-2152A ------- No consent required if emergency §36-2153B(2)	Judicial consent is alternative if in the child's best interest & she is mature enough to make the abortion decision §36-2153B(1)			No hospital employee or hospital is required to perform or participate in abortions. §36-2151		

Chart 1 Continued

	Minors Parental Consent Notice						
State	*Parental*	*Judicial Consent*	*Reporting Requirements Minors*	*Reporting Requirements Adults*	*Hospital's Right to Refuse to do an Abortion*	*Residency Requirements*	*Miscellaneous*
Arkansas Code of 1987					No hospital employee or hospital is required to perform or participate in abortions §20-16-601		Hospitals or other facilities that perform abortions required to register with State Board of Health who sets up specific procedural standards. §20-9-302—*Also* must have license from Department of Health. §20-9-302
Annot. Calif. Stat. Health & Safety Code	Parental Consen §25958(a) Emergency Exception	Judicial alternative if minor sufficiently mature & informed §25958(b)-(c)	Reporting regulated by the State Department of Health. §25955.5	Reporting regulated by the State Department of Health. §25955.5	Refusal permitted §25955		Special rape and incest procedure which requires a committee's review. §25952
Colorado Rev. Stat. 1986					Refusal permitted §18-6-104		
Connecticut Stat. Annot. 1974—Title 53 & 53A	Only Criminal Regs.	Only Criminal Regs.	Only Criminal Regs.				

Chart 1 Continued

State	Minors Parental Consent Notice		Reporting Requirements		Hospital's Right to Refuse to do an Abortion	Residency Requirements	Miscellaneous
	Parental	*Judicial Consent*	*Minors*	*Adults*			
Delaware Code Annot. 1974—Title 13 & 14	Parental Consent §24 §1791(b)(3)	Judicial alternative must be available according to case law.	Report to State Board of Health. §24 §1791(c)	Report to State Board of Health. 24 §1791(c)		120 days (minor exceptions) 14§1793	Minor may consent to therapeutic treatment for pregnancy or contagious disease confidentially. 13§708
	*Delaware requires 2 physicians to verify that appropriate circumstances exist for the aboriton—i.e., death of the mother, defective child, incest, rape or risk of injury or physical or mental health of the mother (See—24 §1790(a))						
D.C. Code of 1981	Nothing Specific Except Criminal Penalties.						
Florida Stat. Annot. 1957	Parental Consent Title 29 §390.001(4)(a)	Judicial alternative if sufficiently mature to give informed consent. Title 29 §390.001(4)(a)	Report to Department of Health and Rehab. 29 §390.002	Report to Department of Health & Rehab. 29§390.002	Refusal Permitted. 29§390.001(8)		Notice to husband. title 29 §390.001(4)(b) Abortion counseling must inform of effects & alternatives. 29§390.025(b)
Code of GA Annot. 1988	Parental Consent §24A-4403(a)(1)(A) Emergency exception §24A-4407	Judicial Alternative §24A-2403(b) Best interest of child & minor is well enough informed. §24A-4405(c)(1)			Criminal Code §26-1202 Not required		

Chart 1 Continued

State	Minors Parental Consent Notice		Reporting Requirements		Hospital's Right to Refuse to do an Abortion	Residency Requirements	Miscellaneous
	Parental	*Judicial Consent*	*Minors*	*Adults*			
Hawaii Rev. Stat. 1976			Report anonymous stats to Bureau of Vital Stats.	Report anonymous stats to Bureau of Vital Stats.		90 days §435-16(a)(3)	Can perform only in licensed hospital. §453-16(a)(2).
Idaho Annot. General Laws 1987	Notice only to parents. §18-610(7)				Not required §18-612		Abortion counseling must inform of effects and alternatives. §18-609(2)
*Idaho laws say if Roe is overturned, then the abortion rights in Idaho laws are repealed. See §18-613.							
Ill. Rev. Stat. 1987	Parental Consent §81-51	Judicial alternative best interest standard and mature enough to understand.	Must report anonymous stats to Department of Public Health §81-15 and 81-30	Must report anoymous stats. to Department of Health. §81-15 and 81-30			Leg. Intent is to reinstate original laws regulatory abortion if *Roe* is overruled. §81-21
Indiana Annot. Code—of 1984	Parental Consent. §35-1-58.5-2.5(a)	Judicial Alternative if best interest or minor is mature enough to make the abortion decision independently. §35-1-58.5-25(D).	Must report anonymous stats to Department of Public Health §35-1-58.5-5.	Must report anomyous stats. to Department of Public Health. §35-1-58.5-5	Refusal Right §16-10-3-2		
Iowa Code Annot. 1972					Refusal Right §146.2		

Chart 1 Continued

	Minors Parental Consent Notice						
			Reporting Requirements				
State	*Parental*	*Judicial Consent*	*Minors*	*Adults*	*Hospital's Right to Refuse to do an Abortion*	*Residency Requirements*	*Miscellaneous*
Kansas Stat. Annot. 1985 "Public Health			Anonymous Records to Secretary of Health. §65-445	Anonymous Records to Secretary of Health. §65-445	Refusal Right §65-444		
Kentucky Rev Stat. 1982	Parental Notice 311.732(2) Medical Emergency Exception §311.732(1)	Judicial Alternative if sufficiently mature and in best interest. §311.732(3)	Anonymous Records to Cabinet for Human Resources. §213.055	Anonymous Records to Cabinet for Human Resources. §213.055			Must be provided information regarding risks, gestation of fetus & other pamphlets regarding Alternatives §311.726 Must be given 2 hours before the abortion. Notice to Spouse 311.735. Note: In Supplement the Atty General held that this Section appears to be unconstitutional.
Louisiana Rev. Stat. 1977	Parental Rights R.S. 40 §1299.33(D)	Judicial Alternative required by case law.	Stats. must be reported to State Registrar. R.S. 40 §64	Stats must be reported to State Registrar. R.S. 40§64	Refusal Rights R.S. 40:1299.33(a)		

Chart 1 Continued

	Minors Parental Consent Notice		Reporting Requirements				
State	*Parental*	*Judicial Consent*	*Minors*	*Adults*	*Hospital's Right to Refuse to do an Abortion*	*Residency Requirements*	*Miscellaneous*
Maine Stat. Annot. 1964	Parental Notice 24 Hours before. 22 §1597(2) Notice is waived if emergency 22 §1597(3) **Notice Not Consent 22 §1597(5)*		Stats. must be reported to Department of Human Services. 22 §1596	Stats. must be reported to Department of Human Services 22 §1596	Refusal Rights Title 22 §1591 Cannot discriminate if refusal. Title 22 §1592		48 Hour waiting period for adult women unless emergency to ensure consent. 22§1598
Annot. Code of Maryland 1987)			Records ______ Annual Report of all requests and actions to State Board of Health. §20-208(c)	Records ______ Annual Report of all requests and actions to State Board of Health. §20-208(c)	Refusal Rights §20-214		Required to be given information before abortion regarding alternatives and financial matters. §20-211
Annot. Law of Mass. 1980	Parental Consent C.112§125	Judicial Alternative if mature enough or in best interest. C.112§125	Records must be filed with Commissioner of Public Health C.112§12R	Records must be filed with Commissioner of Public Health. C.112§12R	Refusal Rights C.272§21B		Dr must do blood test to verify pregnancy prior to abortion C.112§12R Consent form must be signed 24 hrs before abortion C.272§125

Chart 1 Continued

State	Minors Parental Consent Notice: Parental	Minors Parental Consent Notice: Judicial Consent	Reporting Requirements: Minors	Reporting Requirements: Adults	Hospital's Right to Refuse to do an Abortion	Residency Requirements	Miscellaneous
Michigan: No Specific Legislation in These Areas							
Minnesota Stat. Annot. 1988					Refusal Rights Public Health §145.42		
Mississippi Code Annot. 1972							License will be suspended for unlawful abortion. §73-25-29
Vernon's Annot. Missouri Stats.	Parental Consent Title 12 §188.028(1)	Judicial Alternative if best interest. Title 12 §188.028(4)	Anonymous Stats. must be submitted to State Division of Health within 45 days of abortions. title 12 §188.052	Anonymous Stats. must be submitted to State Division of Health within 45 days of abortions. Title 12 §188.052	Refusal Rights 12 §188.020		Written consent 48 hours 12 §188.027 Counseling must include alternatives. Title 12 §188.063
Montana Code Annot.—1987	Notice to parents §50-20-107(b)		Anonymous reporting to Department of Health & Environmental Science. §50-20-110	Anonymous reporting to Department of Health & Environmental Science. §50-20-110	Refusal Rights §50-21-111		Notice to Husband 50-20-107(A) Exceptions for emergencies: No consent or notice §41-1-405

Chart 1 Continued

	Minors Parental Consent Notice		Reporting Requirements				
State	*Parental*	*Judicial Consent*	*Minors*	*Adults*	*Hospital's Right to Refuse to do an Abortion*	*Residency Requirements*	*Miscellaneous*
Rev. Stat. of Nebraska 1943	24 Hour notice to parents §28-347(1) Emergency exception §28-347(3)	Judicial alternative to waive parental notice if minor is mature enough to make abortion decision independently. §28-347(2)					
Nevada Annot. Stat. Revised – 1986	Parental Notice unless necessary to preserve patient's life or health. §442.255(1)	Judicial Alternative if 1. mature enough to make informed decision; 2. financially independent; 3. notice would be detrimental to her best interest. §442.255(2)	Health Division shall adopt Regs. §442.260 *Also* Hospitals must submit monthly report to State Registrar of Vital Stats §442.265	Health Division shall adopt Regs. §442.260 *Also* Hospitals must submit monthly report to State Registrar of Vital Stats. §442.265			Consent §442.253
New Jersey Stat. Annot					Refusal Rights 2A:65A-2 & 2A:65A-3		
New Mexico Stat. 1978			Report anonymously within 5 days to the State Registrar. §24-14-18	Report anonymously within 5 days to the State Registar. §24-14-18			

Chart 1 Continued

	Minors Parental Consent Notice						
			Reporting Requirements				
State	*Parental*	*Judicial Consent*	*Minors*	*Adults*	*Hospital's Right to Refuse to do an Abortion*	*Residency Requirements*	*Miscellaneous*
McKinney's Consol. Laws of New York							Cannot report requests for abortion services unless the party requesting is: 1. a law enforcement agency; 2. the State Department of Health; and 3. court order.
General Stats. of N.C.			Anonymous Stats. to Department of Human Resources. §14-45.1(c)	Anonymous Stats. to Department of Human Resources. §14-45.1(c)			
N. Dakota Century Code (1981)	Parental Consent §14-02.1-03.1(1)	Judicial Alternative of best interest or minor is mature enough to understand. §14-02.1-03.1(2)	Report to Department of Health including all data called for in the US Standard Reprot of induced Termination of Pregnancy as recommended by the National Center for Health. Stats. §14-02.1-07	Report to Department of Health including all data called for in the US Standard Report of Induced Termination of Pregnancy as recommended by the National Center for Health. Stats. §14-02.1-07			Written consent 48 hours before. §14-02.1-03

Chart 1 Continued

State	Minors Parental Consent Notice: *Parental*	Minors Parental Consent Notice: *Judicial Consent*	*Reporting Requirements: Minors*	*Reporting Requirements: Adults*	*Hospital's Right to Refuse to do an Abortion*	*Residency Requirements*	*Miscellaneous*
Ohio Revised Code Annot. – 1987	Parental Notice – 24 hours in person or by phone §2919.12(B)(1)(a) - Alternative notice to sibling, step-parent or grand-parent §2919.12(B)(2) -If fear of abuse by parent or guardian, 48 Hour Notice	Judicial alternative §2919.12(B)(1)(a)(iii)	Within authority of the Public Health Council §3701.341	Within authority of the Public Helath Council. §3701.341	Refusal Rights §4731.91		Informed Consent §2919.12(A)
Oklahoma Stat. Annot. 1984			Confidential Reports to be completed and sent to State Department of Health. 63 §1-738	Confidential Reports to be completed and sent to State Department of Health. 63 §1-738	Refusal Rights 63 §1-741		Abortion can only be performed in hospitals. 63§1-737
Oregon Rev. Stats. 1987			Report to Vital Stats. Must be anonymous. §435.496	Report to Vital Stats. Must be anonymous. §435.496	Refusal Rights §435.475 & 435.485		

Chart 1 Continued

	Minors Parental Consent Notice						
			Reporting Requirements		Hospital's Right to		
State	*Parental*	*Judicial Consent*	*Minors*	*Adults*	*Refuse to do an Abortion*	*Residency Requirements*	*Miscellaneous*
Penn. Stat. Annot. 1983	Parental Consent except emergency. 18 §3206	Judicial alernative if mature enough or best interest. 18 §3214	Report to Department of Health within 15 days after each reporting month. 18§3214	Report to Department of Health within 15 days after each reporting month. 18 §3214	Refusal Rights—Conscience Clause. 18 §3202(d)		Informed Consent includes notice of risks. 18 §3205 Unless emergency —24 hour waiting period.
Rhode Island Code 1956	Parental Consent Health & Safety. §23-4.7-6	Judicial alternative if mature enough to consent or if in best interest Health & Safety. §23-4.7-6					Consent required Health & Safety. §23-4.7-2 Spousal Notice. §23-4.8-2
South Carolina Annot. 1985	Parental Consent if less than 16—§44-41-30 Except emergency		Report of Department of Health & Environmental Control §44-41-60	Report of Department of Health & Environmental Control. §44-41-60	Refusal Rights §44-41-40 & §44-41-50		General Consent Required §44-41-30
South Dakota Codified Laws 1986 *The current abortion rights repealed if states can once again regulate abortion. §34-23A-21	Parental Consent §34-23A-7		Reports to State Department of Health. §34-23A-19	Reports to State Department of Health. §34-23A-19	Refusal Rights §34-23A-13 & §34-23A-14		General consent required §34-23A-7 24 hour waiting period/See—form in statute. §34-23A-10.1 Counseling must provide alternatives. §34-23A-10

Chart 1 Continued

	Minors Parental Consent Notice		Reporting Requirements				
State	*Parental*	*Judicial Consent*	*Minors*	*Adults*	*Hospital's Right to Refuse to do an Abortion*	*Residency Requirements*	*Miscellaneous*
Tennessee Code Annot. 1982	Parental Consent Required *Effective July 1, 1989. §37-10-301	Judicial Alternative *Effective July 1, 1989. §37-4-203	Reports to Commissioner of Public Health. §39-4-203	Reports to Commissioner of Public Health. §39-4-203	Refusal Rights. §39-4-204		Consent Required Risk & Alternatives must be stated/2 day waiting period. §39-4-202
Texas Vernon's Annot. Stat. 1989			Anonymous Report to Texas Board of Health (Annual). 71 §4512.8	Anonymous Report to Texas Board of Health (Annual). 71§4512.8	Refusal Rights Health Public Title 71 §4512.7		
Utah Code Annot. 1978			Reporting to Division of Health. §76-7-313	Reporting to Division of Health. §76-7-313			Written consent – Must be given names of two licensed adoption agencies & details of risks. §76-7-305
Vermont – No Specific Legislation In These Areas							
Virginia Annot. Code 1982					Conscience Clause Refusal §18.2-75		Consent – Risks must be stated. §18.2-76

Chart 1 Continued

	Minors Parental Consent Notice		Reporting Requirements				
State	*Parental*	*Judicial Consent*	*Minors*	*Adults*	*Hospital's Right to Refuse to do an Abortion*	*Residency Requirements*	*Miscellaneous*
Washington Annot. 1988	Parental Consent 18 years. 9.02.070				Refusal OK – §9.02.080	90 Day Residency §9.02.070	Patient consent §9.02.070
West Virginia Code 1985	24 Hour actual notice to parents or 48 hour constructive – Petition to waive notice________If mature enough to make decision or best interest 16-2F-4 – Emergency Exception 16-2F-5	Judicial Alternative – Petition to waive notice. 16-2F-6	*Minors* Reporting to Department of Health.				
Wisconsin Stat. Annot. 1977	Parental Notice – But hospital must have written consent of minor to provide notice. §146.78(4) Emergency Exceptions. §146.78(3)		Report to Department of Health §146.81	Report to Department of Health. §146.81	Refusal Rights. §140.42		Informed Consent – Risks & Alternatives. §146.78(1&2)
Wyoming Stat. Annot. 1988			Reporting to State Office of Vital Record. §35-6-107	Reporting to State Office of Vital Record. §35-6-107	Refusal Rights §35-6-106 & §35-6-114 (No Discrimination if Refusal)		

Statement of Need for Therapeutic Abortion

Form 35

A.M.
Date________________ Time________________ P.M.

We find from observation and examination of________________that she is pregnant and that she is suffering from the following ailment or condition: ________________________

____

Further progress of her pregnancey would gravely endanger or imperil her life. Therefore, we are of the opinoin that it is medically necessary to perform a therapeutic abortion upon her.

(1) ____

(2) ____

(3) ____

(Duty licensed physicians)

Consent to Therapeutic Abortion

Form 36

A.M.
Date________________ Time________________ P.M.

1. I authorize and consent to the performance upon ________________________of a therapeutic abortion to be performed
(myself or name of patient)
by or under the direction of Dr. ________________.

2. I acknowledge that I have been informed by Dr.(s) ____________

____

that in his (their) opinion further progress of
(myself or name of patient)
pregnancy would gravely endanger or imperil the life
of____________________________and that in his (their) opinion, it is
(myself or name of patient)
medically necessary to perform a therapeutic abortion.

3. I consent to the performance of operations and procedures in addition to or different from those now contempleated, whether or not arising from presently unforeseen conditions, which the above-named doctor or his associates or assistants may consider necessary or advisiable in the course of the operation.

4. I consent to the administration of such anesthetics as may be considered necessary or advisable by the physician responsibile for this service, with the exception of ______________________________

____
(state "none", "spinal anesthesia", etc.)

5. The nature and purpose of the operation, possible alternative methods of treatment, the risks involved, the possible consequences, and the possibility of complications have been explained to me by

Dr.________________ and by________________.

6. I acknowledge that no guarantee or assurance has been given by anyone as the the results that may be obtained.

7. I acknowledge that all blank spaces on this document have either been completed or crossed off prior to my signing.

[Cross Out Any Paragraphs Above Which Do Not Apply]

Witness________________ Signed________________________
(Patient or person authorized to consent for patient)

Authorization to Treat Condition of Recent or Partial Abortion

Form 37

A.M.
Date________________ Time________________ P.M.

I authorize Dr. ________________ to treat me for the condition set forth in the following history. ________________________________

____

____

____

____

This condition occurred prior to the time that I visited Dr. ________________ for treatment.

Signed____________________

Witness ________________

Request for First Trimester Abortion

Form 38

1. I hereby request and authorize the performance upon myself of an abortion to be performed by or under the direction of Doctor ________________.
2. I certify that to the best of my knowledge I have been pregnant for 12 weeks or less.
3. I have received a fact sheet containing detailed information on the nature and purpose of an abortion, the risks involved, and the possibility of complications. I have read the fact sheet. It has been explained to me, and I understand it. I am aware, on the basis of this explaination, of the risks involved in an abortion and the possible complications.
4. If any condition arises in the course of the abortion which calls for procedures in addition to or different from those now contemplated, I further request and authorize the above-named doctor or his associates to do whatever is considered necessary or advisable.
5. I understand that a doctor is available to answer any questions I may have concerning the abortion.
6. I acknowledge that I have received no guarantees or warranties with respect to the benefits or results which may be obtained from the abortion.
7. I consent to the administration of a
   (Cross out one) local anesthetic general anesthetic.
8. I acknowledge that I have read this document in its entirety and that I fully understand it and that all blank spaces have been completed prior to my signing.

Date:____________________ ____________________
Signature of Consenting Party

A.M.
Time:________________ P.M.

Witnesses:

____
Signature of Witness

____
Signature of Witness

If Consenting Party Is Other Than Patient:

____
Signature of Consenting Party

____
Relationship

Editor's Note: *This form is reproduced with permission of Michael Reese Hospital and Medical Center, Chicago, Illinois.*

Form 39

1. I hereby request and authorize the performance upon myself of a mid-trimester abortion to be performed by or under the direction of Doctor ________________ or his associates and assistants.
2. I certify that to the best of my knowledge I have been pregnant for more than 12 weeks and no more than 22 weeks (from the last menstrual period).
3. The nature and purpose of this operation, the risks or complications that might result from it and the possible alternative methods of treatment have been explained to me, and I understand the explanation I have received.
4. If any condition arises in the course of the abortion which calls for procedures in addition to or different from those now contemplated, I further request and authorize the above-named doctor, his assistants and associates to do whatever is considered necessary or advisable. I understand that this may include any of the following procedures: suction curettage, dilatation and curettage, hysterotomy and hysterectomy. The nature and purpose of each of these procedures and the risks and complications associated with them have been explained to me and I understand the explanation I have received.
5. I consent to the administration of an anesthetic if necessary.
6. I understand that there is a possibility that I may give birth to a live fetus. I understant that Hospital is obligated by law to make available and utilize life support for any fetus showing visible signs of viability. I understand that I will be responsible for all hospital and medical expenses incurred by this infant.
7. I understand that my doctor is available to answer any questions I may have concerning the abortion.
8. I acknowlege that I have received no guarantees or warranties with respect to the benefits or results which may be obtained from the abortion.

Continued

Form 39 Continued

9. I acknowledge that I have read this document in its entirety and that I fully understand it and that all blank spaces have been completed prior to my signing.

Date:____________________ ____________________________
Signature of Consenting Party

Time:________________ A.M. P.M.

Witnesses:

____
Signature of Witness

____
Signature of Witness

If Consenting Party Is Other Than Patient:

____
Signature of Consenting Party

____
Relationship

15.0 Implied and Oral Consent

If an adult patient is of sound mind and knows that he or she can agree to, or refuse an operation, and if the patient has been fully informed by his or her physician of what the operation will entail, then, by cooperating with the doctor, the patient gives implied consent even though the consent is not in writing.[1] In one such case of implied consent,[2] the patient was told by the surgeon that skin for a grafting operation would probably be taken from his arm. Instead, it was taken from his leg. The court held that consent was implied inasmuch as the patient voluntarily went under anesthesia without knowing definitely from which part of his body the skin would be taken.

In another instance,[3] consent to set a fracture by means of surgery was held to be implied when the surgeon was unable to set a fractured bone by external manipulation.[4]

In a case involving a chiropractor,[5] a patient brought action alleging battery and negligent failure to inform or explain risks. The court held that consent to medical treatment may be express or implied. Implied consent may be inferred from a patient's action in seeking treatment or in some other act indicating a willingness to submit to a particular course of treatment. Implied consent is the consent customarily given in routine office practice. Implied consent to an operation always involves the possibility of a misunderstanding as to the purpose and scope of the undertaking, and proof is often difficult to obtain in the event of a controversy.[6]

The concept of implied consent permits a physician, in an emergency, to operate on or to extend the scope of surgery performed on an unconscious or delirious person who is unable to make his or her own decision. In one such case,[7] a patient's finger had become stiff due to an injury. The surgeon advised an operation on the finger, and the woman consented. When the doctor cut into the finger, he found an adhesion between the tendons. The decision was then made that the best results could be obtained by enclosing the tendons in fascia.

The woman had not been informed prior to the operation that transplantation of tissue might be required. Since she was under an anesthetic (and thus incapable of judging the situation), the surgeon cut into her thigh and removed tissue which was transplanted into the finger. The operation on the thigh resulted in a muscle hernia and other injuries. The court held that the considerations involved in correcting the stiff finger did not present an emergency that would justify an operation on the patient's thigh. Consent, therefore, was not implied.[8]

This situation frequently arises in connection with serious accidents when the patient is unable to act on his or her own behalf. If someone is present who has authority to act for the patient or if such a person can be reached before an operation is undertaken, consent should be obtained.[9]

Oral consent to an operation is, of course, ordinarily supplemented by implied consent. This can occur when a patient, after orally agreeing to an operation, cooperates with the physician in its performance. Like implied consent, oral consent is open to misunderstanding and may be difficult to prove.

---

1 Wilson v. Lehman, *379 S.W.2d 478 (Ky. 1964).*

2 Knowles v. Blue, *209 Ala. 27, 95 So. 481 (1923).*

3 McGuire v. Rix, *118 Nebr. 434, 225 N.W. 120 (1929).*

4 See also Dicenzo v. Berg, *340 Pa. 305, 16 A.2d 15 (1949);* Baxter v. Snow, *78 Utah 217, 2 P.2d 257 (1931);* McClees v. Cohen, *158 Md. 60, 148 Atl. 124 (1930);* Knowles v. Blue, *209 Ala. 27, 95 So. 481 (1923);* Mosslander v. Armstrong, *90 Neb. 774, 134 N.W. 922 (1912);* Van Meter v. Crews, *149 Ky. 335, 148 S.W. 40 (1912).*

5 Jones v. Malloy, *412 N.W.2d 837 (Neb. 1987).*

6 Haywood v. Allen, *406 S.W.2d 721 (Ky. 1966).*

7 Franklyn v. Peabody, *249 Mich. 363, 228 N.W. 681 (1930).*

8 *See also* Wells v. McGehee, *39 So.2d 196 (La. App. 1949).*

9 Doerr v. Movius, *463 P.2d 477 (Mont. 1970).*

16.0

Generally speaking, written consent to an operation is not required by law, and no particular form is necessary to give validity to a written consent.[1] The essential requirements of a written consent are that the consent form state clearly the nature and extent of the operation authorized, and that it be signed by a person legally qualified to give consent.

The authorization should state who is to be responsible for administering the anesthetic[2] and the postoperative care,[3] if these services are to be performed by a physician other than the operating surgeon. The inclusion of the place and date of execution and the signature of a witness[4] are desirable, but only because they tend to facilitate proof. The more vague and indefinite the terms of the consent, the more specifically it will be construed by the court.[5]

State statutes have been enacted which provide that if all the criteria for a consent form are met, the signed document creates a conclusive presumption that the consent is valid.[6] In a recent challenge to such a statute, in Florida the Supreme Court of that state held that the medical consent law does not violate due process if the statutory substantive elements of informed consent are satisfied.[7]

'Blanket" consent forms which purport to give a physician unlimited authority and discretion without specifying the particular operation, should not be used.[8]

The use of the general consent forms may also depart from statutory consent requirements. In one such instance,[9] a woman underwent an exploratory laparotomy and cholecystectomy. She had signed a consent form authorizing the gall bladder operation, and the form described the operation and set forth some general risks. It did not, however, indicate the specific risks as required under state legislation. The court held that the patient must prove that the undisclosed risk actually occurred. Thus, the general consent form does not necessarily protect a physician or hospital.

The use of such forms has given rise to medical liability claims charging that the performance of an operation was different from the one for which oral consent was obtained. Some courts have construed blanket consent forms to permit only the procedures which were orally agreed upon. In the absence of a signed consent that describes the operation to be performed with reasonable accuracy, and permits such extension as may be advisable, a jury can easily choose to believe the patient's recollection of the treatment he or she authorized.[10]

In a Louisiana case,[11] a woman and her husband brought suit against two physicians and their insurer for unauthorized surgery. The woman had consented only to a simple appendectomy, but a total hysterectomy was also performed. The doctor in charge testified that no emergency existed, but stated that he removed the female organs as a precautionary measure because he felt it was good surgical procedure.

The patient had signed the following printed form.

Authority to Operate

Date____________

I hereby authorize the Physician or Physicians in charge to administer such treatment, and the surgeon to have administered such anesthetics, as found necessary to perform this operation which is advisable to the treatment of this patient.

Signed____________________
(Patient or nearest relative)

Witness______________

Witness J.L.T.

The court said:

> We think the above so-called authorization is so ambiguous as to be almost completely worthless, and, certainly, since it fails to designate the nature of the operation authorized, and for which consent was given, it can have no possible weight under the factual circumstances of the instant case . . .
>
> Despite our conclusion, we intend no adverse criticism of the medical judgment of the operating surgeons, but the fact remains that their actions constituted an offense for which, under the law, they are liable in damages. It is a gratuitous observation to declare that protection against such liability in the vast majority of cases is readily available by an exceedingly easy and simple procedure prior to the actual performance of an operation.

In finding for the plaintiff, the court gave particular weight to the fact that the physicians had previously treated the patient because she was unable to conceive, and were therefore aware that she was anxious to have children. Many childless women would prefer to assume the risk of delaying surgery involving the reproductive organs until they have had the opportunity to have children. In any case of abdominal surgery involving a woman of childbearing age, it is wise for the surgeon to have a definite understanding of how he should proceed if he finds a diseased condition that does not constitute a true emergency but that requires corrective surgery which would impair or destroy a patient's ability to procreate. Where the patient has granted a surgeon appropriate authority to proceed under these circumstances, it is desirable that the authorization be set forth in the consent form.

If a patient insists on limiting a surgeon's authority, this fact should also be set forth in the consent form for the doctor's protection in case the limitation should cause an unsatisfactory result. If the patient insists on limitations that are clearly inconsistent with good medical practice — such as refusing a medically preferred anesthetic — the surgeon might feel justified in declining the case.

A prudent physician will insist on a consent in writing that is sufficiently inclusive in both specific and general authority to permit him to follow good medical practices in all eventualities. Physician and patient should have a clear understanding regarding a possible extension of the operation, not only in the event of an emergency, but also where it is medically advisable.

---

1 Maercklein v. Smith, *129 Colo. 72, 266 P.2d 1095 (1954). But see Vernon's Annotated Civil Statutes of Texas, Art. 4590i, Sect. 6.05 and 6.06.*

2 A surgeon is not liable for the Negligence of an anesthetist. The law is well settled that the operating surgeon is not an insurer against the negligent acts of the anesthesiologist. Thompson v. Presbyterian Hospital, Inc., *652 P.2d 260, 265 (1982);* Woodsor v. Huey, *261 P.2d 199 (Oklahoma, 1953);* Wiley v. Whanon, *68 Ohio App. 345, 41 N.E.2d 255 (1941).*

3 In Reed v. Laughlin, *332 Mo. 424, 58 S.W.2d 440 (1983), the surgeon who had performed an appendectomy on the plaintiff failed to give him any postoperative care. The court said: "* * * as a general rule, in the absence of an agreement or understanding limiting the service, or reasonable notice to the patient that he will not undertake the subsequent treatment, when a surgeon is employed to perform an operation, the relation of physician and the patient continues until ended by the mutual consent of the parties, the physician's withdrawal after reasonable notice, the dismissal of the physician or surgeon by the patient or the cessation of the necessity which gave rise to the relation, and the surgeon must not only use reasonable and ordinary care and skill in performing the operation, but during the continuance of the relation of physician and patient exercise ordinary diligence in the subsequent treatment and give, or see that patient is given, such attention as the necessity of the case demands." See also* Saunders v. Lischkoff, *137 Fla. 826, 188 So. 815 (1939);* Gross v. Partlow, *190 Wash. 489, 68 P.2d 1034 (1937);* Hopkins v. Heller, *59 Cal. App. 447, 210 Pac. 975 (1922).*

4 *In* Wheeler v. Barker, *208 P.2d 68 (Cal. 1949) and* Stone v. Goodman, *241 App. Div. 290, 271 N.Y. Supp. 500 (1943), the plaintiff alleged that he signed the consent form while under sedation and that the consent was, therefore, invalid. A witness to the signing testified to the contrary.*

5 *The court in* Valdez v. Percy, *35 Cal. App.2d 485, 96 P.2d 142 (1939), said with respect to a broad, general consent: "However, we do not understand such agreement to constitute a consent to perform operations other than the one for which the operating surgeons were engaged by plaintiff to perform unless necessity therefore arose during the authorized operation as hereinbefore mentioned." See also* Moore v. Webb, *345 S.W.2d 239 (Mo. 1961).*

6 *Fla. Stat. Ann. §786.46; Tex. Civil Stat. §4590i; Utah §78-14-5; Wash. Rev. Code §7.70.060.*

7 Parikh v. Cunningham, *493 So.2d 999 (1986).*

8 *See* Chandler v. Cook, *265 A.2d 794 (Pa. 1970);* Gray v. Grunnagle, *223 A.2d 663 (Pa. 1966);* See also, *Rovosky §1.6.2 (1987 Supp.)*

9 Seals v. Pittman, *499 So.2d 114 (1986).*

10 *In* Danielson v. Roche, *109 Cal. App.2d 832, 241 P.2d 1028 (1952), the defendant surgeon removed a part of the plaintiff's Fallopian tubes during an appendectomy. The plaintiff had signed a general consent. The surgeon was held justified in extending the operation not only because of the "emergency" but for the reason that additional surgery that might be advisable or necessary was authorized by the general consent.*

11 Rogers v. Lambermens Mutual Casualty Co., *119 So.2d 649 (La. 1960); but see* Stafford v. Louisiana State University, *448 So.2d 852 (1984) (emergency exception was applicable to surgeon's decision to amputate patients gangrenous left lower leg where the condition of the patient was acutely threatening.*

Form 40

A.M.
Date________________ Time________________ P.M.

I have been informed by Dr.________________ of the nature, risks, possible alternative methods of treatment, possible consequences and possible complications involved in the treatment by means of ______

____

for the relief of____.

Nevertheless, I authorize Dr.________________ to administer such treatment to me.

Signed__________________________
(Patient or person authorized to consent for patient)

Witness________________

Form 41

1. I have been advised by my physician, Dr.______________ that the following operation or treatment should be performed upon me:

____
(Describe operation of treatment)

2. My physician has explained to me, and I understand the following:
   - A. The nature of the recommended treatment.
   - B. The purpose of and need for the recommended treatment.
   - C. The possible alternatives to the recommended treatment for which I similarly refuse consent.
   - D. The probable consequences of not proceeding with the recommended treatment and/or alternatives.
3. I know that my failure to follow the aforesaid recommendations will endanger my life or health. **I nontheless refuse to consent to the proposed treatment.**
4. My reason for refusal is:______________
5. I personally assume the risks and consequences of my refusal, and release for myself, my heirs, executors, administrators, or personal representatives physicians who have been consulted in my case from any and all liability for ill effects which may result from my refusal to consent to the performance of the proposed treatment.
6. I acknowledge that I have read this document in its entirety and that I fully understand it and that all blank spaces have been either completed or crossed off prior to my signing.

CAUTION – THIS IS A RELEASE OF LIABILITY – READ BEFORE SIGNING

Date: ______________________ ______________________
Signature of Refusing Party

A.M.
Time ______________________ P.M.

Witnesses:

____
Signature of Witness

____
Signature of Witness

If Refusing Party Is Other Than Patient:

____
Signature of Refusing Party

____
Relationship

Consent to Heart Evaluation Exercise Test

Form 42

A.M.
Date________________ Time________________ P.M.

1. I authorize the performance upon myself of a heart and circulation exercise evaluation test to be performed under the direction of Dr.________________.

2. The purpose of the test is to evaluate the condition of my heart and circulation.

3. I have been informed that the test will be performed on a treadmill and the amount of effort which I will expend will be gradually increased. My pulse, blood pressure, oxygen intake and electrocardiogram will be monitored by Dr.________________ or his trained observer.

4. I have been informed that the test may cause abnormal blood pressure, fainting, disorders of heart beat and, in rare instances, heart attack. Every effort will be made to minimize any such occurrences and personnel and equipment will be available to deal with them should they occur.

5. I acknowledge that no guarantee or assurance has been given me by anyone as to the results of the test.

Witness________________ Signed________________________

(Patient or person authorized to consent for patient)

Consent to Radiation Therapy

Form 43

A.M.
Date________________ Time________________ P.M.

I authorize Dr.________________, and such assistants as he may designate, to administer ____
(X-ray, cobalt, radium, etc.)
therapy to ________________ and to continue such treatment from
(name of patient)
time to time as he may deem advisable. The effect and nature of this treatment, possible alternative methods of treatment, and the risks of injury despite precautions have been explained to me. I know that radiation is potent in destroying tissue. No guarantee or assurance has been given by anyone as to the results that may be obtained.

Witness________________ Signed____________________________
(Patient or person authorized to consent for patient)

Form 44a

A.M.
Date________________ Time________________ P.M.

1. I (We) authorize Dr.________________, and assistants of his choice, to administer________________ *(insulin and/or electric)* shock treatment and relaxant drugs and other medication, to ________________ *(name of patient)*; and to continue such treatment at such intervals as he and his assistants may deem advisable.

2. The effect and nature of this treatment and possible alternative methods of treatment have been explained. I (We) understand that shock therapy, like medical and surgical procedures, involves an element of risk despite precautions, and the possibility of complications such as dislocations and fractures of the limbs and vertebrae.

3. In addition to the foregoing, the strict care which will be required immediately following treatment and during convalescence has been fully explained to me (us).

4. No guarantee or assurance has been given by anyone as to the results that may be obtained.

Witness________________ Signed____________________
(Patient or person authorized to consent for patient)

Consent to Electric Shock Therapy

Form 44b

A.M.
Date________________ Time________________ P.M.

1. I authorize Dr.________________, and assistants of his choice, to administer electric shock treatment, and relaxant drugs and other medication, to________________ *(name of patient)* and to continue such treatment at such intervals as he and his assistants may deem advisable.

2. I understand that this treatment consists of passing a controlled electric current between two electrodes applied to the patient's temples. In some instances, the patient may be given medication prior to treatment to reduce tension and produce muscular relaxation. I understand that the patient will not feel the electric current and will feel no pain. When the electric current is administered, the patient becomes unconscious and has strong convulsive muscular contractions which may last from 35 to 50 seconds. The patient gradually regains consciousness and his confusion clears within 15 to 60 minutes. The patient may experience headache and nausea.

3. I understand that the treatments may cause temporary confusion and memory impairment. I also understand that certain risks and complications are involved in the treatment. The most common risk is fracture and dislocation of the limbs and vertebrae. I acknowledge that these and other risks and complications of this procedure have been explained to me.

4. In addition to the foregoing, the strict care which will be required immediately following treatment and during convalescence has been fully explained to me.

5. The alternative methods of treatment have been explained and no guarantee or assurance has been given by anyone as to the results that may be obtained.

Witness________________ Signed________________________
(Patient or person authorized to consent for patient)

Permission to Use Radioisotopes

Form 45

A.M.
Date_______________ Time_______________ P.M.

I authorize Dr._______________, and such assistants as he may designate, to administer a (tracer) (therapeutic) dose of

_______________to_________________________. The uncertainties
(myself or name of patient)
and nature of this treatment, and the risks of injury despite precautions, have been explained to me. I voluntarily accept the risks for the results of this treatment or its interpretation, and agree that the above-named physician, his assistants, the hospital and its personnel shall assume no responsibility for the results of this treatment or its interpretation.

Witness_______________ Signed_________________________
(Patient or person authorized to consent for patient)

Consent to Diagnostic Procedure

Form 46

A.M.
Date_______________ Time_______________ P.M.

I authorize Dr._______________, and such assistants as he may

designate, to perform upon_________________________the following
(myself or name of patient)
diagnostic procedure:____

____

The nature of this procedure, possible alternative methods of diagnosis and the risks of injury despite precautions have been explained to me.

Witness_______________ Signed_________________________
(Patient or person authorized to consent for patient)

Consent to Diagnostic or Therapeutic Procedure

Form 47

Date________________ Time________________

1. I consent to the performance of the following procedure upon the patient named above:

   ____
   (State nature of procedure)

   to be performed by or under the supervision of

   Dr.____
   (Medical Staff Member)

2. A physician has explained the procedure to me and informed me of the risks involved in this procedure. I was informed of the risks involved if the patient named above did not undergo this procedure. I was also informed of possible alternative methods of treatment, and of the risks involved in these alterntive methods. I have had an opportunity to discuss this procedure with a physician, and have received answers to all questions I asked.
3. The possible outcomes of this procedure have been explained to me, and I understand there is NO GUARANTEE that any particular results will be obtained.
4. Dr.________________ the attending physician(s), will perform or supervise the performance of this procedure. I authorize the physician performing this procedure to obtain the assistance of other physicians (including residents and interns) as he considers advisable. In addition, I authorize the physician performing this procedure or his assisting physician to administer anesthesia to the patient named above as required during the course of the procedure.

I have read and fully understand this Consent to Diagnostic Procedure. All the blank spaces were filled in before I signed the form.

________________ ________________________________
Date & Time *Signature of Patient*

________________ ________________________________
Date & Time *OR Signature of Person Authorized to Consent for Incompetent Patient*

Use This Part Only If Patient Is Incompetent.

____
Relationship to Patient

Patient did not sign this Consent because

____

____

Editor's Note: *This form is reproduced with permission of Northwestern Memorial Hospital, Chicago, Illinois.*

Consent to Anesthetic Management

Form 48

Date________________ Time________________

1. I request that Dr.________________ or another anesthesiologist designated by the Hospital Department of Anesthesia, administer anesthesia and provide other required medical care or therapeutic procedure to the patient named above. I understand that the anesthetic care shall be adminstered by or under the supervision of my anesthesiologist or his designate. I authorize the anesthesiologist to obtain the assistance of other physicians (including residents and interns), nurse anesthetists, or other assistants as he considers advisable.
2. It is possible that it may be desirable to administer anesthesia by other methods than the methods that are planned at this time. I authorize the administration of anesthesia by such methods, with the exception of

____
State exception or "None"

3. An anesthesiologist or his designate has explained to me the nature of the anesthetic care to be administered and the risks involved in this. I was also informed of possible alternative methods of anesthesia, and the risks involved in these alternative methods including refusal of anesthesia. I have had an opportunity to discuss this with the anesthesiologist, or his designate, and have received answers to all the questions I asked.

I have read and fully understand the Consent to Anesthetic Management. All the blank spaces above were filled in before I signed this form.

________________ ____________________________
Date & Time *Signature of Patient*

________________ ____________________________
Date & Time *OR Signature of Person Authorized to Consent for Incompetent Patient*

Use This Part Only If Patient Is Incompetent.

____
Relationship to Patient

Patient did not sign this Consent because

____

____

Continued

Form 48 Continued

Statement Of Physician

I believe that at the time the above consent was signed, the person who signed was capable of understanding the nature of the patient's physical condition and of the proposed treatment; the risks involved in the proposed treatment and in any reasonable alternatives to the proposed treatment; and the risks involved in refusal of the proposed treatment.

I certify that I explained to the person siging this consent the items described in Paragraph 3 of the Consent to Anesthetic Management, that I answered the signer's questions concerning them, and that I witnessed the signature of the patient, or other person authorized to consent for the incompetent patient named above.

A.M.
P.M.

Signature of Physician ______ *Date* ______ *Time*

Form 49

A.M.
Date________________ Time________________ P.M.

1. I authorize the performance upon ____________________
(myself or name of patient)

of an ANGIOGRAM to be performed by or under the direction of Dr.________________.

2. I have been informed that an Angiogram is a study of a person's blood vessels. A needle puncture will be made in my arm or groin. A small tube will be introduced into one of my blood vessels through this puncture. A solution will then be injected through this tube, which will enable my blood vessels to be seen on X-rays.

3. I have been informed that minor complications, such as accumulations of blood in the tissues where the tube is introduced or a small outpouching of the artery at the same site, may occur. I have also been informed that other, more serious, complications may occur. These complications are the loss of or damage to an organ or, in rare instances, death may result.

4. The nature and purpose of the procedure, the possible complications, the possible alternative diagnostic procedures, the risks involved and the possible consequences have been explained to me by

Dr.________________ and by ________________.

5. I acknowledge that no guarantee or assurance has been given me by anyone as to the results of the procedure.

6. I further acknowledge that I have read this entire consent form and that all the blank spaces have been either completed or crossed off prior to my signing.

Witness________________ Signed____________________________
(Patient or person authorized to consent for patient)

Consent to Blood Transfusion and Release of Liability

Form 50

1. My doctor has informed me that I need or may need during treatment a transfusion of blood and/or blood products in the interest of my health and proper medical care. The blood/blood products which may be provided to me include:
   - ☐ Autologous (blood donated by me for my own use)
   - ☐ Designated (blood donated by others specifically for my use)
   - ☐ Homologous (volunteer donor pool)
2. I understand that when available, autologous and/or designated blood/blood products will be used first. These units will be reserved for me only for a fixed and specified period of time. In the event that such autologous and/or designated blood is insufficient for my transfusion needs, homologous blood/blood products from the Hospital's usual supply will be used. I further understand that I will not be informed of the identity of the donors of blood/blood products administered to me.
3. The risk and benefits of receiving homologous or designated transfusion(s) have been described to me. The risks include, but are not limited to: a chill, fever, itching and other mild allergic reactions, hemolytic reaction, and possible exposure to infectious agents such as hepatitis, cytomegalovirus infection, infectious mononucleosis, and acquired immune deficiency syndrome. These risks exist despite the careful testing of the blood and blood products.
4. The alternatives to transfusion, including the risks and consequences of not receiving this therapy, have been explained to me.
5. I hereby authorize Doctor________________, his/her assistants or associates, to administer a transfusion(s) to:____________________
   (myself or name of patient)
6. I hereby release for myself, my heirs, executors, administrators, personal representatives and assigns, Doctor________________, ________________Hospital and all their respective agents and employees from any and all claims of any kind and nature that I may have against any of them at any time hereafter as a result of this transfusion or anything arising in connection herewith.

Continued

Form 50 Continued

I Acknowledge That The Foregoing Has Been Presented To Me And Understand Its Contents And Purpose.

Date: ______________________

Time ____________________ A.M. P.M. ______________________________
Signature of Consenting Party

Witnesses:

____
Signature of Witness

____
Signature of Witness

If Consenting Party Is Other Than Patient:

____
Signature of Consenting Party

____
Relationship

This authorization must be signed by the patient. In the case of a minor patient, this authorization must be signed by a parent or guardian. In the case of a patient who is physically unable to sign this authorization, he/she should place an "X" on the signature line and have his/her assent witnessed. In the case of a patient who has been declared mentally incompetent, this authorization may only be signed by a legally appointed guardian.

Editor's Note: *This form is reproduced with permission of Michael Reese Hospital and Medical Center, Chicago, Illinois.*

Agreement for Blood Transfusion

Form 51

To: Dr.__________________and _________________Hospital
(attending physician)

Date ___________________________ Time_______________ A.M. P.M.

1. I authorize the administration of a blood transfusion to____________________________________
(myself or name of patient)
and such additional transfusions as may be deemed advisable in the judgment of the attending physician, or his associates or assistants.

2. It is understood and agreed that the attending physician or his associates or assistants shall be responsible only for the performance of their own individual professional acts, and that the blood typing and the selection of compatible blood are the responsibilities of those who actually perform the necessary laboratory tests.

3. It has been explained that blood transfusions are not always successful in producing a desirable result and that there is a possibility of ill effects, including but not limited to the transmission of infectious hepatitus, or other diseases or blood impairments.

4. Also, it has been explained that emergencies may arise when it may not be possible to make adequate cross-matching tests, and that immediate need may make it necessary to use existing stocks of blood which may not include the most compatible blood types.

5. It is understood and expressly agreed that the blood supplied in accordance with this agreement is incidental to the rendition of services and that no requirement, guarantee, or warranty of fitness or quality shall apply.

Witness________________ Signed________________________
(Patient or person authorized to consent for patient)

Agreement for Blood Plasma Transfusion

Form 52

To: Dr.________________ and________________Hospital
(attending physician)

Date__________________________ Time________________ A.M. P.M.

1. I authorize the administration of blood plasma to

______________________ in such amounts and at such times as
(myself or name of patient)
may be deemed advisable in the judgment of the attending physician, or his associates or assistants.

2. It has been explained that blood plasma is a product manufactured from the pooled blood of many donors and sometimes carries the virus of infectious hepatitus and other diseases. It has been further explained that the administration of blood plasma is not always successful in producing a desirable result.

3. It is understood and expressly agreed that the blood plasma supplied in accordance with this agreement is incidental to the rendition of services and that no requirement, guarantee, or warranty of fitness or quality shall apply.

Witness________________ Signed________________________
(Patient or person authorized to consent for patient)

Refusal to Permit Blood Transfusion

Form 53

A.M.
Date________________ Time________________ P.M.

I (We) request that no blood derivatives be administered to ________________ during this hospitalization, notwithstanding that such treatment may be deemed necessary in the opinion of the attending physician or his assistants to preserve life or promote recovery. I (We) release the attending physician, his assistants, the hospital and its personnel from any responsibility whatever for any untoward results due to my (our) refusal to permit the use of blood or its derivatives.

Witness________________ Signed____________________________

Witness________________ Signed____________________________

Agreement with Blood Donor

Form 54

To: Dr.____________________________and ______________Hospital
(physician in charge of blood bank)

Date ______________________________ Time_______________A.M./P.M.

1. On behalf of ________________, a patient who has been the recipient of blood from the blood bank of the ________________ Hospital, and in order to reduce the obligation which was incurred by this patient in receiving such blood, I request that I be accepted as a blood donor.

2. I represent that I am not now nor have I ever been afflicted with syphilis, tuberculosis, malaria, infectious hepatitus, brucellosis, infectious mononucleosis or any other infectious disease or blood impairment, except as stated in paragraph 3. I am in good health and know no reason or condition which might impair or affect the suitability of my blood or create a danger in any way for the recipient of my blood; nor do I know of any condition, physical or mental, which might impair my own health and well-being as a result of my serving as a blood donor.

3. The following are all the infectious diseases or blood impairments which I have ever had:__________________________________

4. In consideration of the sum of________________dollars ($________________) to be paid me for my services as a blood donor, which I direct you to apply against the bill for services due and owing by the patient referred to in paragraph 1. I agree to assume all of the direct and indirect risks involved, including but not limited to personal injuries which I may sustain.

5. I have been given, understand, and agree to follow the precautionary instructions which are intended to facilitate my own recovery after giving blood. I have also been informed of the possibility of ill effects and the risks involved in serving as a blood donor.

6. The last time that I served as a blood donor was on ________________, 19____.

I Certify That The Above Statements Are True And I Understand The Meaning Of This Agreement.

Witness__________________ Signed______________________________
(Donor)

Accepted: Dr. ____________________ and ____________________ Hospital

By ____
(Duly authorized agent)

Release and Receipt (Blood Donor)

Form 55

A.M.
Date________________ Time________________ P.M.

I acknowledge receipt of the sum of________________dollars ($________________), which I direct you to apply against the bill for services due and owing by ________________, the patient on whose behalf I have given my blood, and in consideration therefor I release

Dr.____________________________and ____________________________
(physician in charge of blood bank)

Hospital and their agents, employees and assistants from all liability of whatsoever nature, whether for personal injuries or in tort or in contract, in connection with or resulting from the services that I have already rendered.

I Understand That This Is Complete Release Of All My Claims.

Witness________________ Signed____________________________
(Donor)

Agreement With Blood Donor

Form 56

To: Dr.______________________________and _______________Hospital
(physician in charge of blood bank)

Date __________________________________Time_________________A.M. P.M.

1. I represent that I am not now, nor have I ever been afflicted with syphilis, tuberculosis, malaria, infectious hepatitis, brucellosis, infectious mononucleosis or any other infectious disease or blood impairment, except as stated in paragraph 2. I am in good health and know no reason or condition which might impair or affect the suitability of my blood or create a danger in any way for the recipient of my blood; nor do I know of any condition, physical or mental, which might impair my own health and well-being as a result of my serving as a blood donor.

2. The following are all the infectious diseases or blood impairments which I have ever had:______________________________________

____

3. In consideration of the sum of _________________ dollars ($_________________) to be paid me for my services as a blood donor, I agree to assume all of the direct and indirect risks involved, including but not limited to personal injuries which I may sustain as a result of the taking of my blood.

5. I have been given, understand, and agree to follow the precautionary instructions which are intended to facilitate my own recovery after giving blood. I have also been informed of the possibility of ill effects and the risks involved in serving as a blood donor.

5. The last time that I served as a blood donor was on _________________, 19____.

I Certify That The Above Statements Are True And That I Understand The Meaning Of This Agreement.

Witness:__________________ Signed________________________________
(Donor)

Accepted: Dr. ____________________ and ____________________ Hospital

By____
(Duly authorized agent)

Release and Receipt (Blood Donor)

Form 57

A.M.
Date_______________ Time_______________ P.M.

I acknowledge receipt of the sum of_______________dollars ($_______________), in hand paid, and in consideration therefore I release Dr.__________________________and_______________
(physician in charge of blood bank)
Hospital and their agents, employees and assistants from all liability of whatsoever nature, whether for personal injuries or in tort or in contract, in connection with or resulting from the services that I have already rendered.

I Understand That This Is Complete Release Of All My Claims.

Witness_______________ Signed____________________
(Donor)

Consent to Use of Prosthesis

Form 58

A.M.
Date_______________ Time_______________ P.M.

I authorize Dr._______________, or his associates or assistants, to install a prosthesis within my body made of the following material:___________________. I know that there is no adequate substitute for normal bone and that there is a possibility of breakage or complications such as infection and pain. I understand, also, that the complications that may arise often require removal of the prosthesis and further surgery. No guarantee or assurance has been given as to the results that may be obtained.

Witness_______________ Signed____________________
(Patient)

Form 59

A.M.
Date________________ Time________________ P.M.

I have been informed that protective siderails should be placed on my bed and raised for my personal protection. I know that a fall from my bed could result in fractured limbs or vertebrae, brain injury or other serious bodily injury. Nevertheless, I instruct the ________________ Hospital and its employees NOT to place or raise protective siderails on my bed. I assume all risks and fully release the hospital, its employees and house staff, and my physician from any liability for any injury or damage to me caused by the failure to place or raise protective siderails on my bed.

Witness________________ Signed______________________________
(Patient)

Authorization for Smallpox Vaccination

Form 60

A.M.
Date______________ Time______________ P.M.

I (We) authorize Dr.______________, the attending physician, to administer smallpox vaccination to ______________, my (our) infant (to myself) to provide immunization against smallpox.

It has been explained to me (us) that the United States Public Health Service "now believes that the risk of smallpox in the United States is so small that the practice of routine smallpox vaccination is no longer indicated in this country." It has further been explained that the Public Health Service has published a statement that the risk of complications resulting from vaccination is greater than the probability of contracting the disease unless travel to and from a country where smallpox is endemic is planned, or unless contact with patients who have the diseases is possible.

Dr.______________ has also explained that the vaccination cannot be administered if (I) my (our) child has eczema or other forms of chronic dermatitis or has household contacts with these conditions or has an altered immune state because of diseases such as ______________ or therapy (or pregnancy if the recipient is a female of child-bearing age) and I (we) have assured him that none of these conditions exist.

I (We) voluntarily consent to the administration of the smallpox vaccination and release Dr.______________ from liability for any results that may occur.

Witness______________ Signed________________________
(Patient or person(s) authorized to consent for patient)

Authorization to School Health Physician

Form 61

I authorize________________, M.D., director of the School Health Department at____________________________or the person acting
(name of college or university)
in his stead in his absence to provide such regular health care including immunization procedures to my child________________, a
(name)
a student at the college, as is necessary for my child's health and best interests as well as the best interests of the student body.

I authorize the director or his representative to act on my behalf in case my child is victim of major accident, injury or illness when immediate medical or surgical care is needed, provided ________________, M.D. or his representative make diligent effort first to notify me of the situation and obtain my preferences. If such efforts to get in touch with me are unsuccessful I authorize ________________, M.D., (or one person designated to act in his stead in his absence) to take such action and give such consent on my behalf as his judgment dictates.

____________________________   ____________________________
Date   *(Signature of parent or guardian)*

Health Examination Form for Student Athlete

Form 62

________________________ (name of student) ________________________ (name of school)

Grade________ Age________ Height___________ Weight_________

Blood Pressure_______________

Significant Past illness or injury____________________________

Eyes____R 20/ ; L20/ ; Ears____Hearing R /15; L /15

Respiratory ____

Cardiovascular ______ Liver ______ Spleen ______ Hernia ______

Musculoskeletal_______________ Skin _______________________

Neurological_______________ Genitalia _____________________

Laboratory: Urinalysis_________________ Other_________________

Comments____

Complete Immunizations:

Polio_______________ (Date) Tetanus_______________ (Date)

Other____ (type and date)

I certify that on this date I made a limited, routine physical examination on _______________ (name of student) at his request and at the request of school authorities in connection with supervised ahtletic activities sponsored by ____________________________ (name of school)

On the basis of my examination together with the medical history furnished to me by the student, I have found no indications of physical or medical reason which would make it inadvisable for him to engage in supervised school athletic activities except those crossed out below:

Names of Sports		
Baseball	Gymnastics	Swimming
Basketball	Rowing	Tennis
Cross Country	Skating	Track
Field Hockey	Skiing	Volleyball
Football	Soccer	Wrestling*
Hockey	Softball	Others____________
Golf	Speedball	

*Estimated desirable weight level:______________________pounds.

Continued

Form 62 Continued

Date of examination:____

Signature of physician:______________________________________

Physician's address:____________________ Telephone:__________________

Student Participation And Parental Consent

Name of Student:________________ Name of School:________________

Date:_________ Date of Birth:_________ Place of Birth:_________

I hereby apply for an opportunity to compete in interscholastic athletics for the above school. This application is entirely voluntary on my part and is made with the understanding that I have not violated any of the eligibility rules and regulations of the __________________ State Association. I join and concur in the Parental Consent set forth below.

Signature of Student____

Parental Consent

I (We) hereby give my (our) consent for the above named student (1) to represent his school in athletic activities, except those crossed out on this form by the examining physician, provided that such athletic activites are approved by the State Association; (2) to accompany any school team of which he is a member on any of its local or out-of-town trips. I (We) authorize the school to obtain, through a physician of its own choice, any first aid or emergency medical care that may become reasonably necessary for the student in the course of such athletic activities or such travel. I (We) also agree not to hold the school or anyone acting in its behalf responsible for any injury occurring to the above named student in the course of such athletic activities or travel.

____

____

(Signature(s) of Parent(s) or Guardian(s)

Date:__________________________ Address:__________________________

Request for Prescription of Oral Contraceptives

Form 63

A.M.
Date________________ Time________________ P.M.

I hereby acknowledge that I have received from________________, M.D., a booklet containing information on the use, effectiveness, and known hazards of oral contraceptives, including

______________________, and that I have been informed by
(insert name of product)

said________________, M.D., of the possible serious side-effects of such oral contraceptives, including but not limited to phlebitis, thromboembolism, breakthrough bleeding and hepatic disease and informed of alternative methods of contraception. I further acknowledge that I understand such information and warnings.

I understand that such oral contraceptives are prescribed for the intended purpose of preventing future pregnancies, but no guarantees or assurances of the results of the use of such oral contraceptives have been given by anyone. I, nevertheless, request________________, M.D., to prescribe for me, or for ________________________________
(insert name and relationship)

the oral contraceptive ________________________.
(insert name of product)

Witness________________ Signed____________________________
(Patient or person authorized)

Request and Consent for Placement of Intrauterine Contraceptive Device

Form 64

I acknowledge that_______________, M.D., has informed me of the nature and purpose of intrauterine contraceptive devices, including

______________________. I understand that such device is placed in
(insert name of device)

the uterus of a female patient for the intended purpose of preventing future pregnancies, but that it is not invariably effective in preventing pregnancy. I further acknowledge that no guarantee or assurance has been given by anyone as to the results to be obtained from the placement and use of such device within the uterus.

I have been informed by_______________, M.D., of alternative methods of contraception and of the risks and possible complications which may arise from the placement and use of such intrauterine contraceptive device, including but not limited to perforation of the uterus by the device, expulsion of the device, infection, pain and cramps.

I, nevertheless, request and consent to the placement of such intrauterine contraceptive device within my uterus or the uterus of

______________________________ by_______________, M.D.
(insert name and relationship)

Witness________________ Signed__________________________
(Patient or person authorized to consent for the patient)

Release for Ritual Circumcision

Form 65

A.M.
Date________________ Time________________ P.M.

We request Dr.________________, the attending physician, and________________ Hospital to permit our son to be circumcised by ____________________________ whom we have selected as a

(person to perform circumcision)

person qualified in the ritual of our faith and by experience to perform this procedure. We assume full responsibility and release the attending physician, the hsopital and its staff from liability for any adverse results that my occur.

Witness________________ Signed________________________

(Father)

Signed________________________

(Mother)

Consent to Gynecological Examination and Treatment Following Sexual Assault

Form 66

Patient ____
(Last Name) *(First Name)* *(Middle)*

Address ____

______________________________ Age ______________

1. I request and authorize Doctor ______________ and his assistants to perform a gynecologic examination. I authorize the above-named doctor and his assistants to administer medications as described below.
2. The above-named doctor has explained the following to me:
   - ☐ Gynecological examination, including vaginal examination.
   - ☐ Antibiotic injection to prevent venereal disease. I understand that there is a slight chance of an allergic reaction with the administration of any antibiotic.
   - ☐ Ovral ("the morning-after") pills prescribed to prevent conception. I understand that certain side effects might appear while taking this drug, such as nausea, vomiting, headaches, irregular bleeding, dizziness and breast tenderness, and that these side effects should disappear after I have taken all of my pills. I understand that if they do not, I should return to the hospital or see my doctor. As a result of taking Ovral, I understand that I may have a slightly greater chance than non-pill users of developing certain serious problems in rare cases. These include the following: Blood clots; stroke; heart attack. I also understand that if any of the following more serious symptoms occur, I should seek immediate medical attention: chest or arm pain; shortness of breath; unusual pain/swelling in legs; severe headache.

     I understand that taking these pills does not prevent pregnancy 100%. I further understand that if I do not have a menstrual period within four weeks, it is imperative that I see my doctor.
3. I acknowledge that I have received no warranties or assurances with respect to the benefits to be realized or consequences of the aforementioned procedure(s).
4. I acknowledge that I have read this document in its entirety and that I fully understand it and that all blank spaces have been completed prior to my signing.

Date: ______________________

Time ____________________ A.M. P.M. ______________________________
Signature of Consenting Party

Witnesses:

If Consenting Party Is Other Than Patient:

______________________________ ______________________________
Signature of Witness *Signature of Consenting Party*

______________________________ ______________________________
Signature of Witness *Relationship*

Editor's Note: *This form is reproduced with permission of Michael Reese Hospital and Medical Center, Chicago, Illinois.*

Reproductive Technology

17.1 Artificial Insemination

Artificial insemination procedures may be carried out in two ways. If the sperm of the husband is used, the procedure is known as AIH (Artificial Insemination Homologous). AIH is generally used when the husband is impotent. If the sperm of a donor other than the recipient's husband is used, the procedure is known as AID (Artificial Insemination Donor).[1]

The identity of an AID donor is usually kept from the recipient and her husband, and vice versa. It appears, however, that doctors are occasionally approached by couples who wish to have the wife inseminated with the sperm of someone they know. Most of the states that have passed AID statutes failed to anticipate such an arrangement.[2]

The typical AID situation is one in which the recipient's husband is sterile. Couples may also request AID when the husband and wife have Rh incompatibilities, or when the husband fears that he might pass along a potential genetic defect, such as the inheritable forms of Down's syndrome or Tay-Sachs disease.[3]

An emerging issue is whether AID should be made freely available to unmarried women. With the shift away from the traditional family, a growing number of unmarried women are seeking to be inseminated with the sperm of an anonymous donor, but this use of this procedure remains controversial.

AIH, by contrast, poses few legal problems since the child is the biological offspring of husband and wife. There is greater uncertainty about the legal rights of parties in the AID setting.[4] Most AID-related disputes concern the parental rights or obligations of the recipient's husband. These questions arise in a number of legal contexts, including divorce,[5] child visitation[6] and support,[7] and adoption proceedings. While the cases fall far short of establishing a coherent doctrine, resolution of the underlying legitimacy issue generally turns on whether the recipient husband consented, actually or by implication, to the insemination procedure.

A more important legal development has been the intervention of state legislatures seeking to clarify the rights of parties affected by AID. At this time, most states have passed AID statutes.[8] The primary concern of these statutes is to legitimize the AID-conceived child. Each statute makes the offspring of the donor's sperm the legal offspring of a consenting husband for the purpose of legitimacy, inheritance and support.

The statutes focus on the husband's (rather than the wife's) consent to AID. Most statutes require the husband's consent in writing. Some require that both he and his wife sign.[9] Others direct the physician to file the husband's consent confidentially with the state health department.[10] The statutes, however, contain no correlative requirement that a man secure his wife's consent before donating sperm.

The statutes leave some important questions about the AID-conceived child unanswered. They do not, for instance, resolve the question of the child's legitimacy in a situation in which a married woman is artificially inseminated without her husband's consent. A case presenting these facts was recently litigated in Illinois.

The Illinois AID statute requires a husband's written consent, seemingly as a prerequisite to legitimization. No written consent had been obtained in the case in point. The court nevertheless, found "actual consent", as evidenced by the husband's acts in acknowledging the child, and held that the AID-conceived child was his legal offspring.[11]

A second ambiguity plagues twenty-one of the thirty state statutes. In those twenty-one states,[12] the AID offspring is considered to be the legitimate child of the consenting husband when the insemination is performed by a physician.[13] The question remains whether insemination by a person other than a physician invalidates the legitimacy provisions.[14]

The statutes fail to clarify the rights of parties when an AID child is born to an unmarried woman.[15] [16]

Generally, the statutes do not address the doctor's responsibility to screen sperm for genetic and sexually transmitted diseases. Idaho and Ohio require physicians to quarantine frozen sperm and to screen donors for the HIV virus. Ohio also requires a full physical examination and a medical and genetic history from would-be donors.[17]

In the absence of statutory directives, physicians are held to reasonable standards of care. The American Fertility Society guidelines on sperm screening, although voluntary, might be admissible in a malpractice action as evidence of minimal standards of care.[18] As do the AFS guidelines, the Center for Disease Control recommends that the use of all fresh sperm be discontinued and that donor sperm be frozen and quarantined so that testing for HIV may take place at the time of donation and six months later. A doctor's failure to comply with this federal recommendation might be considered negligence by a court.[19]

As in other medical interventions, AID triggers the need for a fully informed consent. The physician's discussion with the recipient and her husband should include an explanation of the procedure and its risk, as well as an exploration of alternative methods of achieving conception[20] (the physician should thus establish to his or her own satisfaction that the husband is sterile). The patient may have questions about the thoroughness of donor screening and the number of pregnancies a particular donor has been permitted to create. She is entitled to candid responses to these questions.[21]

The doctor's agreement with the parties should include:

(1) The recipient's written consent to the procedure.

(2) The husband's written consent.

3) The donor's written consent to the unrestricted use of the semen he supplies, and certification that he will make no effort to ascertain the identity of the recipient or her husband.

(4) Permission for the physician to select the outside donor.

(5) A statement that the doctor does not guarantee that pregnancy will occur.

---

1 A third type of artificial insemination, AIC, is mentioned from time to time in the literature. In AIC, the sperm of the recipient's husband and an unrelated donor are combined. The primary benefit of AIC seems to be the psychological one it may bestow on an oligospermic husband. But the procedure has its drawbacks: recent studies suggest that the addition of the husband's semen may diminish the fertility of the unrelated donor's sperm. L. Andrews, New Conceptions 180 (1984).

2 New Jersey, New Mexico and Washington appear to contemplate the possibility of a nonanonymous donor in the portions of their AID statutes that permit the donor and recipients to contract privately regarding the donor's rights and duties.

3 Andrews, supra note 1, at 162.

4 Presumably, AIC raises all the same legal problems as AID.

5 K.S. v. G.S., 182 N.J. Super. 102, 440 A.2d 64 (Super. Ct. 1981).

6 Brooks v. Fair, 40 Ohio App. 3d 202, 532 N.E.2d 208 (Ohio Ct. App. 1988).

7 In re Baby Doe, 291 S.C. 389, 353 S.E.2d 877 (1987); People v. Sorensen, 68 Cal. 2d 280, 437 P.2d 495, 66 Cal. Reptr. 7 (1968).

8 Ala. Code Sec. 26-17-21 (Supp. 1986); Alaska Stat. Sec. 25.20.045 (1983); Ark. Stat. Ann. Sec. 61-141(c)(1971); Cal. Civil Code Sec. 7005 (West 1983); Cal. Penal Code Sec. 270 (West Supp. 1987); Col. Rev. Stat. Sec. 19-6-106 (1986); Conn. Gen. Stat. Ann. Sec. 45-69(f-m)(West 1981); Fla. Stat. Ann. Sec. 742.11

(West 1986); Ga. Code Ann. Sec. 43-34-42 (Michie 1984); Ga. Code Ann. Sec. 19-7-21 (Michie 1981); Idaho Code Secs. 39-5401 to 39-5408 (1985, Supp. 1986); Ill. Ann. Stat. ch.40, paras, 1452-1453 (Smith-Hurd 1987); Kan. Stat. Ann. Secs. 23-128 to 130 (1981, Supp. 1986); La Civ. Code Ann. art. 188 (West Supp. 1987); Md. Est. & Trust Code Ann. Sec. 1-206b (1974); Md. Health Gen. Code Ann. Sec. 20-214 (1987); Mich Comp. Laws Secs. 333.2824 to 700.111 (West 1980); Minn. Stat. Ann. Sec 257.56 (1987); Mont. Code Ann. Sec. 40-6-106 (1985); Nev. Rev. Stat. Sec. 126.061 (1985); N.J. Stat. Ann. Sec. 9:17-44 (West Supp. 1987; N.M. Stat. Ann. Sec. 40-11-6 (1986); N.Y. Dom. Rel. Law Sec. 73 (West 1977); N.C. Gen. Stat. Sec. 49A-1 (1984); Ohio Rev. Code Ann. Secs. 3111.30-38 (Page Supp. 1986); Okla. Stat. Ann. tit. 10, Secs. 551-553 (West Supp. 1985); Or. Rev. Stat. Secs. 109.239-243, and 109.247 (1985); Or. Rev. Stat. Secs. 677.355-677.370 (1985); Tenn. Code Ann. Sec. 68-3-306 (1987); Tex. Fam. Code Ann. Sec. 12.03 (Vernon 1986); Va. Code Ann. Sec. 64.1.7.1 (1986); Wash. Rev. Code Ann. Sec. 26.26.050 (1986); Wis. Stat. Ann. Sec. 767.47 (West 1981); Wis. Stat. Ann. Sec. 891.40 (West Supp. 1987); Wyo. Stat. Sec. 14-2-103 (1986). For a comparative analysis of these statutes, see U.S. Congress, Office of Technology Assessment, Infertility: Medical and Social Choice , *OTA-BA-358 (Washington, DC: U.S. Government Printing Office, May 1988), at pp. 242-50.*

9 *Alabama, California, Illinois, Ohio.*

10 *Alabama, California, Connecticut, Idaho, Kansas, Montana, New Mexico, Nevada, Ohio, Oklahoma, Oregon, Washington, Wisconsin, Wyoming.*

11 Adams. v. Adams, *174 Ill. App. 3d 595, 528 N.E.2d 1075 (Ill. App. Ct. 1980).*

12 *Alabama, Arkansas, California, Colorado, Connecticut, Georgia, Idaho, Illinois, Minnesota, Montana, Nevada, New Jersey, New Mexico, New York, Ohio, Oklahoma, Oregon, Virginia, Washington, Wisconsin, Wyoming.*

13 *Three states, Georgia, Florida and Idaho, make it a crime for a person other than a physician to do AID.*

14 *Ohio's statute eliminates any confusion by providing expressly that nonphysician insemination does not cancel the legitimization sections.*

15 *Ohio, again, is the exception. Its statute strips the donor of any claim to the child regardless of the mother's marital status.*

16 Jhordan C. v. Mary K., *179 Cal. App. 2d 386, 224 Cal. Rptr. 530 (1986);* C.M. v. C.C., *152 N.J. Super. 160, 377 A.2d 821 (1977).* See also Kaiser, Artificial Insemination: Donor Rights in Situations Involving Unmarried Recipients, *26 J. Fam. L. 793 (1987-88).*

17 *In addition to these requirements, the Idaho and Oregon statutes contain provisions directed at the donor, rather than his physician, which make it a violation of law for him to give sperm if he knows he has a venereal or genetic disease.*

18 *U.S. Congress, Office of Technology Assessment,* supra *note 8, at 248-49.*

19 Id. *at 249.*

20 *F. Rozovsky,* Consent to Treatment *§ 3.7 (1984).*

21 *Andrews,* supra *note 1, at 167.*

Consent to Artificial Insemination

Form 67

A.M.
Date________________ Time________________ P.M.

We,________________ and ________________, being husband and wife and both of legal age, authorize Dr.________________ and such assistants as he may designate, to inseminate the wife artificially, and to use the semen of (the husband) (the husband and a donor or donors) (a donor or donors) for this purpose. We authorize him to employ such assistants he may desire to assist him.

We understand that even though the insemination may be repeated as often as recommended by Dr.________________, there is no guarantee on his part or assurance that pregnancy or full term pregnancy will result.

We agree to rely upon the sole discretion of Dr.________________ in the selection of qualified donors and never to seek to discover the identity of any donor. We agree that following the insemination, Dr.________________ may destroy all records and information concerning the identity of the donor or donors.

We, and each of us, acknowledge our obligation to care for and support and otherwise treat any child born as the result of such artificial insemination in all respects as though it were our natural born child.

We understand that if pregnancy shall result, there is the possibility of complications of childbirth or delivery, or the birth of an abnormal infant or infants, or undesirable hereditary tendencies of such issue, or other adverse consequences.

(CROSS OUT ANY WORDS ABOVE WHICH DO NOT APPLY)

Signed______________________________
(Husband)

Signed______________________________
(Wife)

Witness________________

Agreement and Consent to Artificial Insemination (Donor)

Form 68

THIS AGREEMENT entered into this__________day of __________, 19____ by and between________________*(Husband)* and________________*(Wife)* both jointly and severally, both of ________________ and ____________Hospital and Medical Center *(Hospital)* witnessth that:

WHEREAS, Husband and Wife, both jointly and severally, desire to use the services of the Hospital and its doctors, agents and employees to perform one or more artificial insemination procedure(s) with sperm from an unknown donor and,

WHEREAS, the hospital has the facilities and ability to perform said procedure(s),

NOW THEREFORE IT IS AGREED

1. The Doctor is hereby authorized to and shall peform the procedure of artificial insemination upon the Wife. The Doctor shall obtain the necessary sperm from a donor who shall never be told the identity of Husband and Wife; nor shall Husband and Wife ever be told the identity of the donor. Husband and Wife shall rely upon the judgment and discretion of the Doctor, to choose a donor whose physical and mental characteristics are compatible with those of Husband and Wife and shall never seek to discover the identity of any donor.
2. On occasion, the Doctor will use donor sperm that has been frozen for the purpose of storage, over periods of weeks to months.
3. Husband and Wife understand that if pregnancy does result, the normal possibility exists of complications during pregnancy and childbirth, of the birth of an abnormal infant, of undesirable hereditary tendencies of such infant and of other adverse consequences.
4. Husband and Wife understand that neither the Hospital nor its doctors can be responsible for the physical or mental characteristics of any child or children so produced; and therefore do jointly and severally release and forever discharge the Hospital, its officers, doctors, agents, employees, successors and assigns from any and all claims, demands, costs, expenses, and loss of services incurred as a result of the physical or mental nature or character of any child or children so produced.
5. From the moment of conception Husband and Wife, both jointly and severally accept the act of conception as their own act and ac-

Continued

Form 68 Continued

knowledge the child or children produced as their own legitimate child or children and as the heir or heirs of their bodies with all the rights and privileges accompanying such status. Husband and Wife jointly and severally waive forever any right which they might have to disclaim such child or children as their heir.

6. The nature of this agreement is such that it must remain confidential. Therefore, Husband and Wife agree that the sole copy of the same may be given to the Hospital for its confidential files.

WHEREFORE: the parties hereto have executed this agreement on the date first written above.

____________________ Husband   ____________________ Wife

____________________ M.D.   ____________________ Date

Editor's Note: *This form is reproduced with permission of Michael Reese Hospital and Medical Center, Chicago, Illinois.*

Offer to Serve as a Donor of Semen

Form 69

A.M.
Date________________ Time________________ P.M.

To Dr.________________:

1. I offer my services as a donor of semen with the understanding that the identity of any recipient shall not be disclosed to me, nor shall you voluntarily reveal my identity to any recipient.
2. To the best of my knowledge:
   (a) I am in good health; I have no communicable disease; and I do not now, nor have I ever suffered, from any physical or mental impairment or disability, whether inherited or as a result of any disease or ailment, except as follows:

   ____.

   (b) I am not now nor have I ever been afflicted with syphilis or any other venereal disease, except as follows:____________

   ____

   (c) None of my grandparents, parents, brothers, sisters, or children, if any, nor their lineal descendants, have ever been afflicted with emotional illness or any inherited mental or physical disabilities or disease, except as follows:____________
3. For the purpose of determining whether I am acceptable as a donor of semen, I consent to a physical examination, including the taking of blood and other body fluids, by you or any other physician whom you may designate.

Signed________________________
(Donor)

Witness________________

Consent of Wife of Donor

Form 70

Date________________

To Dr.________________:

1. I have read my husband's offer to serve as a donor of semen and to the best of my knowledge the statements he has made are true.

2. If my husband is accepted as a donor, I understand that it is your intention to use his semen for purposes of artificial insemination, but not with respect to myself.

3. I know that artificial insemination is a medical procedure intended to cause pregnancy through the use of semen introduced by means other than sexual intercourse.

4. I agree that I shall not attempt to discover the identity of any recipient of my husband's semen.

5. In serving as a donor of semen, I know that my husband may become the father of a child or children of which I am not the mother, but I nevertheless consent to the performance of such services by him.

Signed____________________________

Witness________________

17.2 In Vitro Fertilization

In vitro fertilization (IVF) is a process in which an egg is surgically removed from a woman's ovary and fertilized in a petri dish with her husband's sperm. The embryo thus created is then implanted in the woman's uterus.[1] Even though the procedure is now being performed in quite a few IVF clinics and programs,[2] it is still sufficiently novel to be surrounded by a great deal of legal uncertainty. The most important question still awaiting definitive resolution is one of terminology: which applications of IVF technology are 'therapeutic" and which constitute "research?"

At issue are the rights of couples to use basic IVF to initiate pregnancy, or to decide not to transfer an abnormal embryo, or to cyropreserve embryos for later transfer.[3] This question matters at the federal level because the Department of Health and Human

Services' guidelines on research on human subjects, impose detailed consent and reporting requirements on researchers who receive HHS funding, and thus control human IVF "research."[4] Under these guidelines, IVF includes "any fertilization of human ova which occurs outside the body of a female, either through a mixture of donor human sperm and ova or by any other means."[5] The federal government has not funded IVF and seems unlikely to involve itself any time soon.[6]

At the state level, in the wake of *Roe v. Wade*, twenty-four states[7] passed laws that restrict experimentation on fetuses. Fifteen[8] of the twenty-four use language such as "embryo" and "unborn child" that might be construed to include preimplantation IVF embryos.[9] The Congressional Office of Technology Assessment predicts that the fetal research statutes will not be construed as banning nonexperimental therapeutic techniques that aim at bringing healthy offspring into being, but the issue remains open.[10]

Meanwhile states may move to regulate IVF directly, as they have in the case of artificial insemination. Five states currently have laws that refer specifically to IVF.[11] Pennsylvania's law seeks only to monitor the procedure.[12] Louisiana's, on the other hand, seems intended to constrain the choices of IVF participants. It grants an embryo that is outside the body the status of a 'juridical person," able to sue and be sued.[13] The implication is that actions adverse to the embryo (such as discard) are subject to legal consequences.[14] Louisiana's law has yet to be tested, but the decision of a federal court entertaining a challenge to Illinois' fetal research law (which specifically mentions IVF) may be instructive.

This court held that an IVF woman is pregnant the moment her egg is fertilized, even though the fertilization occurs outside the body.[15] It would seem to follow that a decision to discard the embryo would be treated as any other form of pregnancy termination, i.e., it would require the woman's consent.[16]

At least until IVF becomes established as a common technique for human conception, it calls for high standards of care and consent.[17] A physician should explain the process and disclose all likely results, benefits and risks. Alternative methods of conception should be explored.[18] Finally, the doctor should obtain the consent of both of the prospective parents throughout the process. In a case in which a preimplantation embryo was destroyed without the patient's consent, a jury awarded the would-be mother $50,000 in damages for her mental anguish.[19]

1 *L. Andrews,* New Conceptions *289 (1984).*

2 *U.S. Congress, Office of Technology Assessment,* Infertility: Medical and Social Choices, *OTA-BA-358 (Washington, DC: U.S. Government Printing Office, May 1988), at p. 250.*

3 Id.

4 *45 C.F.R. §46.201 (1980).*

5 *45 C.F.R. §46.201 (1980).*

6 *U.S. Congress, Office of Technology Assessment,* supra *note 2, at 178.*

7 *Ariz. Rev. Stat. Ann. Sec. 36-2302 (1986);Ark. Stat. Ann. Secs. 82-436, 442 (Supp. 1985); Cal. Health & Safety Sec. 25956 (West 1984); Fla. Stat. Ann. Secs. 390.001(6), 873.05 (1987); Ill. Ann. Stat. ch. 38, paras. 81-26, 32 (1987); Ind. Code Ann. Sec. 35-1-58.5-6 (West 1987); Ky. Rev. Stat. Sec. 436.026 (1985); Key. Rev. Stat. Sec. 311.720 (1983); La. Rev. Stat. Ann. Secs. 14:87, 121-133 (1987); Me. Rev. Stat. Ann. tit. 22, Secs. 1593-95 (1980); Mass Gen. Laws Ann. ch. 112, Secs. 12J,K (1983); Mich. Comp. Laws Secs. 333-2685-2692 (1980); Minn. Stat. Ann. Secs. 145-421, 422 (Supp. 1986); Mo. Rev. Stat. Secs. 188.015,037 (Vernon 1983); Mont. Code Ann. Sec. 50-20-108 (1987); Neb. Rev. Stat. Sec. 28-346 (1985); N.M. Stat. Ann. Secs. 24-9A-1 to 6 (1976); N.D. Cent. Code Sec. 14.02.2-01 (1981); Ohio Rev. Code Ann. Sec. 2919.14 (Page 1987); Okla. Stat. Ann. tit. 63, Sec. 1-735 (1984); Pa. Stat. Ann. tit. 18, Secs. 3203, 3216 (1983); R.I. Gen Laws Sec. 11-54-1 (Supp. 1987); S.D. Cod. Laws Ann. Sec. 34-23A-17 (1986); Tenn. Code Ann. Sec. 39-4-208 (1982); Utah Code Ann. Sec. 76-7-310 (1978); Wis. Stat. Ann. Sec. 51.61 (Supp. 1986); Wyo. Stat. Sec. 35-6-115 (1977).*

8 *Arizona, California, Illinois, Louisiana, Maine, Massachusetts, Michigan, Minnesota, New Mexico, North Dakota, Ohio, Oklahoma, Pennsylvania, Rhode Island, Utah.*

9 *For an analysis of the probable impact of these statutes on IVF, see U.S. Congress, Office of Technology Assessment,* supra *note 2, at 324 (Appendix C).*

10 *Note that the validity of the fetal research statutes themselves — as distinguished from their application to IVF — is by no means firmly settled. In the only challenge to date, the Louisiana statute was struck down for vagueness.* Margaret S. v. Edwards, *794 F.2d 994 (5th Cir. 1986).*

11 *Kentucky, Illinois, Louisiana, New Mexico, Pennsylvania. For a description of these laws, see U.S. Congress, Office of TEchnology Assessment,* supra *note 2, at 252 (Box 13-A).*

12 *Pa. Stat. Ann. tit. 18, Sec. 3203.*

13 *La. Rev. Stat. Ann. Sec. 9:124 (1986).*

14 *U.S. Congress, Office of Technology Assessment,* supra *note 2, at 253.*

15 Smith v. Hartigan, *556 F. Supp. 157 (N.D. Ill. 1983).*

16 *U.S. Congress, Office of Technology Assessment,* supra *note 2, at 253.*

17 *F. Rozovsky,* Consent to Treatment *§8.11 (1984).*

18 Id.

19 Del Zio v. Manhattan's Columbia Presbyterian Medical Center, *No. 74-3558 (S.D.N.Y. 1978). The* Del Zio *case is discussed in Andrews,* supra *note 1, at 155-57.*

18.0

After the death of a patient, the right to freedom from interference automatically passes in modified form to the spouse or next of kin. Any unauthorized interference with the dead body exposes the offender to a suit for damages by the person entitled to its custody.[1] The damage award is based not on a theory of property rights in the body, but on a concept of injury to the sensibilities of the survivors.[2] Anyone who participates in an autopsy that is not approved by the surviving spouse or next of kin, or that is not authorized by law, is subject to criminal prosecution.[3]

The person entitled to possession of a body for the purpose of burial is generally entitled to authorize an autopsy upon it to determine the cause of death. The right to the body, and the attendant right to give or withhold consent to an autopsy, is not vested in the executor.[4] It is vested in the surviving spouse, provided he or she was living with the deceased at the time of death in the normal relationship of a marriage unless statutes to the contrary exist.[5] If the surviving spouse is not living with the deceased at the time of death,[6] or was legally separated,[7] consent is vested in the next of kin.

If the surviving spouse asserts the right to the body and does not abuse it, the next of kin has no rights to the body and has no cause of action for the performance of an unauthorized autopsy.[8] If there is no surviving spouse, the right is vested in the next of kin in order of kinship.[9] Under such circumstances, a child of the deceased usually has rights superior to those of anyone else except the coroner or medical examiner.[10]

If the deceased is not survived by any children, authority over the dead body normally is vested in the parents.[11] It is not clear in cases where the deceased child is a minor whether the father's consent alone is sufficient, or whether the mother is also necessary.[12] Few states have clarified this by statute.[13]

If the parents of a deceased, minor child are divorced or separated, consent to an autopsy should be obtained from the parent who has custody of the child.[14] *Where no parents or children are involved, authority over a dead body is normally vested in brothers and sisters and so on through various degrees of family relationship.*

Some states have statutes that define the sequence in which the right to control a dead body occurs.[15] Some states have laws that determine how many people in the same class may give a valid consent,[16] while in other states consent is implied.[17]

The deceased may have left directions that an autopsy should be performed. The trend in American cases is to honor the deceased's directions regarding the disposition of his or her body.[18] There are statutes in a number of states providing that a person may, during his lifetime, direct what is to be done with his body after death.[19] California, Nebraska, Nevada, and Utah allow a decedent to authorize an autopsy in his or her will.[20]

In some states the workmen's compensation commission is permitted to order an autopsy when there is a claim that death resulted from an occupational cause.[21] Sometimes an insurance policy will permit an autopsy, and in states recognizing such consents, a physician acting under such authority will be protected.[22]

---

1 Jackson v. Rupp, *228 So.2d 916 (Fla. 1970);* French v. Ochsner Clinic, *200 So.2d 371 (La. 1967);* Trammell v. City of New York, *82 N.Y.S.2d 762 (1948);* Steagall v. Doctors Hospital, *171 F.2d 352 (D.D.C. 1948);* Beller v. City of New York, *58 N.Y.S.2d 112 (1945);* Simpkins v. Lumbermens Mutual Casualty Co., *20 S.E.2d 733 (S.C. 1942);* Alderman v. Ford, *72 P.2d 981 (Kan. 1937);* McPosey v. Sisters of the Sorrowful Mother, *57 P.2d 617 (Okla. 1936);* Aetna Life Ins. Co. v. Lindsay, *69 F.2d 627 (7th Cir. 1934);* Darcy v. Presbyterian Hospital in City of New York, *95 N.E. 695 (N.Y. 1911).*

2 Darcy v. Presbyterian Hospital, *95 N.E. 696 (New York 1911); Alderman v. Ford, 72 P.2d 981 (Kansas 1937).*

3 *All states have statutes making the unauthorized disturbance of a dead body, or interference with a dead body, a crime.*

4 In re Estate of Mgurdichian, *291 N.Y.S.2d 453 (1968);* Burney v. Children's Hospital in Boston, *47 N.E. 401 (Mass. 1897).*

5 Foley v. Phelps, *37 N.Y.S. 471 (1896);* Larson v. Chase, *50 N.W. 238 (Minn. 1891);* See *Ariz. Rev. Stat. Ann. §36-832; Haw. Rev. Stat. §453-15; Md. Ann. Code Health General art. 5, §501; Mich. Comp. Laws Ann. §333.2855; Miss. Code Ann. §41-37-25.*

6 See *S.C. Code §44-43-710.*

7 Donaldson v. Holcomb, *396 S.W.2d 281 (Ark. 1967);* Morrow v. Cline, *190 S.E. 207 (N.C. 1937). See Indiana Code Ann. §16-8-1-4 (Burns);* Southern Life & Health Ins. Co. v. Morgan, *105 So.161 (Ala. 1925).*

8 Trammel v. City of New York, *82 N.Y.S.2d 762 (1948);* Steagall v. Doctors Hospital, *171 F.2d 352 (D.D.C. 1948);* Aetna Life Ins. Co. v. Lindsay, *69 F.2d 627 (7th Cir. 1934).*

9 Beller v. City of New York, *58 N.Y.S.2d 112 (1945);* O'Donnell v. Slack, *55 P.906 (Cal. 1899).*

10 Koerber v. Pakte, *102 N.W. 40 (Wis. 1905).*

11 Stephenson v. Duke University, *163 S.E. 698 (N.C. 1932);* Coty v. Baughman, *210 N.W. 348 (S.D. 1926);* Darcy v. Presbyterian Hospital in City of New York, *95 N.E. 695 (N.Y. 1911);* Palenzke v. Bruning, *98 Ill. App. 644 (1901).*

12 *In* Stephenson v. Duke University, *163 S.E. 698 (N.C. 1932), it was held that, since the father has the primary duty to support the child, support that would include burial, only he had a cause of action for the performance of an unauthorized autopsy on the child. So long as the father is alive, the*

mother has no cause of action for the wrongful act. In Coty v. Baughman, *210 N.W. 348, 350 (S.D. 1926), however, the court said: "We think the rights of the father and mother are equal in the body of their deceased child, and that the consent of both to an autopsy would be necessary where the father and mother were living together and both were within this state."* See *Miss. Code Ann. §41-37-25 (either parent may consent unless the other objects.)*

13 See *S.C. Code §20-7-270 (allows a married minor or, if necessary, the spouse of a married minor to consent to an autopsy on the minor or any child of the minor).*

14 Rader v. Davis, *134 N.W. 849 (Iowa 1912).*

15 See e.g., *Cal. Health and Safety Code Ann. §7100 (Supp. 1984) that provides the following order of the right to control: (1) surviving spouse (2) child or children (3) parent or parents (4) those persons in next degree of kinship (5) the public administrator.* See also *Iowa Code Ann. §144.56; Pa. Stat. Ann. tit. 35. §1111 (Purdon); N.C. Gen. Stat. §130A-398 Neb. Rev. Stat. §71-1339,* See generally, *Consent for Autopsies, JAMA, Vol. 250, No. 9, pages 1161-64 (Sept. 2, 1983).*

16 Ark. Code Ann. §20-17-303; Colo. Rev. Stat. Ann. §12-36-133; Conn. Gen. Stat. Ann. §199-286; Del. Code Ann. Tit. 16, §2701; Fla. Stat. Ann. §872.04(2); Ga. Code Ann. §21-206; Hawaii Rev. Stat. §435-15; Idaho Code §54-1817; Ill. Rev. Stat. Ann. ch. 31 Sec. 42(2)(a) (Smith-Hurd Supp.); Ind. Code Ann. §16-8-1-4 (Burns); Kan. Stat. Ann. §65-2893; Ky. Rev. Stat. Ann. §72.070; Md. Ann. Code Health-General art. 5, §501; Mich. Comp. Laws §333.2855; Miss. Code Ann. §41-37-25; Mo. Ann. Stat. §194.115(3); N.J. Stat. Ann. §26:6-50; N.D. Cent. code 23-06.1-02; Ohio Rev. Code Ann. §2108.50: Okla. Stat. Ann. tit. 21, §1154; Pa. Stat. Ann. tit. 35, §1112 (Purdon); S.C. Code §44-43-710; Tenn. Code Ann. §68-4-111; Tex. Code Crim. Pro. Ann. art. §49.05 (Vernon); Wis. Stat. §155.05.

17 Ariz. Rev. Stat. Ann. §36-832; Cal. Health & Safety Code Ann. §7113 (Supp.); Iowa code Ann. §144.56; Neb. Rev. State. §§71-1339, 1341; N.M. stat. Ann. §24-12-4; N.C. Gen. Stat. §§130-A-398 to 400; N.D. Cent. code§23-0601-02; Or. Rev. Sat. §97.130; S.D. Codified Laws §34-26-2; Utah Code Ann. §264-13; Va. Code §54-325.8 (1979 Supp.); Wash. Rev. Code Ann. §68.08.101; W.Va. Code §16-4B-1. Many statutes, particularly in states that imply that consent from one of several persons ith a right to custody of the body is sufficient, provide that another person of the same or higher priority class may object, usually in writing. See Ill. Ann. Stat. ch. 31, Sec. 42 (Smith-Hurd); Iowa Code Ann. §144.56; Can. TStat. Ann. §65-2893 (written objection by certain persons); Miss. Code An.. §41-37-25; S.C. Code §44-43-710; S.D. codified Laws §34-6-2; Va. Code §54.325.8 (1979 Supp.); W.V.A. Code Ann. §164B-1.

18 Beller v. City of New York, *58 N.Y.S.2d 112 (1945);* Wales v. Wales, *190 A. 109 (Del. 1936);* Painter v. United States Fidelity & Guaranty Co., *91 A. 158 (Md. 1914);* Darcy v. Presbyterian hospital in City of New York, *95 N.E. 695 (N.Y. 1911).*

19 Ill. Ann. Stat. ch. 31, §42(a)(Smith-Hurd); Ark. Code Ann. §20-17-303; Cal. Health & Safety Code §7113; Kan. Stat. Ann. §65-2898; Ky. Rev. Stat. §72.072(2); Miss. code Ann. §41-37-25; Mo. Stat. Ann. §194.115; Mont. Code Ann. 50-21-103; N.M. Stat. Ann. §24-12-4; N.C. Gen. Stat. §130A-398 §90-217(3); N.D. Cent. Code §26-06-13(4); Ohio Rev. Code Ann. §2108.50 (Page); Pa. Stat. Ann. Title 35, §1111(1)(Purdon); S.C. Code Ann. §44-43-710; S.D. Codified Laws Ann. §34-26-3.

20 Cal Health & Safety Code 7113; Neb. Rev. Stat. 451.010(1); Utah code Ann. 26-15-18(2)(a), 24-4-24(b). See also, NC Gen Stat. 130A-398 (which allows a personal representative of the descendant's estate to request an autopsy).

21 Vermont Stat. Ann. title 21, §1018.

22 Palmquist v. Standard Accident Ins. Co.; *3 F. Supp. 358 (S.D. Cal. 1933).* See also, *Fla. Stat. Ann. §627.615.*

18.1 Authority of Coroner or Medical Examiner

In all jurisdictions, a public official, either the coroner or medical examiner, has legal authority to perform autopsies in cases where death has resulted from something other than natural causes. There is no basis for action against a coroner, medical examiner or examining physician when statutorily authorized autopsy or postmortem examination is performed in good faith without negligence or wanton disfigurement of the cadaver. When death is due to violence or a casualty, or when there is reasonable ground to believe that it occurred in that way, the right to custody of the dead body is vested immediately in the coroner or the medical examiner. Most statutes also vest authority in the coroner or medical examiner in cases where death occurs in a state prison or county jail.

When the coroner or medical examiner has legal control of a dead body that authority is supreme. The official is, moreover, entitled to the body in the same condition it was in at the moment of death. In general, a coroner or medical examiner is authorized to perform or procure an autopsy on any body lawfully coming into that official's custody.[1]

If a coroner or medical examiner authorizes the performance of an autopsy on a body that is not properly within the legal jurisdiction of the coroner or medical examiner, the official and those who perform the autopsy are liable to the surviving spouse or next of kin.[2]

1 Chaparro v. Jackson & Perkins Company, *346 F.2d 677 (Cir. 1965);* Sturgeon v. Crosby Mortuary, *299 N.W. 378 (Neb. 1941);* Kingsley v. Forsyth, *257 N.W. 95 (Minn. 1934).*

2 Gurganious v. Simpson, *197 S.E. 163 (N.C. 1938);* Streipe v. Liberty Mutual Ins. Co., *47 S.W.2d 1004 (Ky. 1932).*

18.2 Limitations on Autopsy

All autopsies must be performed in a manner that shows decent respect for the body of the deceased.[1] By statute, many states provide immunity from civil or criminal liability for persons who in good faith order or perform an autopsy.[2] In the absence of a specific restriction, consent to an autopsy by implication authorizes a physician to conduct the procedure in the usual and approved manner of the medical profession, and to remove for examination and study such parts of the body as are necessary to accomplish the purposes of the autopsy.[3]

Authority to remove parts or organs for study does not, in the absence of a specific agreement, include the authority to retain them permanently.[4] If there is no specific authorization for retention of parts of the body, those that have been removed must be replaced in the body cavity before interment.[5]

The person who has the right to authorize an autopsy has the right to state the limits within which it shall be performed, and the autopsy must be undertaken strictly within those limits.[6] Some statutes also preclude performing an autopsy because of a decedent's religious beliefs or affiliations.[7]

---

1 Hill v Travelers' Insurance Co., *294 S.W. 1097 (Tenn. 1927);* Young v. College of Physicians & Surgeons of Baltimore City, *32 A. 177 (Md. 1895).*

2 See Cal. Health & Safety Code §§7113, 7114; Del. Code Ann. tit. 16, §2701; Idaho Code §19-4301B (performed by a person pursuant to a coroner's order); Ind. Code Ann. §17-3-17-015; Ky. Rev. Stat. Ann. §72.070; Me. Rev. Stat. Ann. tit. 22, §3033 (for medical examiner unless caused by gross negligence); Miss. Code Ann. §41-37-7; Mont. Code Ann. §50-21-103, 104 (if pursuant to Coroner's Act); N.Y. Pub. Health Law §4211 (McKinney)(if performed in good faith without knowledge of the existence of an autopsy objection card, no criminal or civil liability); Ohio Rev. Code Ann. §2108.5; Tenn. Rev./ Code Ann. §38-712 (pursuant to medical examiner's act); Tex. Code Crim. Pro. Ann. art §49.04 (pursuant to court order); Utah code Ann. §26-4-13 (pursuant to Workmen's Compensation Act), §26-4-20 (pursuant to Medical examiner Act), §26-4-24 (pursuant to consent statute); Va. Code §54.325.8.

3 Lashbrook v. Barnes, *437 S.W.2d 502 (Ky. 1969);* Palmquist v. Standard Accident Ins. Co., *3 F.Supp. 358 (S.D. Cal. 1933).*

4 Hendriksen v. Roosevelt Hospital, *297 F.Supp. 1142 (N.Y. 1969);* Lashbrook v. Barnes, *437 S.W.2d 502 (Ky. 1969);* Palmquist v. Standard Accident Ins. Co., *3 F.Supp. 358 (S.D. Cal. 1933).* See *Neb. Rev. Stat. 71-1341; Haw. Rev. Stat. §453-15. Particular organs are often subject to special retention requirements. Kan. Stat. Ann §19-1033; Ohio Rev. Code Ann. §2108.53 (pituitary glands).*

5 Code of Va. §19.1-46.1; Bonilla v. Reeves, *267 N.Y.S.2d 374 (1966).*

6 Tackett v. Terrill, *404 S.W.2d 158 (Tex. 1966);* Hill v. Travelers' Ins. Co., *294 S.W. 1097 (Tenn. 1927);* Koerber v. Patek, *102 N.W. 40 (Wis. 1905);* Winkler v. Hawkes & Ackley, *102 N.W. 418 (Iowa 1905). See Mont. Rev. Code Ann. §69-5103; Nev. Rev. Stat. §451.010; N.Y. Public Health Law §4210(3)(McKinney).*

7 Ariz. Rev. Stat. Ann. 11-593(c); Cal Health and Safety Code 7113; La. Rev. Stat. Ann. §3:1561(c); Md. Ann. Code 5-310; NY County Law 674 (3)(b) as applied in Atkins v. Medical Examiner of Westchester County, 418 NYS 2d 839 (1979).

18.3 Forms for Consent

A number of states have statutes that provide that consent to an autopsy must be in writing.[1] In other states, several types of consent are permissible,[2] including oral authorizations that are recorded[3] or witnessed.[4]

1 *Conn. Gen. Stat. §19a-386; Fla. Stat. Ann. §872.04; Iowa Code Ann. §144.56 (Supp.); Neb. Rev. Stat. §1341; N.Y. Pub. Health Law §4210(3)(b)(McKinney)(if not for determining the cause of death); Ohio Rev. Code Ann. §2108.50; Pa. Stat. Ann. tit. 35, §1111 (Purdon).*

2 *Ky. Rev. Stat. Ann. §72.070 (written or telegraphic); Cal. Health & Safety Law §7113 (written, telegraphic, or recorded oral); Fla. Stat. §872.04 (Supp.)(witnessed telephone consent if undue delay otherwise).*

3 *Cal. Health & Safety Law §7113; W.Va. Code §16-4B-1; Md. Code Ann. Health-General arts, §501; S.D. Codified Laws Ann. §34-26-2.*

4 *Fla. Stat. §872.04; Ill. Ann. Stat. ch. 31 §42(2)(Smith-Hurd); Ind. Code Ann. §16-8-1-2 (Burns)(from person outside the country).*

Authorization for Autopsy

Form 71

A.M.
Date_______________ Time_______________ P.M.

I (We) request and authorize the physicians and surgeons in attendance at the_______________Hospital to perform a complete autopsy on the remains of_______________and I (we) authorize the removal and retention or use for diagnostic, scientific, or therapeutic purposes of such organs, tissues, and parts as such physicians and surgeons deem proper.

This authority is granted subject to the following restrictions:

____

____
(If no restrictions, write "None")

The following special examinations shall be made:

____

____

I (We) wish the remains to be released to:

_______________________________, ______________, ______________.
(Name of undertaking establishment) *(City)* *(State)*

I (We) represent that I am (we are) the_______________
(relationship)
of the deceased and entitled by law to control the disposition of the remains.

Signed_______________________

Signed_______________________

Witnesses:

____

____

Name of person obtaining Authorization:

____

Authorization to Retain and Dispose of Body

Form 72

A.M.
Date________________ Time________________ P.M.

We request and authorize the release of the body of baby ________________ to the Pathology Staff of the Laboratory at ________________Hospital, for scientific purposes and study with privilege of ultimate disposal.

Signed____________________________
(Mother)

Signed____________________________
(Father)

Witnesses:

____

____

Authorization to Use Eyes (Donor)

Form 73

A.M.
Date________________ Time________________ P.M.

I authorize, at the time of my death, the removal of both or either of my eyes for donation to any eye bank serving the area in which my death occurs and for such purpose as the eye bank may see fit.

Signed____________________________
(Donor)

Witness________________

Authorization to Use Eyes (Next of Kin)

Form 74

A.M.
Date______________ Time______________ P.M.

I authorize any member of the medical staff of the

______________Hospital to remove both or either of the eyes of

______________, the deceased, for donation to any eye bank serving the area and for such purpose as the eye bank may see fit.

Signed____________________
(next of kin)

____
(relationship to deceased)

Witness______________

Authorization for Release of Body to Funeral Home

Form 75

Patient________________________ Date______________

I hereby authorize the__________________ to release the remains
(name of institution)

of ______________________________
(name of decedent)

to the______________________________
(name of funeral home)

Signature ____________________

Relationship to Patient ______________

Witness____________________

I certify that the remains of the above named patient was, after proper identification, received by me for the purpose of burial.

Signature ____________________

Funeral Home____________________

Consent to Disposal of Amputated Part or Organ

Form 76

A.M.
Date________________ Time________________ P.M.

I authorize________________to preserve for scientific purposes, or for use in grafts in living persons, or to otherwise dispose of the following named tissues, parts or organs, ________________, of

__________________________, in accordance with
(myself or name of patient)
customary medical practice.

Signed____________________________

Witness________________

Transplantation

19.0

A large variety of organs and tissues can presently be used in transplantation procedures.[1] Such organs include kidneys, heart and liver. Examples of commonly transplanted tissues include corneas, skin and bone.[2]

Any person who dies is a potential tissue donor, but only one who has been declared brain dead is a potential organ donor.[3] Organs or tissues may sometimes be procured from living as well as dead donors. Kidneys and skin may be obtained from both. Cadaver donation is now regulated by statute in every state. The law governing live donation procedures is less well developed.

Gifts by deceased donors are covered in all 50 states and the District of Columbia by some version of the 1968 Uniform Anatomical Gift Act (UAGA).[4] A survey of the UAGA's salient features suggests, however, that there are significant variations in the law among states. A physician will, therefore, need to know the details of his jurisdiction's enactment.[5]

The UAGA provides that any person over 18 and of sound mind may donate all or part of his body for transplantation, research or medical education. Some states vary the age of capacity to 19 or 21. Six states permit minors to make anatomical gifts with written parental consent.[6]

The UAGA also authorizes gifts by survivors of the decedent. The act ranks survivors by classes for this purpose. The decision to authorize a gift is first given to the decedent's spouse. If there is no spouse, the decision passes to an adult son or daughter, then to either parent; then to an adult brother or sister, and then to the decedent's guardian. Finally, it passes to any person authorized or under obligation to dispose of the decedent's body.

Survivors cannot authorize gifts if there is evidence that the decedent had a contrary intent. On the other hand, if a donor authorizes a gift to be made after his or her death, no survivor can bar the gift.

In cases of donor authorization, the gift may be made by personal will or by the Uniform Donor Card. If the gift is made by will, it is not necessary to wait for the will to be probated; the gift takes effect upon the donor's death. If the gift is made via a Uniform Donor Card, the UAGA in most states requires the signatures of two witnesses.[7]

Fewer formalities are required when survivors authorize gifts. Gifts may be made by a signed writing, by telegraph, or by recorded telephone message. This provision is intended to facilitate donations by out-of-town survivors.[8]

A gift may be made to a specific donee, though this is not required. The UAGA specifies the persons or institutions that may receive the gift. The list includes hospitals, surgeons, physicians, medical or dental schools, organ and tissue banks or storage facilities and individuals who need the gift for therapeutic purposes.

If no donee is specified, or if a designated donee is not available, the attending physician may serve as donee. To avoid any apparent conflict of interest, the UAGA prohibits a physician-donee from participating in any transplant-related procedure.

Under the UAGA, the time of death is determined by the physician who tends the donor at his death. If no physician is in attendance, time of death is determined by the doctor who certifies the death. Once again, the physician who makes the determination of death is precluded from participating in the removal or transplanting of any part of the dead body.

The UAGA does not attempt to establish statutory standards in determining the donor's time of death. Death has, however, been legally defined as brain dead either by statute[9] or by high court judicial precedent[10] in 47 states. These developments track contemporary medical practice, which equates human death with brain death.[11] Accordingly, this definition is implied even when it is not explicitly included in state anatomical gift laws.[12]

In both the 1968 and the 1987 versions of the UAGA, "the decedent" is defined as including stillborn infants and fetuses. This represents a fairly conservative approach to the controversial cluster of issues that surround the use of organ tissue from aborted fetuses for medical purposes. Fetal brain tissue transplants have already been performed on adult patients who suffer from Parkinson's disease,[13] and researchers are now exploring the possibility of using fetal brain implants to treat many other neurological diseases, including Alzheimer's disease.[14]

These developments, controversial in themselves, give rise to the even more perplexing problem that fetuses may be aborted solely for the purpose of harvesting tissues and organs.[15] Fetal research statutes may, however, be construed to prohibit these practices.[16] It remains for state and federal legislation to address these issues directly.[17]

Section 7(c) of the UAGA affords protection from civil liability for health care providers "who act in good faith in accord with the terms of this Act or with the anatomical gift laws of another state . . . . " To date, this language has been construed in only one reported decision. In that case,[18] a woman's body was kept functioning through life support techniques for some 48 hours after her husband had been told by a physician that she was dead, and had given his consent to the removal of his wife's kidneys. The Wisconsin Supreme Court held that Sections 7(c) imunized the defendant physicians against their actions in connection with the transplant operation, but did not constitute a defense for actions taken while the patient was still alive.

In a similar case[19] presenting facts not implicating the language of the UAGA, the New Jersey Supreme Court ruled that a decedent's parents could recover damages when a hospital refused for two days to disconnect their son's life support machines although the parents had informed the hospital that they would not consent to an organ donation.

When Congress passed the National Organ Transplant Act in 1984, the legislation outlawed the buying and selling of human organs and created the Task Force on Organ Transplantation and the Organ Procurement and Transplantation Network. In April, 1986, the Task Force, published a widely acclaimed report that focused on measures to increase the supply of organs available for transplant. Congress responded to some of the Task Force's recommendations in its Omnibus Budget Reconciliation Act of 1986. Under the law, hospitals receiving Medicare and Medicaid reimbursements were required to establish protocols for "required requests" or routine inquiries about tissue and organ donation to families of potential donors.[20]

In the wake of the federal legislation, some 30 states have passed "required requests" statutes.[21] These statutes leave the indication of suitable donors to a physician's discretion. When a doctor identifies a potential donor, he or she must inquire whether the patient has a Uniform Donor Card and, if not, whether the survivors will authorize a donation.[22] So far, no comparable regulations control the donation of organs and tissues in living donors. The legal ramifications of transplantation in this circumstance are generally the same as those that apply to other surgical procedures (e.g., negligence, informed consent, warranty, etc.).[23]

The few reported court decisions involving transplantations mainly address the issue of the consent of the donor. Although the outcomes vary, the results are not necessarily inconsistent. In one case,[24] a 28-year old man suffering from chronic glomerulus nephritis could no longer be maintained on artificial kidney machine treatments. His mentally incompetent brother was found to be an acceptable donor for a kidney transplant. Finding that the incompetent was emotionally and psychologically dependent on his brother, the court permitted the transplantation on the grounds that the procedure was in the best interest of the incompetent, who would otherwise be jeopardized by the death of his brother.

In another instance[25] a physician was held liable for performing a skin transplant on a minor donor when it appeared that the child's mother neither knew about nor consented to the surgery. Yet in another situation,[26] when a mother donated a kidney to her son after the defendant surgeon negligently removed one of the boy's kidneys, the woman was not permitted to recover for the adverse affect she sustained from the loss of the organ. In dismissing the suit, the court ruled that the "rescue doctrine" did not apply to the transplant donor because she had had full knowledge of the consequences of her actions.

The theories of liability, breach of warranty and strict liability that have been applied to blood transfusions may also apply to organ transplants. State statutes, however, prevent the use of these theories of liability by declaring that blood transfusions are a service and not a sale. These statutes have generally included organ transplants in their legislative definition of services.

---

1 *P. Williams,* Life from Death: The Organ and Tissue Donation and Transplantation Source Book with Forms *3 (Contemporary Public Health Issues Vol. 2, 1989).*

2 *Bernat,* Ethical and Legal Aspects of the Emergency Management of Brain Death and Organ Retrieval, *5 Emergency Medicine Clinics of North America No. 4 661, 671 (Nov. 1987).*

3 Id.

4 *An amended version of the UAGA was drafted in August 1987. The amendments, a response to the continuing shortage of organs and tissues available for transplant, are designed to facilitate donation and procurement. Williams,* supra *n. 1, at 10. Although most state statutes are modeled on the old act, the amended UAGA is important today as a precursor of future directions in anatomical gift law. The text and the 1987 UAGA is contained in Williams,* supra *n. 1, at 209 (Appendix B).*

5 *The state anatomical gift laws are reprinted in Willaims,* supra *n. 1, at 27-203 and in South-Eastern Organ Procurement Foundation,* Statutory Regulation of Organ Donation in the United States, *(2d ed. 1986). The following citations are to the sections that commence each state's treatment of anatomical gifts: Ala. Code §22-19-40; Alaska Stat. §13.50.010; Ariz. Rev. Stat. Ann. §36-841; Ark. Stat. Ann. §20-17-601; Cal. Health & Safety Code §7150.5; Colo. Rev. Stat. §12-34-101; Conn. Gen. Stat. Ann. §19a-272; Del Code Ann. tit. 24, §2710; D.C. Code Ann. §2-1501; Fla. Stat. Ann. §732.910; Ga. Code Ann. §44-5-140; Hawaii Rev. Stat. §327-1; Idaho Code §39-3401; Ill. Ann. Stat. ch. 110 1/2, §301; Ind. Code Ann. §29-2-16-1; Iowa Code Ann. §142A.1; Kan. Stat. Ann. §65-3209; Ky. Rev. Stat. Ann. §311.165; La. Rev. Stat. Ann. §17:2351; Me. Rev. Stat. Ann. tit. 22, §2901; Md. Est. & Trusts Code Ann. §4-501; Mass. Gen. Laws Ann. ch. 113, §7; Mich. Comp. Laws Ann. §333.10101; Minn. Stat. Ann. §525.921; Miss. Code Ann. §41-39-11; Mo. Ann. Stat. §194.210; Mont. Code Ann. §72-17-101; Neb. Rev. Stat. §71-4801; Nev. Rev. Stat. §451.500; N.H. Rev. Stat. Ann. §291-A:1; N.J. Stat. Ann. §26:6-57; N.M. Stat. Ann. §24-6-1; N.Y. Pub. Health Law §4300; N.C. Gen. Stat. §130A-402; N.D. Cent. Code §23-06.0-01; Ohio Rev. Code Ann. §2108.01; Okla. Stat. Ann. tit. 63, §2201; Or. Rev. Stat. §97.250; 20 Pa. Cons. Stat. Ann. §8601; R.I. Gen. Laws §23-18.5-1; S.C. Code Ann. §44-43-310; S.D. Codified Laws Ann. §34-26-20; Tenn. Code Ann. §68-30-101; Tex. Stat. Ann. art. 4590-2; Utah Code Ann. §26-28-1; Vt. Stat. Ann. tit. 18, §5231; Va. Code §32.1-289; Wash. Rev. Code Ann. §68.50.340; W. Va. Code §16-17-1; Wis. Stat. Ann. §157.06; Wyo. Stat. §35-5-101.*

6 *Connecticut, Delaware, Minnesota, North Dakota, Utah and Wisconsin.*

7 *Utah requires only one witness; California does not require any. The amended UAGA dispenses with the attestation requirement.*

8 *Williams,* supra, *n. 1, at 15.*

9 *Alabama, Alaska, Arkansas, California, Colorado, Connecticut, Delaware, District of Columbia, Florida, Georgia, Hawaii, Idaho, Illinois, Indiana, Iowa, Kansas, Kentucky, Louisiana, Maine, Maryland, Michigan, Mississippi, Missouri, Montana, Nevada, New Hampshire, New Mexico, North Carolina, Ohio, Oklahoma, Oregon, Pennsylvania, Rhode Island, South Carolina, Tennessee, Texas, Vermont, Virginia, West Virginia, Wisconsin and Wyoming.*

10 *Arizona, Massachusetts, Nebraska, New Jersey, New York and Washington.*

11 *Bernat,* supra *n. 2, at 669-70.*

12 *Williams,* supra *n. 1, at 14.*

13 *Note,* The Intentional Creation of Fetal Tissue for Transplants: The Womb As a Fetus Farm?, *21 J. Marshall L. Rev. 853, 855-59 (1988).*

14 *Williams,* supra *n. 1, at 14.*

15 *Note,* supra *n. 13.*

16 *Davis,* Fetal Tissue Transplants: Restricting Recipient Designation, *39 Hastings L. J. 1079-80 (1988).*

17 *Williams,* supra *n. 1, at 14.*

18 Williams v. Hoffman, *66 Wis.2d 145, 223 N.W.2d 844 (1974).*

19 Strachan v. John F. Kennedy Memorial Hospital, *538 A.2d 346 (N.J. 1988),* discussed in *Annas,* Brain Death and Organ Donation: You Can Have One Without The Other, *1988 Hastings Center Rep. 28 (June/July).*

20 *Bernat,* supra *n. 2, at 673.*

21 *Alabama, Arizona, Arkansas, California, Connecticut, Delaware, Florida, Georgia, Hawaii, Illinois, Indiana, Kansas, Kentucky, Louisiana, Maine, Maryland, Massachusetts, Michigan, Mississippi, Missouri, New Hampshire, New Jersey, New York, Ohio, Oregon, Rhode Island, Tennessee, Washington, West Virginia and Wisconsin.*

22 *Bernat,* supra *n. 2, at 673.* See also AMA Report of the Board of Trustees:

Organ Procurement System, 71 R.I. Med. J. 357 (1988).

23 But see *Adams,* Live Organ Donors and Informed Consent, *8 J. of Legal Medical, No. 4, at 555 (1987) for an argument that donation by live donors is not like traditional medical intrusions and thus deserves novel legal analysis.*

24 Strunk v. Strunk, *445 S.W.2d 145 (Ky. 1969).*

25 Bonner v. Moran, *126 F.2d 121 (D.C. 1941)*

26 Sirianni v. Anna, *285 N.Y.S.2d 709 (1967).*

Anatomical Gift by a Living Donor

Form 77

I am of sound mind and 18 years or more of age.

I hereby make this anatomical gift to take effect upon my death. The marks in the appropriate squares and words filled into the blanks below indicate my desires.

I give: ☐ my body; ☐ any needed organs or parts;

☐ the following organs or parts________________;

to the following person (or institution):

☐ the physician in attendance at my death;

☐ the hospital in which I die;

☐ the following named physician, hospital, storage bank or other medical institution____________;

☐ the following individual for treatment__________;

for the following purposes:

☐ any purpose authorized by law; ☐ transplantation;

☐ therapy; ☐research; ☐ medical education.

Dated______________ City and State____________________

Signed by the donor in the presence of the following who sign as witnesses:

____
(Signature of Donor)

____
Witness

____
(Address of Donor)

____

____

Anatomical Gift by Next of Kin or Other Authorized Person

Form 78

A.M.
Date________________ Time________________ P.M.

I hereby make this anatomical gift of or from the body of

________________who died on________________at the

________________in________________. The marks in the appropriate squares and the words filled into the blanks below indicate my relationship to the deceased and my desires respecting the gift.

I am the surviving:

☐ spouse; ☐ adult son or daughter; ☐ parent;
☐ adult brother or sister; ☐ guardian; ☐ ________________,
authorized to dispose of the body;

I give ☐ the body of deceased; ☐ any needed organs or parts;
☐ the following organs or parts________________________________;
to the following person (or institution)____________________________

(insert name of a physician, hospital, research or educational institution, storage bank or individual),

For the following purposes:

☐ any purpose authorized by law; ☐ transplantation;
☐ therapy; ☐ research; ☐ medical education.

Dated________________ City and State____________________________

____
(Signature of Survivor)

____
(Address of Survivor)

Form 79

Uniform Donor Card

of ____
(name of donor)

In the hope that I may help others, I hereby make this anatomical gift, if medically acceptable, to take effect upon my death. The words and marks below indicate my desires.

I give: (a) ☐ any needed organs or parts
(b) ☐ only the following organs or parts

____
Specifiy the organ(s) or part(s)

for the purposes of transplantation, therapy, medical research or education:

(c) ☐ my body for anatomical study if needed.

Limitations or special wishes, if any______________________

Signed by the donor and the following two witnesses in the presence of each other:

______________________	______________________
(Signature of donor)	*(Date of Birth of Donor)*
______________________	______________________
(City and State)	*(Date Signed)*
______________________	______________________
(Witness)	*(Witness)*

Consent to Transplant

Form 80

A.M.
Date_______________ Time_______________ P.M.

1. I hereby authorize and consent to the performance upon

______________________________of a___________________
(myself or name of patient) *(name of organ)*

transplant to be performed by or under the direction of

Dr.______________.

2. I understand that________________________ will attempt
(person or instituiton procuring)

to obtain a______________________ from whatever source is
(name of organ)

available.

I understand that because the organ which is obtained may have to be transplanted immediately and because certain tests, if performed to determine whether or not the organ was defective, would render the organ useless for transplantation purposes, the organ which is transplanted may be defective.

3. I understand that this operation involves a greater degree of risk than other types of surgery, that there is a serious risk of infection, and that my body may reject the organ.

4. The other risks of this operation, my prognosis, the nature of the operation, the purpose of the operation, the alternative methods of treatment, the possible complications, and the possible consequences have been fully explained to me by Dr.______________.

5. I consent to the administration of such anesthetics as may be considered necessary or advisable by the physician responsible for this service, with the exception of________________________.
(state "none," "spinal anesthesia," etc.)

6. I acknowledge that no guarantee or assurance has been given by anyone as to the results that may be obtained.

7. I acknowledge that all blank spaces on this document have been either completed or crossed off prior to my signing.

(CROSS OUT ANY PARAGRAPHS ABOVE WHICH DO NOT APPLY)

Signed__________________________
(Patient or person authorized to consent for patient)

Witness______________

Consent to Remove Organ for Transplant (Living Donor)

Form 81

A.M.
Date________________ Time________________ P.M.

1. I hereby authorize and consent to the removal of my ______________________ *(name of organ)* for the purpose of transplanting it into the body of________________ (or into the body of another human being or into the storage facilities maintained by________________for transplantation into the body of another human being at a later time).

2. I authorize the performance of this operation by or under the direction of Dr.________________.

3. The nature and purpose of the operation, the risks involved, the possible consequences and the possible complications have been explained to me to my satisfaction by Dr.________________ and by ________________.

4. I consent to the administration of such anesthetics as may be considered necessary or advisable by the physician responsible for this service, with the exception of ______________________________ *(state "none," "spinal anesthesia," etc.)*.

5. I acknowledge that no guarantee or assurance has been given by anyone as to the results that may be obtained.

6. I consent to the photographing or televising of the operations or procedures to be performed, including appropriate portions of my body, for medical, scientific or educational purposes, provided my identity is not revealed by the pictures or by descriptive texts accompanying them.

7. For the purpose of advancing medical education, I consent to the admittance of observers to the operating room.

8. I acknowledge that all blank spaces on this document have been either completed or crossed off prior to my signing.

(CROSS OUT ANY PARAGRAPHS ABOVE WHICH DO NOT APPLY)

____
(Patient or person authorized to consent for patient)

Witness________________

20

In recent years, the incidence of AIDS has generated a flurry of state legislative and administrative activity. In 1987 and 1988, over 600 AIDS-related bills were introduced in state legislatures.[1] State public health departments and insurance commissioners have responded to the disease with reporting requirements and other regulations.[2] With so much yet to be learned about the disease, state lawmaking efforts will doubtless continue, particuarly as AIDS travels into the heterosexual population and affects children.[3] Since it is not possible in this short space to track this disparate, evolving body of law in its entirety, the focus here is on representative state action in three areas of special concern to physicians: informed consent, confidentiality and reporting requirements.

1 *The American Medical Ass'n,* AIDS: 1988 State Legislative Update *v (1989).*

2 *Lewis,* Acquired Immunodeficiency Syndrome: State Legislative Activity, *258 J. Am. Medical Ass'n No. 17 (Nov. 6, 1987).*

3 *Gostin and Ziegler,* A Review of AIDS-Related Legislative and Regulatory Policy in the United States, *15 Law, Medicine & Health Care No. 1-2, at 5 (Summer 1987).*

20.1 Informed Consent

The question of informed consent takes on special urgency in the context of HIV testing because of the possible adverse ramifications of a seropositive result on a person's employment, insurability and housing situations.[1] These concerns have prompted a number of state legislatures to pass specific AIDS laws to supplement the more general informed consent statutes enacted elsewhere. These states require the written informed consent of a test subject before a test for the presence of the AIDS antibody may be performed by a health care facility, physician or other health care provider. The states with such legislation include California, Colorado, Hawaii, Illinois, Indiana, Kentucky, Maine, Massachusetts, Oregon, Washington and Wisconsin.[2]

Even in these states, however, the principle of informed consent to HIV testing is not monolithic. Some states[3] permit an exception when the testing is done in connection with a transplant or is related to research under the Uniform Anatomical Gift Act.[4] A number of others[5] recognize an exception covering a general situation (the details vary) in which a physician determines that HIV testing is medically necessary to appropriate diagnosis and treatment, and the test subject has otherwise consented to medical treatment.[6] Still others[7] permit HIV testing in the absence of written informed consent if a designated individual or committee finds that a health care provider has been or could be exposed to the test subject's blood or bodily fluids.[8]

A Florida statute eliminates the writing requirement if the subject's medical record shows that the test was explained and consent obtained.[9] California law authorizes parental or conservator consent where the test subject is a minor under twelve or incompetent.[10] A Wisconsin statute permits the medical director of either a center for the developmentally disabled or a mental health institute to treat a patient under specified circumstances.[11]

---

1 The American Medical Ass'n, AIDS: 1988 State Legislative Update (1989).

2 Id.

3 California, Indiana, Massachusetts, and Wisconsin.

4 The American Medical Ass'n, supra *note 1, at 7.*

5 Illinois, Indiana, Hawaii.

6 The American Medical Ass'n, supra *note 1, at 8.*

7 Illinois, Louisiana, Texas.

8 The American Medical Ass'n, supra *note 1, at 8.*

9 Id.

10 Id. *at 7.*

11 Id.

Informed Consent for HIV Antibody Test

Form 82

I voluntarily give my consent to be tested for exposure to the Human Immunodeficiency Virus (HIV). HIV is the term used for the virus that is thought to cause AIDS. I understand that my blood will be drawn for the purpose of determining whether I have been exposed to this virus.

I understand that the exact meaning of an HIV antibody test result may not be clear in my case. A positive result does not mean that I will come down with AIDS. A negative result does not ensure that I do not have early HIV infection or that I cannot transmit the infection.

I understand that all reasonable efforts to provide confidentiality and/or anonymity to the extent provided by law will be made. However, I understand that the results of this test will be recorded in my medical record. As medical record information, these tests results will be regarded as confidential, and the Hospital will not disclose these test results to unauthorized third parties without my express written authorization. I understand, however, that confidentiality cannot be absolutely guaranteed, and that the results wil be available to physicians and other health care professionals responsible for my care and treatment.

I understand that Illinois law requires that if this test result in combination with other data leads my physician to make a presumptive diagnosis of AIDS, then my case must be reported to the public health authorities and may be investigated by them.

I have been informed that if this test is positive a physician will provide counselling for follow up care and for precautions against transmitting this infection.

I understand that if I refuse this test my exposure to the HIV will remain unknown. My ability to infect others with this virus will also remain unknown.

I warrant that I freely give my informed consent and that I have not been forced, coerced or subjected to any constraint or inducement. I understand that I may withdraw this consent anytime prior to having my blood drawn.

______ I hereby give consent for the performance of the HIV antibody test.

______ I refuse consent for the performance of the HIV antibody test. I understand that this refusal may limit the clincial data available to my physician. However, this refusal will not affect my access to further care.

______________________________ ______________________________
Signature Date

____
Witness

Editor's Note: *This form is reproduced with permission of Northwestern Memorial Hospital, Chicago, Illinois.*

Consent to Withdrawal of Blood for Autologous Transfusion for High Risk Patients

Form 83

Name of Patient:______________________ Date:______________

Name of Physician:____

Reason for High Risk:______________________________________

I consent to the withdrawal of my blood by authorized staff members of __________Hospital for autologous transfusion purposes (i.e., to be used later if needed in the course of my surgery). My physician named above has explained to me the purpose, nature and advantages of autologous transfusion, the risk involved, and the possibility of complications.

Withdrawal of Blood

The procedure for withdrawing blood for autologous use is similar to routine blood donation. The usual risks of withdrawing blood are lower blood volume and low blood pressure.

Because of my medical problems, I am at greater risk than most patients for complications from blood withdrawal. Symptoms may include feeling faint, lightheaded or weak. In addition, those patients with angina (chest pain) may have an acute exacerbation of their symptoms. To minimize these risks, fluid will be administered intravenously during withdrawal to replace lost blood volume during withdrawal.

Transfusion of Blood

It is anticipated that the units of blood withdrawn will be used during my surgery and hospitalization. If I do not require transfusion of all of the blood withdrawn from me, I consent to the use or disposal of the remaining units of blood in any manner deemed appropriate by the hospital.

If my blood is withdrawn more than once in preparation for my surgery, this consent applies to each occasion when my blood is withdrawn for autologous transfusion. I also consent to such additional procedures related to withdrawal of blood and autologous transfusion as may be necessary or desirable.

If my requirements are greater than the number of autologous units that I have donated, then I will receive non-autologous blood.

I have read and understand this consent form, and have had an opportunity to ask questions about this procedure. All blanks on this form were filled in when I signed it.

______________________ ______________________
Patient Witness

____
Person authorized to consent for patient

Patient did not sign this consent because______________________

Editor's Note: *This form is reproduced with permission of Northwestern Memorial Hospital, Chicago, Illinois.*

20.2 Confidentiality

Many of the concerns that underlie the AIDS informed consent statute are more directly addressed in state laws that specifically protect the confidentiality of AIDS-related information. About half the states have passed such laws. A number of them[1] have codified the general proposition that information that identifies a person who may be infected with the AIDS virus is confidential, and may not be revealed to any third party except with the written authorization by the infected person.[2]

The preponderance of legislative effort has specified exceptions to the general rule. One of the most common exceptions, addressed by a number of states,[3] relates to emergency medical care. The laws ensure that emergency medical technicians will be informed if they have been exposed to an HIV-infected individual (although the identity of the patient remains confidential). These laws also provide for notifying persons who must take body fluid precautions, i.e., coroners, funeral directors and medical examiners, when an infected person dies.[4]

A second category of exceptions involves the communication of AIDS-related information between health care personnel. Twenty-one states[5] permit disclosures of AIDS information to protect a named individual's life or health. Eleven of these states[6] specifically authorize disclosure to facilitate the continued care and treatment of the patient, even in a nonemergency situation.[7]

1 *California, Colorado, Hawaii, Kentucky, Maryland, Rhode Island, Texas.*

2 *The American Medical Ass'n,* AIDS: 1988 State Legislative Update (1989).

3 *California, Georgia, Illinois, Indiana, Kansas, Kentucky, Louisiana, Maryland, Massachusetts Michigan, Mississippi, Missouri, Rhode Island, Tennessee, Texas, Utah, Virginia, Washington, Wisconsin.*

4 *The American Medical Ass'n,* supra *note 2, at 9-10.*

5 *Alabama, California, Colorado, Delaware, Florida, Georgia, Hawaii, Illinois, Indiana, Kentucky, Louisiana, Mississippi, Missouri, New Hampshire, New York, North Carolina, Rhode Island, South Carolina, Tennessee, Texas and Wisconsin.*

6 *Alabama, California, Florida, Georgia, Hawaii, Illinois, Mississippi, New Hampshire, New York, North Carolina, Texas.*

7 *The American Medical Ass'n, supra* note 2, at 10.

20.3 Reporting Requirements

One of the most contentious questions in the AIDS debate is whether physicians have a "duty to warn" sexual partners or those who share intravenous drug paraphernalia with an infected person if that person refuses to reveal his or her HIV status. In ten states,[1] doctors or health care facility personnel are permitted, but not required, to give the information to affected persons after counseling with the infected individual.[2] Thus, state legislatures have declined to elevate disclosure into a duty. The laws of five of the ten states[3] expressly immunize health care providers against liability, either for disclosure or for failure to disclose to interested third parties.[4]

All fifty states, acting through statute or administrative regulation, require that confirmed cases of AIDS be reported to state public health officials.[5] In thirteen states,[6] a seropositive test result also constitutes a reportable condition.[7] These state reporting regulations contain their own set of confidentiality strictures. Individuals are reported either by name or by patient identifiers.[8]

---

1 *Alabama, California, Florida, Georgia, Kansas, New York, South Carolina, Texas, Washington, Wisconsin.*

2 *The American Medical Ass'n,* AIDS: 1988 State Legislative Update (1989).

3 *California, Florida, Georgia, New York, Texas.*

4 *The American Medical Ass'n,* supra *note 2, at 10-11.*

5 Id. *at 11.*

6 *Arizona, Arkansas, Georgia, Hawaii, Idaho, Indiana, Iowa, Minnesota, Mississippi, Missouri, New Hampshire, South Carolina and Virginia.*

7 *The American Medical Ass'n,* supra *note 2, at 11.*

8 Id.